STREET NAMES
OF
VANCOUVER

BY
ELIZABETH WALKER

To Terry
Elizabeth Walker
14 May, 1999 -

©

Vancouver Historical Society

Vancouver Historical Society
PO Box 3071
Vancouver, British Columbia v6b 3x6.

Canadian Cataloguing in Publication Data

Walker, Elizabeth
        Street Names of Vancouver
Includes bibliographic references and maps.
isbn 0-9692378-7-1 : (pbks.) $24.95
        1. Street Names– British Columbia– Vancouver
2. Vancouver (BC)– History.
I. Vancouver Historical Society   II. Title
FC3847.67.W34 1999   971.1'33   c99-900358-5
F1089.5V22W34 1999

Street Names of Vancouver by Elizabeth Walker
Editing and colour maps: Bruce Macdonald
Production management and design: Carlyn Craig
Cover design: Teresa Gustafson
Printing and binding by Hignell Printing Ltd.
Printed and bound in Canada

Published with the assistance of the Government of British Columbia through the British Columbia Gaming Commission.

To order single copies of **Street Names of Vancouver,** mail $24.95 for each softbound edition (in Canada please add $2.10 GST) plus $5 each for shipping to: Vancouver Historical Society, PO Box 3071, Vancouver, BC, Canada v6b 3x6.

Booksellers: Retail discounts are available from Gordon Soules Book Publishers Ltd.
Tel: (604) 688-5466 or (604) 922-6588; Fax (604) 688-5442; Email: books@gordonsoules.com

PRINTED IN CANADA

First printing, April 1999.

Contents

Acknowledgements

This book, like all books, owes its existence to the help, encouragement, and work of many people.

My first thanks to to the staff of the City of Vancouver Archives, who unfailingly assisted me and introduced me to the arrangement of civic records. My endless requests to see South Vancouver Voters Lists were patiently met.

Staff of the Vancouvers Public Library, particularly the Special Collections Division, maintained its record for good service.

Confronted with the technicalities of land surveys, I turned for help to Noel Petes, Vancouver City Surveyor. He and his staff, especially Paul Neely and Jean Yamashita, explained the system and located various surveys. The staff at the Land Titles Office in New Westminster unearthed many early surveys for my perusal.

Bruce Macdonald edited my text, gathered photographs, and prepared the maps. While preparing the maps he clarified ambiguities in my text and identified the location of several streets – a great contribution to this reference work.

Peggy Imredy, co-author of my article on Kitsilano street names, prodded me to continue my research, as did Gordon Elliot, Helen and Philip Akrigg's work on British Columbia place names provided me with an excellent example to follow.

I am grateful that the executive and members of the Vancouver Historical Society had sufficient faith in the value of my reseach to undertake its publication. Adrian Clark deserves special mention for all his work in organizing the casino night, obtaining the production manager, and chairing the publications committee. Thanks are extended to Robert McDonald and Nancy Stubbs, members of this committee. I applaud Jean Barman, Chuck Davis, Yvonne Klan, Cyril Leanoff, Bruce Macdonald, Kathleen Mackinnon, Nancy Stubbs, and John Spittle who toiled long hours at the casino night granted by the British Columbia Gaming Commission. Through their efforts sufficient funds were raised to publish this book.

Teresa Gustafson ably converted nebulous ideas into an attractive cover design, and Jerry Eberts patiently turned a rough draft into a preliminary manuscript.

Last, but not least, Carlyn Craig, production manager and designer, brought her enthusiasm, interest, and knowledge to bear upon the task of putting my research into a publishable format.

Elizabeth Walker

Abbreviations and Explanatory Notes

BCER   British Columbia Electric Railway
CPR   Canadian Pacific Railway
CVA   City of Vancouver Archives
DL   District Lot
OGT   Old Granville Townsite
THSL   Townsite of Hastings Suburban Lands

Plan with numbers only (e.g., Plan 3845) refers to a registered survey plan for land in Group 1, New Westminster Land District, and held in Land Registry Office, New Westminster

Plan with an alphabetical prefix (e.g., Plan LE 3742B) refers to a marginally numbered working plan of the Vancouver Engineering Department. Those referred to in the text are in City Surveyor's Office, Vancouver City Hall. Many are attached to individual street-naming by-laws.

Introduction

My interest in the 773 current Vancouver street names and the 400 that have fallen into disuse was piqued by the many questions people asked me about them when I was working in the North West History collection at the Vancouver Public Library. Though not always successful, I would do my best to locate streets with unknown names or differentiate between the various "Boundary" streets or "Victoria" streets. Little did I know what byways my research would lead me into or how much I'd learn about surveys and other technical aspects of street naming. Because surveys are the basis of street patterns, one needs to know a bit of history about them.

In 1858, apart from the Hudson's Bay Company post at Fort Langley, New Westminster was the only non-Native settlement in the Lower Mainland. But by December 1859 people were seeking land on Burrard Inlet. Anticipating possible development, around 1860 the colonial government created a reserve for a townsite near the Second Narrows of Burrard Inlet, later known as Hastings Townsite.

In 1863, under instructions from Colonel Moody, George Turner (a Royal Engineer) made the first survey on the inlet. Beginning at the Townsite reserve, he surveyed westerly along the south shore, laying out District Lots (DLs) 184, 183, 182, 181, 185, and a townsite that appears to have included the original naval reserve in the vicinity. District Lot map (Map no. 14258) of Vancouver shows the original parcels of land in the shape in which they were granted by the Crown.

Between the 1860s and the arrival of the Canadian Pacific Railway (CPR) at Vancouver in 1887, speculation in these District Lots was rampant. Bruce Macdonald, author of *Vancouver: An Illustrated History*, indicates the wheeling and dealing that went on and the changing ownership of these various District Lots. The names of many of these property owners (such as Dunlevy and Vernon) were perpetuated when streets were surveyed and street names assigned. Streets were also named after Oppenheimer, Barnard, Dupont, Powell, Keefer, Harris, Jackson, and Prior – all shareholders of the Vancouver Improvement Company, which owned DL 196.

Although he was only here two years, Lauchlan Hamilton, the CPR's surveyor and, later, a land commissioner, is considered to be the "father" of Vancouver. His detailed plans shaped the layout of much of the city, especially the downtown peninsula. He served on the city council in 1886 and 1887 and proposed the creation of Stanley Park.

In surveying Vancouver he faced two problems. First, he had to reconcile existing streets in the old Granville townsite and in DL 185, the future West End, with streets he'd created in DL 541. Second, he had to name a great many streets in a hurry.

A *Plan for the City of Liverpool, Burrard Inlet, DL 185, Group 1, New Westminster District* (Plan no. 92) had been deposited in the Land Registry Office in 1882 by the owners, the so-called "Three Greenhorns" – Samuel Brighouse, William Hailstone, and John Morton. Hamilton planned to extend the east-west streets in DL 541 into DL 185, but one of the owners, a Mr. Spratt, had had a disagreement with the other land owners and wanted no change to Plan no. 92 (Matthews *Early Vancouver* v.3:209).

Hamilton could not wait for a court decision, and, consequently, in the final city plan only alternate streets were through streets, with the break occurring at Burrard Street. For example, Robson and Nelson Streets are through streets but Haro and Barclay are not.

The townsite of Granville, popularly known as "Gastown," established in 1870, was surveyed in 1885 (Plan no. 168). A small logging settlement of a few streets, it sprawled along the waterfront. The fire insurance map published by Sanborn Map and Publishing Company in 1885 indicates the layout, although the street names differ (See Map of Street Names, 1870-99, page 78-9). Hamilton plotted the alignment of the three east-west streets – Water, Cordova, and Hastings – so that they would lead into the new Granville Street, the dominant north-south street that ended at the new CPR station.

Hamilton used simple and speedy methods to solve his second problem with regard to naming the streets. For DL 185, now the West End, he applied names from an admiralty chart of the Pacific Coast. For DL 541, the CPR land grant, he used the names of men prominent in government: Dunsmuir, Richards, Smithe, and A.E.R. Davie. The streets in DLs 183 and 184, named later, commemorate other prominent people. In DL 200A and DL 302 Dr. Israel Powell, one of the owners, was likely the person who suggested the names of Canadian provinces, as he had championed British Columbia's entry into Confederation. A resurvey of DL 264A, Plan 1771 (1905) confirmed many names that had been shown earlier on Hermon and Burwell's 1902 *Plan of the City of Vancouver, BC* (Map 14171).

In anticipation of settlement along the south shore of False Creek, Hamilton named the streets from Heather to Vine as shown in his 1887 survey, *City of Vancouver Canadian Pacific* town site (Map 14160). On 27 April 1936, Hamilton wrote to Major Matthews: "The streets I called after trees as Alder Street, Birch Street, Cedar Street, preserving them as [sic] possible according to the arrangement of the alphabet." Matthews comments that "it is quite possible that Mr. Hamilton did intend to name the 'tree' streets in alphabetical order but that after selecting names he handed them to his draughtsman but forgot to mention their order." However, it was not until 1889 that Donald Charleson signed a contract with the CPR to clear the Fairview slopes, and the official survey was registered in 1891, Plan no. 590.

The city of Vancouver then covered only about one-third of the peninsula west of Boundary Road and did not include Hastings Townsite or scattered settlements in the heavily treed remainder of the peninsula. In 1861-2 Hugh McRoberts slashed a trail along the North Arm of the Fraser River from New Westminster as far as the present Musqueam Indian Reserve; called the River Road, it is now known as South East and South West Marine Drive. Another trail, later known as Kingsway, developed between New Westminster and False Creek. The poet Michael Turner aptly described it as "this road, this way diagonal, in opposition to the grid."

In 1890 a group of New Westminster and Vancouver businessmen – anticipating settlement – built the fourteen-mile long Westminster and Vancouver tramway. The route lay roughly parallel to the present Kingsway from New Westminster to Central Park and Cedar Cottage and then swung north along Park Drive – now Commercial Drive – to Hastings Street and west into a terminal at Carrall Street.

The existence of this interurban tram – later called the Central Park line of the British Columbia Electric Railway Company – hastened the settlement of DL 37 and the formation of the new municipality of South Vancouver, incorporated in 1893. Figure 1, an advertisement for Collingwood, emphasizes the location of the tram line – only one and a half miles from the city boundary. The two stations, one being Cedar Cottage and the other being Collingwood, became the foci of rural-suburban neighbourhoods where real estate developers quoted prices by the acre rather than by the lot. Settlement was further hastened when the Westminster and Vancouver Land Bonus Act, 1894, granted the tramway company 169 acres in the adjoining DL 36 and DL 51.

Figure 1: *Daily News Advertiser*, 26 April 1891.

Figure 2: *Daily News Advertiser*, 5 July 1892.

Under the provisions of the Land Amendment Act, 1894, surveyor E.B. Hermon subdivided Crown lands in DL 36 and DL 49 into small leaseholdings of five to eight acres. In 1900 W.C. Wells, Chief Commissioner of Lands and Works, submitted a report to the Legislative Assembly regarding these holdings, known as the Burnaby and South Vancouver Small Holdings. Descriptions of properties showed the size of houses and barns and the acreage cleared. Settlers whose names were given to the developing road system were John Grant, J.H. Bowman, J. Wilbers, and W.J. Battison.

Just south and east of DL 37, the owners of the scattered clearings had their names perpetuated in the road system of South Vancouver and now Vancouver: Robert Knight and George Kerr through South Vancouver Road By-law 1893; Thomas and Henry Earle, George Wales, and the Doman family by South Vancouver Highway By-law 1903; Abraham Joyce and William Vivian by Highway By-law, 1905.

Subdivisions proliferated as developers moved in. An 1891 advertisement for the "town" of Gladstone likely took its name from the nearby Gladstone Inn (Figure 2). The one-acre lots that fronted on the New Westminster Road – now Kingsway – were only fifteen minutes from the tram line.

Many of the plans were "paper plans" drawn up and registered without the benefit of a prior ground survey. In the 1890s the province lacked available and competent surveyors, and speculation increased the pressure to subdivide. Plans for a subdivision, including paper ones, had to be submitted for approval to the council of South Vancouver municipality. After approval, the plans would be registered at the Land Registry Office in New Westminster. Consideration of these plans often dominated the agenda of council meetings. For instance, the South Vancouver council meeting of 21 August 1909 moved and carried that a surveyor be engaged to find the correct corner of Westminster Avenue at River Road – now Main Street at South East Marine Drive. At a meeting on 16 October 1909, the plan for a proposed subdivision of the easterly 194 feet of Block 8, DL 657, was not approved until the owner had the roads and lanes conform to those in Block 10, presently at St. George Street and East 56th Avenue. By 1910, the South Vancouver street system was chaotic: dead end roads, roads not meeting, and a proliferation of names. To rectify this situation council passed Street-Naming By-law No. 141 on 1 December 1910, which renamed 209 streets.

The task of identifying all of Vancouver's street names proved challenging for several reasons. One was that I had never heard of a great many of the names! Another was that I did not know what part of a street had been renamed. For example, four streets – Thynne Road, Waters Road, Daly Road, and Ferrisdale Boulevard – became sections of Dumfries Street. My first step was to examine plates 91 and 95 of *Goad's Atlas of the City of Vancouver and Surrounding, Municipalities,* published in 1912 by Chas. E. Goad Company. Charles Edward Goad (1843-1910), an English engineer, dominated fire insurance cartography in Canada. His atlas is a major source for our region's urban geography, particularly that of South Vancouver. Each plate not only indicates buildings, lot sizes, and street widths, but also former street names and survey-plan numbers that provide access to the original plans held at the Land Registry office in New Westminster.

Thynne Street lay between the present East 21st and East 31st Avenues, but I had to identify Thynne and establish his connection to the street bearing his name. From various South Vancouver records – voters lists, assessment rolls, and by-laws, I discovered that Thynne Road was officially named in 1903 by South Vancouver By-law 65, after William F. Granville Thynne, first listed in the first South Vancouver Voters List of 1893. The 1895 assessment roll confirms that he owned a half-acre in Block 32 and an improved half-acre in Block 45, DL 352. The 1894 Provincial Voters List shows William F. Granville Thynne as a nurseryman at Cedar Cottage Nursery.

Waters Road appears on plate 91, *Goad's Atlas,* and on Survey Plan 3142, (1910). Jno. Waters, or J.R. Waters, appears in the 1910 Voters List as owning property in DLs 756 and 757, which adjoin DLs 748 and 749; he is last listed in 1918 at Campbell River. South Vancouver Road Loan By-law 6, 1911, allocated $4,000 to Dumfries, formerly Waters Road, from 15th to 18th Avenues.

Daly Road was surveyed but not named in plan 2318, (1909), which surveyed the easterly three-quarters of DL 705. Using present-day maps and working backwards, I found that DL 705 lies between the present East 31st and East 33rd Avenues. The owner, E.A.C. Studd, was in the investment firm of Studd and Daly. Harold Mayne Daly, previously in the law firm of Burns and Daly, was last listed in the 1914 city directory. However, South Vancouver By-law 141 was incorrect in naming Daly Street as part of Dumfries Street because Daly paralleled Dumfries and should have been renamed as part of Fleming Street.

Ferrisdale Boulevard does not appear on any maps or surveys. Plan 2551, (1910), shows a subdivision plan for a Lauderdale Park that had an unnamed street between the present East 45th and 49th Avenues. Because Lauderdale Park was owned by Herbert Ferris there may have been a partial transfer of names between Ferris Road – now East 49th Avenue – and Lauderdale Park. Ferris was evidently pressuring South Vancouver council for a road, for the council minutes of 21 August 1910 record that "Mr. Ferris [should] be informed that the 40 chains on Ferris Road provided by the by-law had already been built and that council [can]not promise any further extension this year"

Looking again at Plate 95 one can see both new and old names: Inverness, formerly Dorchester and Thomas; Culloden, formerly Montana and O'Connor; and Argyle, formerly Earl. These new names are all Scottish place names. Did homesick Scots dominate the Street Naming Committee or was it influenced by the existence of Duff and Stirling Streets, both Scottish-sounding names? It is dangerous to assume too much! Further research reveals that Stirling Street bears the name of an English lawyer, Archibald William Stirling, who was entrusted with the estate of T.W. Duff of London, England.

Many pioneer names also vanished when South Vancouver reworked its street names in December 1910. Draper Street, now part of St. George, had been named after James Draper, who had settled in Hatzic as a rancher in 1889 but had come to South Vancouver in 1906. Grimmett Avenue, now part of Sophia Street, was named for John F. Grimmett, who came to South Vancouver in 1905. A Grimmett Post Office existed until 1918, and John Grimmett's son, Daniel, was a South Vancouver councillor. Creery Road, now part of East 58th Avenue, was named after the Creery family, one of whom, Andrew M. Creery, owned property in South Vancouver in 1895, was manager of the insurance department of Bell-Irving and Company, and served as MLA for the Provincial Party in 1924. Paonessa Avenue, now part of East 38th Avenue, is the only Italian name in the street system. It commemorates Giuseppe Paonessa, born in Italy, who owned property in South Vancouver from 1899 until the 1930s.

Obtaining information on individuals was not always possible. The owner might be listed with initials only or might just appear a few times in the voters lists before selling his/her property. Vancouver city directories, until about 1914, included few listings for South Vancouver or Point Grey residents. Of these many disappeared from the Vancouver city directories after 1914, possibly because of the upheaval caused by the First World War. Reference to provincial voters lists and the 1901 Census of Canada helped considerably. But most revealing was the detailed information in the death certificates, 1872-1976, recently made available on microfilm by the British Columbia Division of Vital Statistics.

South Vancouver By-law 141 also changed east- and west-running streets into numbered avenues, but the numbering did not always jibe with that in the adjoining newly created Point Grey municipality, which had seceded from South Vancouver in 1908. Hence anyone doing research in the period before 1929 must remember that 33rd Avenue in Point Grey joined 34th Avenue in South Vancouver. Not until the 1929 amalgamation of the three jurisdictions – Vancouver, South Vancouver, and Point Grey – did avenue numbering become continuous.

In Point Grey, the "Westerners," many of them of the professional and managerial class, wanted to change the municipal tax structure in order to have a policy of land improvements that would provide adequate street and sewer facilities. Because "Easterners" wanted as little taxation as possible, many of them chose to work on the roads rather than to pay taxes. As a result, South Vancouver grew in a more helter skelter manner than did Point Grey.

By 1910 Point Grey electors approved the raising of $300,000 for opening up, constructing, and improving roads within the municipality. With the experience gained from seeing how inefficient the pattern of streets in South Vancouver was, the new municipality passed a Subdivision Plans Approval By-law that regulated the process of submitting plans for approval. One clause stated that "the naming of all roads, streets and public places shall rest with the municipal council, but this shall not prevent owners from making suggestions" (Point Grey By-law 34, 1912).

Point Grey By-laws 17, 1912, and 17, 1914, changed the names of many roads running north and south to make them agree with adjoining roads in the City of Vancouver. Thus Johnston Road became part of Blenheim Street and York Road became part of Carnarvon. These same by-laws changed east-west street names into numbered avenues, extending southward Vancouver's numbering from the Point Grey boundary at 16th Avenue. Bodwell Road became 33rd Avenue; Whitehead, 37th Avenue; and Wilson, 41st Avenue. Another group of street names that were changed included those in the Eburne Townsite: Townsend, Alberta, Saskatchewan, and Moosomin became 70th to 73rd Avenues.

Meanwhile, back in Vancouver, the city had increased its area by almost 50 per cent with the 1911 annexation of two parcels of land administered by the provincial government: the 2,950 acres of Hastings Townsite and the 350-acre DL 301, which was described as "a squared bit of No Man's land." Henry V. Edmonds, the original owner of DL 301, had named the streets therein after members of his own family. Of these twenty-five names, only Sophia Street remains. The provincial government, which administered Hastings Townsite, had named its streets after BC mining districts such as Skeena; after BC towns such as Nanaimo; and after universities such as Yale, McGill, and Cambridge.

The next major change occurred with the reclamation of the shallow False Creek tidal flats east of Main Street for the purpose of providing space for a railway passenger station and rail yards. Figure 3, a diagram published in the *Vancouver Daily Province*, 4 May 1912, shows the proposed plan for the Great Northern Railway site. The filling in of the northern shore of the creek absorbed many old streets, obliterating the names: Grove Crescent, Grove and Bayview Streets, and Crabtree and Park Lanes.

Figure 3 also shows the city-owned land as a shipping basin (but actually tidal flats, shallow and smelly), but eventually the city filled it in to become part of the yards of the Canadian Northern Pacific Railway, later the Canadian National Railways. New streets with obvious names appeared: Station and National Streets and Industrial and Terminal Avenues.

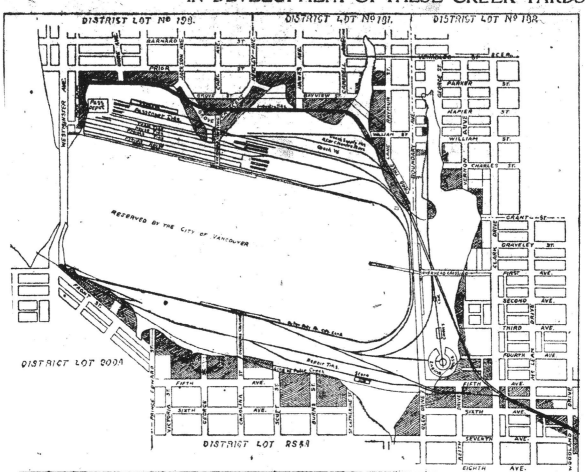

Figure 3: *Daily Province,* 4 May 1912.

On 1 January 1929, the enlarged City of Vancouver came into existence when the three municipalities, South Vancouver, and Vancouver, were amalgamated. Prior to amalgamation, committees had begun to plan the incorporation of the suburban police and fire departments into the Vancouver system, but the coordination of street names was deferred. By-law 2014 (7 October 1929), By-law 2028 (2 January 1930), and By-law 2082 (14 July 1930) renamed various streets in order to remove duplications and renumbered all the South Vancouver avenues south of East 33rd Avenue to the river, making them continuous with those of Point Grey.

These three major street-naming by-laws were the work of the special Street Naming Committee that continued to function under the Building, Civic Planning and Parks Committee, a standing committee of the civic government. Recommendations concerning street names are recorded in the minutes of the standing committee.

On 15 May 1940, the Street Naming Committee recommended that it would be advisable for the city engineer to prepare an official street names map; to repeal all existing street name by-laws; and to adopt a new by-law embodying the proposed map. On 22 December 1941 – two weeks after the Pearl Harbor attack of 7 December – the chairman of the Street Naming Committee, Alderman Buscombe, reported that, although progress had been made, "owing to war conditions it would be inadvisable to make any drastic changes in the arrangement of names, and therefore requested the committee be dismissed and not re-appointed until a more opportune time." This report was tabled.

Indeed it was not until April 1963 – twenty-two years later and after tremendous postwar growth in Vancouver – that By-law 4054, which repealed all sixty-four previous street naming by-laws and made Plan L 325 the official street naming map, was passed.

The creation of new subdivisions had added new streets. Those to the north of Queen Elizabeth Park have a literary flavor – Nigel, Peveril, Talisman, and Midlothian – all taken from the novels of Sir Walter Scott, as suggested by William B. Young of the city's engineering staff. Decisions to improve traffic flow resulted in the creation of connectors such as the Kitsilano and Boyd diversions. The old names of Scott and Burns disappeared in 1948 and 1950, respectively, to become extensions of Prince Albert and Fraser Streets. One can still see the old names stamped in the sidewalk near East 15th Avenue. Major additions since Second World War were veterans' housing subdivisions: Renfrew Heights in 1948 and Fraserview in 1950-2. The original suggestion was to name streets in Renfrew Heights after animals, but on 13 March 1948, Alderman Halford Wilson, Chairman of the Street Naming Committee and a well-known veteran of the Second World War, announced that those streets would bear the names of campaigns and battles conducted in the two world wars: Vimy, Anzio, and Normandy amongst them. Because the Fraserview subdivision is adjacent to Fraserview Golf Course, at the suggestion of James A. Walker, Secretary of the Town Planning Commission, its streets took on the names of well-known golf courses. In the late 1970s, the False Creek Development Group, responsible for the development of city-owned lands in the False Creek basin, suggested names such as Foundry Walk and Sawyers Lane, in keeping with the area's industrial and lumbering history.

All of the streets so far mentioned are "dedicated roads"; that is, roads on city property for which the city is responsible. However, private roads or thoroughfares can be found on private property, such as Granville Island, where the Vancouver Harbour Commission, original administrators of the island, created a few private roads in the 1920s. It later named them Anderson, Duranleau, and Johnston after officials in the Department of Marine and Fisheries, under whose jurisdiction the commission fell. Present administrators of the island, the Central Mortgage and Housing Corporation, gave newer roads (such as Old Bridge Road and Railspur Alley) their names.

The city's policy on the naming of private roads was stated in the Board of Administration meeting of 14 January 1957 (City Council Minutes, v. 66, p. 360). The Department of National Defence requested that four names be assigned to roads within the military housing project at 4th Avenue and Highbury

Street. The board pointed out that since the four roads were not public streets they could not be dedicated, but there would be no objection to the federal government giving them names as long as they not be classed as city streets, that the names not conflict with the master list of street names for Greater Vancouver, and that the Department of National Defence erect the necessary signs. The streets are Antwerp and Ghent Lanes, and Ortona and Salerno Crescents.

This policy for naming private thoroughfares in the many new condominium developments still exists. Developers choose names and submit them to the Street Naming Committees for approval. This committee is comprised of the city surveyor, representatives of the Permits and Licences, Fire, Planning, and Law departments, and the city clerk (who is its chair). The committee considers whether a proposed name could be easily confused with another; whether it could sound garbled in an emergency 911 call; whether it is duplicated in an adjacent municipality; and whether it fits in with the history of the area.

The area with the greatest number of private thoroughfares – eighty-seven in seventeen enclaves – is Champlain Heights, the last large piece of city-owned land to be developed. In 1970 By-Law 4770 deleted most of the grid system of streets between East 48th Avenue and South East Marine Drive, and between Boundary Road and Kerr Street, and substituted a new layout of dedicated roads, shown on Plan LF 4530. Many of the old street names in south east Vancouver disappeared.

There was much discussion in city council and in the planning department about how to develop Champlain Heights. New ideas about city planning favour the concept of distinct neighbourhoods linked to each other by a system of pedestrian walkways rather than the conventional grid layout of a typical subdivision. In 1978 By-law 5195 changed the road system shown in the 1970 by-law. Seventeen enclaves were formed to accommodate various types of housing – for-profit market housing, cooperative housing, and social housing. Within each enclave the private thoroughfares were named by the developer or owner and approved by the Street Naming Committee.

Choosing names for housing developments is a serious business because developers must consider marketing: a good catchy name can lure a potential buyer. In Champlain Heights the idea of having a park-like setting for a home is conveyed by names such as Dartmoor, Lynmoor, and Weymoor – all located in the Moorpark development. Park Place thoroughfares bear names of provincial parks, among them Appledale, Garibaldi, and Kokanee. Community Builders, the developers of Ashleigh Heights, wanted names with a "soft, elegant sound and ... associated with history in a sophisticated manner." To this end they chose Brahms, Handel , Strauss, and Vivaldi .

Sometimes requests are made to change existing street names in order to commemorate an important person or event. Examples include wanting to change Commercial Drive to Via Garibaldi; Rosemont Drive to Kopernik Drive; and Union Street to Victory Street. While it might be sympathetic to the motives behind such requests, city council must consider the cost involved (e.g., changing all the street signs, maps, tax forms, postal addresses, stationery, and computer data) and usually denies them.

Although Vancouver is now a multicultural society, its street names do not reflect this reality. Most are of British origin and replicate the names of places in the "Old Country" or important people or events in British history: all indicate the dominant, founding culture. Although Canada is, officially, a bilingual country, French street names are rare in Vancouver. The few that do exist (e.g., Montcalm, Champlain, and Quesnel) relate to the New France and fur-trade eras in Canadian history. A few Spanish names commemorate early Spanish explorers – Narvaez, Galiano, and Valdez. Other European names (such as Bismarck, Oppenheimer, Paonessa, and Rosenberg) have disappeared. There is one Chinese street name – Sotao Avenue, a private thoroughfare named by the developer and approved by the city in 1996 – even though in 1996 over 24 per cent of Vancouver's population was Chinese. Prior to that time, Canton and Shanghai Alleys in "Chinatown" acknowledged the geographic origin of most of the Chinese immigrants. An important group is almost totally ignored in the city's street names. Here long before the Europeans, First Nations peoples had given names to the area in which they lived; but, as these names were only recorded orally, they were replaced with European ones. A few streets bear Native names – Cree, Haida, and Kamloops amongst them – that were assigned by Europeans; but none of these is relevant to this region and its language. Until recently, Kitsilano, an Anglicization of Khahtsahlano, the name of a chief of the Squamish band, was the only street name drawn from the local Squamish and Halkomelem languages. In 1966, with the creation of the Musqueam Park subdivision, the city proposed that area streets be given names of well-known professional golfers because the subdivision abuts Shaughnessy golf course. However, the Musqueam Band, from which the subdivision is leased, rejected this and suggested instead Halss, Semana, Sennock, and Tamath – the names of former Musqueam settlements.

The origins of the seventeen existing female street names are difficult to verify. Some are family names bestowed by the property owner: Marguerite (Lord Shaughnessy's daughter) and Sophia (Edmonds). Others are of indeterminate origin: Lily, Rose, and Ruby. Alexandra, Elizabeth, and Victoria are royal family names. In a male-dominated civic government it is hardly surprising that few names of female origin have been bestowed. In 1929, Frances Street was named after Sister Frances Redmond, and, in 1996, Gaston Street was named after Sadie Gaston, a community leader in the Collingwood district.

In researching the origin of street names I used three main sources: survey plans, civic documents, and social history. All survey plans are at the Land Registry Office in New Westminster, while duplicates of those in current use are also found at the City Surveyor's Office in Vancouver. The civic documents of Point Grey, South Vancouver, and Vancouver – by-laws, council minutes, voters lists – are well arranged and readily available at the City of Vancouver Archives or in various civic departments. And social and cultural history! A wealth of it exists in the holdings of the City of Vancouver Archives: manuscripts, maps, pamphlets, photographs, and city directories. Many Vancouver companies and societies have donated their records. Finding aids and inventories help to give access to the information contained in them.

Much of the earlier material was collected by the indefatigable Major James Skitt Matthews, a Welshman who came to Vancouver by way of New Zealand in 1898. Around 1920 he started collecting the private papers – and recording the memories – of pioneers. He was appointed the city's first official archivist from June 1933 until his death on 1 October 1970, at the age of ninety-two. He made Vancouver aware of the importance of its past before it had forgotten or destroyed much of the documentary evidence. The major's extensive collection of lore about Vancouver street names, held at the City of Vancouver Archives, reinforced my interest to unearth and verify their origins.

From all the information gathered I had to decide what to include and what to omit. All streets named to the end of 1996 are included, however obvious the origin of the name; the date of naming is part of the history of city development. Due to space limitations the colourful details of individual lives do not appear – only sufficient information to identify them properly. The history of various streets – their physical, commercial, and residential development – is beyond the scope of this project. My hope is that the information contained in this work will lead others to wander the byways of Vancouver history in order to uncover and reveal other interesting facets of its past.

Street Names of Vancouver

A

"A" ROAD. Now West 70th Avenue between Granville and Ash Streets. A survey designation listed in *B.C. Gazette*, 25 January 1900, p. 198.

ABBOTT STREET. Named after Harry Braithwaite Abbott (1820-1915), first general superintendent of the Pacific Division, CPR, 1886-97.

   Wood Street. A short street named arbitrarily on a fire insurance plan of Granville, British Columbia, August 1885, and published by Sanborn Map and Publishing Company (Map 14258), it lay approximately where the present Abbott Street is, just south of the present Water Street.

Harry Abbott, as portrayed in *British Columbians as We See 'Em, 1910 and 1911,* (Vancouver: Newspaper Cartoonist Association of British Columbia, 1911).

Before the arrival of the CPR, "Vancouver" was a logging village one block long. The influence of the CPR is reflected in the many street names with CPR associations: Abbott, Baillie, Beatty, Bodwell, Cambie, Hamilton, Manson, Salsbury, Shaughnessy, Stephens, Strathcona, Angus, Hosmer, Matthews Nanton, Osler, Creelman, McNicoll, Ogden, and Whyte.

ABERDEEN STREET. Named 1910, South Vancouver By-law 146, perhaps after Aberdeen, Scotland, or after John Campbell Gordon, seventh earl of Aberdeen and Governor-General of Canada, 1893-8. This by-law renamed Beauchoux Road and Theta Street.

   Beauchoux Road. Between Kingsway and Foster, named after French-born Alphonse Beauchoux (1872-1936), who owned property shown on Plan 1678 (1907). He became a storekeeper at Agassiz, where he died 3 November 1936.

   Theta Street. Named on Plan 1477 (1907) and shown in *Goad's Atlas*, Plate 113, between Dudley and Cromwell Streets south of the CPR. Theta is the eighth letter in the Greek alphabet and may refer to the eight survey posts needed for the six acreages shown on Plan 1477. Now closed.

   Almas Street. Named Almas Road until 1910 after Alfred Ernest Almas (1862-1960), in 1907 a councillor in South Vancouver. Became Almas Street, South Vancouver By-law 141, 1910, reconfirmed by South Vancouver By-law 251, 1913. Changed to Aberdeen Street between Vanness and Wellington in 1929, Vancouver By-law 2014.

   On 24 October 1995 the Street Naming Committee approved an extension to Aberdeen Street between Euclid Avenue and Crowley Drive (Plan LF 11676).

ACKERY ALLEY. The alley behind the Orpheum Theatre, 884 Granville Street, named after Ivan Ackery (1899-1989), prominent Vancouver theatre manager. On 30 October 1985 Mayor Michael Harcourt proclaimed the day as Ivan Ackery Day and presented him with a centennial plaque naming the alley in his honour.

ADANAC STREET. Named 1930, By-law 2082, when Union Street between Vernon Drive and Boundary Road were renamed. An article about the death of Mrs. Mary Ann Galbraith stated that she had been active in a campaign that succeeded in changing Union Street to Adanac Street because, in those days, disreputable activities had taken place on Union Street (near Main Street) (*Vancover Sun*, 15 October 1974, p. 58). "Adanac" is Canada spelled backwards.

ADERA STREET. Named by Point Grey By-law 17, 1914, after an unidentified person or place. The street extended from 41st Avenue West to 57th Avenue West. Now extends to South West Marine Drive.

Howe Street. Shown on Plans 1982 (1909) and 3563 (1911) between West 62nd and West 65th Avenues. A survey name after Samuel Lyness Howe (1864-1939), first reeve of Point Grey municipality in 1908. Later provincial secretary and minister of mines in the Tolmie government, 1928.

Hon. S.L. Howe. From group photo of the Reeves of Point Grey, 1908-1928. CVA, Port. P. 188, N. 306 #3.

AEGEAN CRESCENT. Private thoroughfare in Champlain Heights first listed in 1982 city directory. Henriquez and Partners, architects, chose Mediterranean place names for the enclave.

AGNES ROAD. Now East 22nd Avenue between Knight Street and Victoria Drive. Named by South Vancouver By-law 65, 1903, after Agnes Livingstone Fowler, donor of the land on which St. Margaret's Anglican Church now stands (Hamilton 1957). First listed in 1902 South Vancouver Voters List, she died 27 June 1912. Changed to East 22nd Avenue in 1910, South Vancouver By-law 141.

AISNE STREET. Unnamed on Plan 3038 (1910) but named December 1914 as Aines [sic] by Point Grey By-law 17, 1914. Point Grey By-law 32, 1919, corrected the spelling to Aisne, which commemorates the first of three battles of the Aisne fought in the valley of the Aisne River, France, in September 1914.

ALAMEIN AVENUE. Named 1946, By-law 2961, to commemorate the Battle of El Alamein, fought in 1942 near El Alamein, Egypt. This part of West 25th Avenue between Puget Drive and Trafalgar Street was renamed to avoid confusion with King Edward Avenue West, which, elsewhere, is synonymous with 25th Avenue.

ALBERNI STREET. Named after the Alberni Canal, shown on the map that L.A. Hamilton used when assigning street names in DL 185, now the West End of Vancouver. Alberni Canal was named after Don Pedro de Alberni, who was with the Eliza expedition to Nootka Sound in 1790.

ALBERT ROAD. See Nanaimo Street.

ALBERT STREET. See Franklin Street.

ALBERTA AVENUE. Now West 71st Avenue between Granville and Selkirk Streets. Named on Plan 1749 (1908), a plan of Eburne Townsite, likely after the newly formed province of Alberta (created in 1905). Changed to West 71st Avenue by Point Grey By-law 14, 1914.

ALBERTA STREET. Named on Plan 1530 (1907), although surveyed on Plan 177 (1884), after the recently created province of Alberta. The name maintains the theme of Canadian provinces established by Dr. I.W. Powell. South Vancouver By-law 141, 1910, changed *Centre Street* to Alberta Street between present West 59th and West 62nd Avenues (an area since absorbed by Winona Park). Named after its position in the centre of three blocks shown on Plan 1765 (1908). In 1945, By-law 3081 changed Yukon Street between West 37th and West 41st Avenues to Alberta and extended it to West 45th. The existing Alberta Street became Elizabeth Street. In 1976, By-law 5010 extended Alberta Street 500 feet south of West 49th Avenue. A short portion exists between West 58th and West 59th Avenues.

ALDER BAY COURT AND ALDER BAY WALK. Private thoroughfares at Alder Bay on the south side of False Creek. Names were approved by the Street Naming Committee on 15 August 1974.

ALDER CROSSING. Named 1976, By-law 5010, for the overhead crossing above the CPR right of way, it connects West 6th Avenue with Lamey's Mill Road on False Creek lands and lies west of Alder Street.

ALDER STREET. Officially registered on Plan 590 (1891) but named on an 1887 map (Map 14160) by L.A. Hamilton, who chose tree names for the large block of land between Cambie and Yew Streets.

ALEXANDER STREET. Shown on Plan 196. Named by L.A. Hamilton after Richard Henry Alexander (1844-1915), one of the "Overlanders" of 1862, who started as an accountant at Hastings Sawmill and became its manager in 1882.

R. Alexander. From group photo of Commissioners and Pilots of Vancouver Pilotage District, 1879-1916. CVA Port. P. 189, N. 138.

ALEXANDRA STREET (DLs 36 and 51). See Ann Street.

ALEXANDRA STREET. Named after Queen Alexandra (1894-1925), widowed consort of King Edward VII, by the CPR, which developed Shaughnessy Heights. Shown on Plan 4502 (1913). Extended to Connaught Drive in 1926, Plan 6011.

ALICE STREET (DL 352). Named 1913, South Vancouver By-law 251, after an unknown woman.

Mills Avenue. Unofficial name shown in *Goad's Atlas*, Plate 91. South Vancouver Road Loan By-law, 1911, allocated $400 to Mills Avenue, south of 22nd Avenue. Clement and Elizabeth Mills each owned property in DL 352 from 1908 to 1913, according to South Vancouver Voters Lists.

ALLAN ROAD. Now East 29th Avenue, one-half block west from Fraser Street to St. George Street. Named on Plan 1220 (1906), after owner Thomas Allan, who appears in South Vancouver Voters Lists, 1908-10. Survey name only.

ALMA STREET. Named Alma Road in 1907, By-law 573, when Campbell Street was renamed after the Alma River in the Russian Ukraine, the site of the first battle of the Crimean War in 1854. One of the "battle" names suggested by Miss Doris Bulwer, when T.H. Calland, an alderman in 1907, remarked that several streets in Kitsilano should be renamed. Other battle names chosen were Balaclava, Blenheim, Trafalgar, and Waterloo.

Campbell Street (DL 540). Named on "Plan of Provincial Government Property to Be Sold at Victoria by Public Auction, Monday, January 18, 1886" (Map CVA 743). Origin of name unknown.

ALMAS STREET. See Aberdeen Street.

ALVES ROAD. Now East 28th Avenue between Welwyn and Commercial Streets. Unnamed on Plan 1540 (1907). Hector Alves, joiner, listed in Vancouver city directory, 1911-4, on Alves Road (an unofficial name).

ALVIN NAROD MEWS. Private thoroughfare near Pacific Boulevard (Plan LF 11478 [1991]). Named after Alvin Jackson Narod (1921-83), founder of Narod Construction Company, which built large projects such as Langara Gardens, Arbutus Village, and the George Massey Tunnel.

AMBERLEY PLACE. Private thoroughfare between South East Marine Drive and Marine Way (Plan LF 11464 [1991]). Named by Redekop Properties Limited. Origin of name unknown.

AMBREY ROAD. Now East 24th Avenue between Gladstone and Brant Streets. A survey name only, origin unknown, shown on Plan 4492 (1913), owner Mary Hanbury. Also known as Hanbury Avenue. Shown in *Goad's Atlas*, Plate 92.

ANACONDA AVENUE. Now East 34th Avenue between Culloden and Commercial Streets. Named on Plan 1522 (1907), after Anaconda, Montana. Dr. S.E. Flemings, care of Panton and Hutchison, owned property in DL 700 in 1907. Samuel Panton connected with the Montana Company, a real estate firm, hence the street name.

Changed to East 35th Avenue, South Vancouver By-law 141, 1910, and to East 34th Avenue in 1929, By-law 2028.

ANCASTER CRESCENT. Named 1952, By-law 3330. J. Alexander Walker, secretary, Vancouver Town Planning Commission, suggested that streets in the Fraserview development, adjacent to the Fraserview Golf Course, bear names of well-known golf courses. Hamilton Golf and Country Club is located at Ancaster, Ontario.

ANDERSON STREET consists of a private thoroughfare on Granville Island and a dedicated street between Granville Street and the boundary of Granville Island.

In 1923 the Vancouver Harbour Commission decided to replace the plank roads on Granville Island with permanent roads. Anderson Street was probably named after Frederick Anderson, chief hydrographer, Department of Marine and Fisheries, 1926-31, to which the Harbour Commission reported.

The dedicated roadway between Granville Street and the boundary of Granville Island was named Anderson Street in 1984, By-law 5741 (Plan LF 9615). In 1996, By-law 7590 (LF 11681) renamed the part of Granville Street under the Granville Bridge north of West 3rd Avenue Anderson Street to remove confusion (Administrative report to city council, 30 April 1996).

ANGLER'S PLACE. Private thoroughfare on the Angus Lands (Plan LF 11138). The name, approved by the Street Naming Committee on 27

August 1987, suggests the marine activity on the nearby Fraser River.

ANGUS DRIVE. Originally named Angus Street by Point Grey By-law 18, 1910, after Richard Bladworth Angus (1831-1922), a director of the CPR who had extensive holding in DL 526 (the CPR land grant). It went south from King Edward Avenue to Marine Drive. Point Grey By-law 17, 1912, confirmed Angus Street as being, at that time, between King Edward Avenue and West 27th Avenue and between West 41st and 49th Avenues.

In 1913, the CPR developed Shaughnessy Heights and named one of the streets therein Angus Avenue (Plan 4502), which joined Angus Street at King Edward Avenue.

Inconsistencies had appeared and some parts of Angus Street were called Angus Avenue. Point Grey By-law 585, 1925, stated that the street in its entirety was to be known as Angus Drive. Evidently inconsistencies still appeared because in 1950 Vancouver By-law 3195 reiterated that Angus Avenue, Angus Drive, and Angus Street were to be known as Angus Drive.

ANGUS ROAD. Now the Grandview Highway between Skeena Street and Boundary Road. A survey name, of unknown origin, shown on Plans 1377 and 1616 (1907), it became East 13th Avenue. In 1946 By-law 2961 changed this part of East 13th Avenue to Grandview Highway.

ANGUS ROAD. Now East and West 45th Avenue. Named by South Vancouver Highway By-law, 1905, after Richard Bladworth Angus (1831-1922), a director of the CPR, who had extensive holdings in DL 526 (the CPR land grant). It lay between the present Granville Street and Angus Drive and gradually extended east and west. When Point Grey and South Vancouver municipality separated in 1908, Angus Road lay in two jurisdictions.

Point Grey By-law 17, 1912, changed its part of Angus Road to 45th Avenue. South Vancouver By-law 141, 1910, changed its part to 47th Avenue East and West. With amalgamation in 1929, 47th Avenue became 45th Avenue, Vancouver By-law 2028, 1929.

ANN STREET. Named as "Anne" Street in South Vancouver By-law 252, 1913. Origin of name unknown. Changed from *Alexander Street* [sic], an incorrect spelling of Alexandra Street, named on Plans 3159 and 3262, (1910), after Queen Alexandra (1844-1929), consort of Edward VII.

ANTWERP LANE. Private thoroughfare in the Canadian Forces Base near Jericho Park, first listed in the 1958 Vancouver directory. Named after Antwerp, Belgium, captured and occupied by German troops in two world wars and liberated by Allied troops.

ANZIO DRIVE. In Renfrew Heights subdivision, developed by Central Mortgage and Housing Corporation as low rental housing for Second World War veterans. On 23 March 1948, Vancouver City Council approved the recommendations of the Vancouver Town Planning Commission that the streets in Renfrew Heights be named after personalities, battles, and events of the two world wars. Anzio, Italy, was the scene of a fierce battle in January 1944.

APPLEDALE PLACE. Private thoroughfare in Champlain Heights named after Appledale Provincial Park on Slocan Lake. Developers of Park Place named thoroughfares after provincial parks. Name approved by the Street Naming Committee on 21 June 1978.

AQUA DRIVE. Private thoroughfare in the Marin Vista development. Name approved by the Street Naming Committee on 21 January 1985.

ARBOR AVENUE. Named 1970, By-law 4770, Plan LF 4530, after adjacent Arbor Street in Burnaby, named 1917, Burnaby By-law 218. In 1978, By-law 5195, Plan LE 3742B, retained the name but changed the alignment.

ARBUTUS DIVERSION. Named 1948, By-law 3081. The diagonal connection between West 53rd and West 54th Avenues made to facilitate traffic along Arbutus Street and West Boulevard to South West Marine Drive.

ARBUTUS STREET. Officially registered on Plan 590 (1891) but named on an 1887 map (Map 14160) by L.A. Hamilton, who chose tree names. Point Grey By-law 6, 1912, extended it from West 16th Avenue to West 37th Avenue. Point Grey By-law 17, 1914, further extended it from West 49th Avenue to the Fraser River and also renamed Stewart Road from West 53rd Avenue to the Fraser River.

Stewart Road. Named by Point Grey By-law 35, 1911, after William Francis Stewart (1853-1926), operator of a steamboat on the Fraser River. In 1908, Stewart was elected to the first council for the newly formed Point Grey municipality and served two years; became police magistrate for Point Grey in 1912. Married Jane McCleery, widow of Samuel McCleery.

See also *Boulevard, East and West.*

ARCHIMEDES STREET. First named on Plan 2362 (1908) as Archimedes Avenue. Probably named because of its proximity to Euclid Avenue. Archimedes was a Syracusan mathematician famous for his discoveries in applied mechanics.

ARGYLE DRIVE. Named 1952, By-law 3330, Plan Ga 49, when the Fraserview subdivision was developing. Branching northeast from Argyle Street at East 58th Avenue, it perpetuates an old South Vancouver street name.

ARGYLE PLACE. Now East 46th Avenue between Argyle and Bruce Streets. Named by South Vancouver By-law 251, 1913, after its location adjacent to Argyle Street. South Vancouver By-law 1956, 1928, changed it to 47th Place, but this name was probably not used because of the impending 1929 amalgamation with Vancouver. Listed as Argyle Place until 1950, when By-law 3195 changed it to East 46th Avenue.

ARGYLE STREET. Named by South Vancouver By-law 141, 1910, probably after Argyle, Scotland. The same by-law also renamed Earl, Herbert, Rugby, McFarlane, and McRae Streets.

Earl Street. Between East 33rd and East 37th Avenues, shown on Plans 3889 and 4197 (1912) as Earls. Origin of name unknown.

Herbert Road. One-third of the way between East 47th and East 49th Avenues. Named on Plan 3161 (1909) after one of the owners, George Herbert Dawson (1866-1940), a surveyor in Vancouver and later, in 1911, surveyor-general of British Columbia.

Rugby Avenue. Between East 45th and East 49th Avenues, named on Plan 1966 (1909). Origin of name unknown.

McFarlane Road. Not named on any map. A 1910 map of South Vancouver (Map 14083) shows an unnamed street in District Lot 728 between the present East 56th and East 58th Avenues. The name was in use in 1909 when South Vancouver council minutes, on 18 September 1909, instructed the road foreman for Ward I to clear boulevard on McFarlane Road on north side for laying sidewalk.

McRae Road. Between South East Marine Drive and the Fraser River. George Wallace McRae (1852-1913) cosigned Plan 1660 (1907), as one of the trustees for the Mary Rowling estate. Principal of Fairview School for twelve years before going into real estate, at his death on 20 April 1913 in North Vancouver, he was secretary-treasurer of United Western Property Company, Vancouver, and an alderman in North Vancouver.

ARLINGTON STREET. Named 1930, By-law 2082, when it was changed from Minto Street to remove duplication with Minto Crescent in Shaughnessy. Origin of name unknown. It lay between East 45th and East 65th Avenues. When Champlain Heights was replotted, By-law 4470, 1970, Plan LF 4530, changed its alignment below East 48th Avenue.

Minto Street. Named by South Vancouver By-law 251, 1913, probably after 4th Earl of Minto, Governor-General of Canada, 1898-1904.

ARMSTRONG STREET. See Sophia Street.

ARMYTAGE ROAD. See Stirling Street.

ARNOLD AVENUE. Now East 23rd Avenue between Rupert and Cassiar Streets. After Albert Frederick Arnold (1877-1965), signature shown on Plan 1769 (1907), associated with Canadian Financiers Limited from 1908 to 1931.

ARNOLD AVENUE. Now East 33rd Avenue between Victoria Drive and Slocan Street. Named on Plan 1955 (1909), probably after Albert Frederick Arnold (1877-1965), owner of property in the vicinity and associated with Canadian Financiers Limited, 1908-31. Changed to East 34th Avenue in 1910, South Vancouver By-law 141, and to East 33rd Avenue in 1929, By-law 2028. A survey name.

ARTHUR STREET. Now East 23rd Avenue between Main and Knight Streets. Shown on Plan 187 (1885) and named by the owner of DL 301, H.V. Edmonds, after a family member, Arthur Black. When Vancouver absorbed DL 301 in 1911, the street became part of East 23rd Avenue.

ASCOT PLACE. Private thoroughfare shown on Plan LF 11504 (1992). The developer, Vancouver Land Corporation, arbitrarily chose the English place name of Ascot, site of the fashionable two-mile racetrack.

ASH CRESCENT. Private thoroughfare between West 54th and West 57th Avenues in Langara Gardens development. First listed in 1969 city directory, it derives its name from nearby Ash Street.

ASH STREET (DL 540). See Simpson Avenue.

ASH STREET. Officially registered on Plan 590 (1891) but named on an 1887 map (Map 14160) by L.A. Hamilton, who chose tree names. By-laws that extended it to its present length were Point Grey By-law 17, 1912, and Vancouver By-laws 3250 (1951) and 3731 (1958).

Martin Street (DL 311). Name proposed in a motion from South Vancouver Board of Works, 19 November 1915, to rename portion of Ash Street from Marine Drive to the Fraser River. No action was taken, however. George Martin (1853-1929), property owner in DL 311 according to South Vancouver Voters List, 1910, was a partner in the real estate firm of Martin and Shannon.

"B" Road. Now Ash Street between West 59th Avenue and the Fraser River. A survey designation only, described in *B.C. Gazette*, 25 January 1900, p. 198.

ASHBURN STREET. Named 1961, By-law 3937, follows the golf course theme established in the Fraserview development. Ashburn Golf Club is at Armdale, Nova Scotia, near Halifax.

ASPEN AVENUE. Named by Point Grey By-law 483, 1926, to continue the pattern of naming streets after trees.

ASQUITH AVENUE (Deleted). Changed from the former East 61st Avenue of South Vancouver between Nanaimo and Vivian Streets and between Kerr Street and Boundary Road in 1929, Vancouver By-law 2028. Named after Herbert Henry Asquith (1852-1928), prime minister of Great Britain, 1908-16. Asquith Avenue disappeared with the replotting of Fraserview (By-law 3330, 1952, Plan Ga 49) and Champlain Heights (By-law 4470, 1970, Plan LF 4530). The last year a resident was listed on Asquith Avenue was 1968.

ATHLONE STREET. Named 1950, By-law 3195, after the Earl of Athlone (1874-1957), Governor-General of Canada, 1940-6.

Willingdon Place. Named by Point Grey By-law 294, 1928, after the Marquis of Willingdon (1866-1941), Governor-General of Canada, 1926-31, who visited the Municipality of Point Grey on 13 April 1927. Changed to Athlone Street in 1950 to remove duplication with Willingdon Avenue in Burnaby.

Rt. Hon. The Earl of Athlone Governor General. CVA Port. P. 1427, N. 748.

ATLANTIC STREET. Named after the Atlantic Ocean in 1916, By-law 1278. Filling in the easterly part of False Creek altered the pattern of streets to the north; Grove Avenue and Bayview became part of Atlantic Street.

Bayview Street. Shown on "Plan of the city of Vancouver, British Columbia," compiled in 1886 by H.B. Smith, and in *Goad's Atlas*, Plates 72 and 75. Name descriptive of its location on an arm of False Creek.

Grove Crescent and *Grove Avenue.* Shown on Plan 196, Grove Crescent was a crescent that lay at the end of a point of land extending south into False Creek between Heatley and Jackson Avenues. When False Creek was filled in, Grove Crescent disappeared. Grove Avenue lay south of Prior Street between Heatley and Jackson Avenues and became part of Atlantic Street, By-law 1278. Name probably descriptive of a grove of trees in the locality.

ATLIN STREET. Named after Atlin Mining Division in 1915, By-law 1230, which renamed Cedar Street. Atlin is derived from a Tlingit word "aht-lah," meaning "big lake" (Akrigg 1997).

Cedar Street (THSL). Shown on Plan 1259 (1906). Changed to Atlin Street to remove duplication with Cedar Street (DL 526), now part of Burrard Street.

AUBREY PLACE. Changed from 29th Place in 1929, By-law 2014. See page 135. According to Spencer Robinson, former South Vancouver municipal official, named after George Aubrey (1859-1943), bookkeeper and accountant who came to Vancouver around 1890 and, according to South Vancouver Voters List, owned acreage in 1905. He died 4 March 1943, when he was trapped by a running fire on his property on Capilano Road, North Vancouver.

29th Place. Named after its location between East 29th and East 30th Avenues. Unnamed on Plans 2558 (1910) and 3493 (1911). First listed in 1917 city directory.

AUGUSTA AVENUE. Now East 37th Avenue, between Culloden and Commercial Streets. Named on Plan 1522 (1907), after Augusta, Montana. Dr. S.E. Fleming, care of Panton and Hutchison, owned property in DL 700 in 1907. Samuel Panton was connected with the Montana Company, a real estate firm, hence the street name. Changed to East 38th Avenue by South Vancouver By-law 141, 1910, and to East 37th Avenue in 1929, By-law 2028.

AUSTREY AVENUE. Surveyed but not named on Plans 1889 (1909), 2177 (1909), and 2741 (1910). First listed in 1914 city directory. Origin of name unknown.

AVERY AVENUE. Changed from Robinson Avenue in 1929, By-law 2014. Origin of name unknown.

Robinson Avenue/Place (DL 318). Named by Point Grey By-law 32, 1919, as Robinson Avenue. However, Point Grey By-law 232, 1924, named the same street Robinson Place. South Vancouver Voters List, 1906, shows Richard Robinson owning property in DL 318. Plan 2978 (1910) shows R. Robinson subdividing Block F, DL 318, where present Avery Street lies.

AVISON WAY. Private thoroughfare in Stanley Park, Plan LF 11621. Named by Vancouver Board of Parks and Recreation, 4 July 1994, after the first employee of the Parks Board, Henry Avison (1855-1924), who cut the first trails and roadways in the park. He became a constable at Prince George, British Columbia, where he died 2 April

Henry Stanley Avison, first white child born in Stanley Park after it was opened in September 1888 and son of Henry Avison, first "Park Ranger," 1888-1898; was present with other family members at the formal naming of "Avison Trail," 8 December 1947. CVA Port. P. 200, N. 61.

1924. Its naming came in response to a request from the Vancouver Public Aquarium, which needed an officially recognized address for postal delivery.

B

"B" ROAD. See Ash Street.

BAILLIE STREET. Named 1951, By-law 3250, after George Henry Baillie, vice-president for operations for CPR in Vancouver.

BALACLAVA STREET. Named by By-law 573, 1907, after the Battle of Balaclava, 1854, scene of the famous charge of the Light Brigade, as suggested by Miss Dora Bulwer (see Alma Street). Formerly *Richards Street*, from English Bay to West 16th Avenue, shown on Plan 229 (1887), and named after the Honourable Albert Norton Richards (1822-97), lieutenant-governor of British Columbia, 1876-81. Renamed to remove duplication with Richards Street in downtown Vancouver.

Point Grey By-law 17, 1912, extended Balaclava south from West 16th Avenue to the Fraser River and changed *Stirling Road* between West 53rd and West 55th Avenues to Balaclava. Named on Plans 2213 and 2242 (1909), probably after Stirling, Scotland, in association with other British street names in the area.

BALDWIN STREET. Named 1950, By-law 3195, after Robert Baldwin (1804-58), who twice served as joint premier of the United Provinces of Upper and Lower Canada and was an advocate of responsible government. Formerly *Buller Street*. Named 1913, South Vancouver By-law 251, after Edmund Ridley Buller (1846-1918), property owner shown on Plan 3086 (1910). In 1967, By-law 4311, Plan LF 2839, extended the street from Galt to Brock.

BALFOUR AVENUE. Named on Plan 4502 (1913), after Arthur James Balfour (1848-1930), prime minister of Great Britain, 1902-5.

BALKAN STREET. Named 1913, South Vancouver By-law 251. Probably to commemorate the Balkan Wars of 1912 and 1913. Unverified.

AVONDALE AVENUE. Named by Point Grey By-law 232, 1924, and reconfirmed by Point Grey By-law 483, 1926. Shown on Plan 5552 (1926). Origin of name unknown.

BALMORAL ROAD. See Wales Street.

BALMORAL STREET. Named on Plan 4049 (1912), probably in association with Victoria Drive and Queen Victoria's Balmoral Castle in Scotland. It lay between the present East 53rd and East 55th Avenues. When Fraserview area was developed, the street was extended to Argyle Drive, By-law 3330, 1952 (Plan 8393).

BALSAM LANE. See Joyce Street.

BALSAM STREET. Named on Plans 848 (1902) and 1058 (1905), which continued the pattern of tree names established by L.A. Hamilton. Point Grey By-law 17, 1912, and By-law 17, 1914, extended it between West 37th and West 41st Avenues and from West 49th Avenue to South West Marine Drive.

BALSAM PLACE. Cul-de-sac north of West 49th Avenue and east of Vine Street. Named by By-law 7474, 1995, Plan LF 11650.

BANKS STREET. See Beatrice Street.

BARCLAY STREET. Named after Barkley Sound, shown on the map used by L.A. Hamilton. Spelling changed when name transferred to street map. In 1787 Barkley Sound named by Captain Charles Barkley (1759-1832), of the trading ship *Imperial Eagle*, after himself.

BARNARD STREET. See Union Street.

BARNARD STREET (DL 318). Named 1947, By-law 3002, after Sir Francis Stillman Barnard (1856-1936). The BCER, owners of the property, suggested the name because Barnard was early and actively engaged in the organization and construction of street railways and other public utilities on the mainland. He served as lieutenant-governor of British Columbia, 1914-9.

BARTLETT ROAD. Now East 32nd Avenue between Fraser and St. Catherines Streets. Changed to East 32nd by South Vancouver By-law 141, 1910. Not shown in *Goad's Atlas* or on other contemporary maps. According to South Vancouver Voters Lists, 1907-9 inclusive, F. Bartlett owned property in DL 391-2, wherein lies East 32nd Avenue.

BARTON ROAD. See Yew Street.

BATH ROAD. Now West 30th Avenue between Blenheim and Carnarvon Streets. Survey name only on Plan 2213 (1909), probably after Bath, England, but not verified.

BATTISON STREET. Named by South Vancouver By-law 251, 1913, after William John Battison (1853-1942), one of the settlers in Burnaby Small Holdings, owning seven acres in DL 36-49. Born in Quebec, he came to British Columbia in 1886. The street lay between present East 45th Avenue and Kingsway and later extended to East 47th Avenue.

In 1921 South Vancouver By-law 558 changed Stuart Street (East 49th to East 54th Avenues) and Cromwell Street (East 54th Avenue to Fraser River) to Battison Street, but maps of 1930 still show Stuart and Cromwell Streets.

BAUER STREET. Named after William Alfred Bauer (1867-1932), original surveyor of Block 146, DL 264 A, in 1894, Plan 722. Born in Australia, he came to Vancouver in 1891 and received his commission as a BC land surveyor in 1892. After a sojourn in the Klondike he returned to Vancouver in 1899, where he practised as a surveyor until 1910.

When McSpadden Park was created, an access road was needed to the west side of the park, so Bauer Street was surveyed (Plan 14827 [1972]).

BAY STREET. See Parker Street.

BAYSHORE DRIVE. Named 1995, By-law 7474, Plan LF 11648, because of its proximity to the Bayshore Hotel.

BAYSWATER STREET. Named on Plan 851 (1902). Probably named for the nearby streams that entered English Bay on either side of the present Bayswater Street (Proctor 1978, 7-9). It may have been named after Bayswater Street in London, England, which is a corruption of Bayard's Water.

BAYVIEW STREET. See Atlantic Street.

BEACH AVENUE. Descriptive name given by L.A. Hamilton when he named the streets in DL 185. It is the only designated avenue in the West End.

BEADNELL COURT. A private thoroughfare in Earl Adams Village, Champlain Heights, a project of the Greater Vancouver Housing Corporation (Development Permit 78705), first listed in 1979 city directory. Streets in this project were named after places in Northumberland County, England. Beadnell is a fishing village and resort on the North Sea.

BEAGLE COURT. A private thoroughfare in Champlain Heights, named by the developers of "Huntingwood," who chose names to fit the theme of hunting with the hounds (beagles among them). Name approved by the Street Naming Committee on 27 May 1983.

BEAMISH COURT. A private thoroughfare in Earl Adams Village, Champlain Heights. Named after William "Ran" Beamish (1911-68), reeve of Burnaby, who also served on Greater Vancouver Water Board and Greater Vancouver Metropolitan Industrial Commission.

BEATRICE STREET. Named by South Vancouver By-law 141, 1910, after an unknown woman. This by-law also renamed Banks Avenue and Suffolk Road.

Banks Avenue. Between East 22nd and East 32nd Avenues, probably named after George E. and H. Muriel Banks, who, according to South Vancouver Voters Lists, 1909 and 1910, owned property in DL 352.

Suffolk Road. Between East 48th and East 49th Avenues, was named on Plan 2199 (1909), probably after Suffolk County, England, in association with Norfolk County on the same plan.

In 1952, Fraserview development absorbed the section of Beatrice Street between East 54th Avenue and South East Marine Drive. In 1954, By-law 3487 changed the section of Victoria Drive lying between the former BCER Central Park line and Stainsbury Avenue to Beatrice Street.

BEATTY STREET. Named by L.A. Hamilton when surveying and naming the streets in DL 541. Henry Beatty (1834-1914) was in charge of the Great Lakes steamer line, organized by the CPR, until his retirement in 1892.

BEAUCHOUX STREET. See Aberdeen Street.

BEAVER STREET (DL 339) (Deleted). Short street between Tyne and Toderick Streets and between East 49th and East 54th Avenues. Changed from Stuart Street in 1930 by By-law 2082 to remove duplication with Stewart Street on the Vancouver waterfront. Last listed in 1968 city directory, By-law 4470, 1970, deleted it from the official Vancouver street plan when Champlain Heights was developed. It is not known if the street was named after the animal or the Hudson's Bay Company steamship, *SS Beaver*.

Stuart Street. Named by South Vancouver By-law 251, 1913, possibly after Duncan W. Stuart, Central Park Post Office, listed in 1915 South Vancouver Voters List as a property owner in DL 339. Although South Vancouver By-law 558, 1921, renamed it Battison Street, the change did not take, as it was still called Stuart Street when changed to Beaver Street.

BEECH STREET. See Beechwood Street.

BEECHIE STREET. Now East 20th Avenue between Main and Knight Streets. Shown on Plan 187 (1885), named by H.V. Edmonds, the owner of DL 301, after his daughter Beatrice Elvina "Beechie" (1874-1961), who married W.A. Munro and lived in Winfield, British Columbia. When DL 301 was absorbed by Vancouver in 1911, Beechie became part of East 20th Avenue.

BEECHWOOD STREET. Named 1929, By-law 2014, which renamed Beech Street because it sounded just like Beach Avenue (in Vancouver's West End).

Beech Street. Named by Point Grey By-law 17, 1914, retained the pattern of tree names. Point Grey By-law 232, 1924, extended the street north from West 33rd Avenue to its intersection with Valley Drive, shown on the map accompanying the by-law. This latter portion not in use when By-law 2014 changed the name.

BEGBIE STREET. See Charles Street.

BEGG STREET. Named 1947, By-law 3002, Plan LF 579, when Canadian National Railways suggested the name after Begg Brothers, who had a plant at 845 Terminal Avenue. F.R. and F.B.

Begg were the first automobile distributors in Vancouver in 1905.

BELL ROAD. See Tanner Street.

BELLA VISTA STREET. Named in South Vancouver Voters List, 1911, which shows Mrs. E.E. Vosper, Bella Vista, Cedar Cottage, DL 750. The name of her house means "beautiful view." South Vancouver Road Loan By-law 151, 1911, allocated $300 to Buena Vista [sic].

> Some streets were named after the homes on them: Bella Vista Street, Cedar Cottage Road, Glendalough Place, Kerrisdale Avenue, Southlands Place

BELLEVUE CRESCENT (DL 320) (Deleted). Shown on the map attached to Point Grey By-law 17, 1914, it ran west from Crown Street below South West Marine Drive to Georgia Drive (now deleted). The land was never developed, and in 1922 Blocks 10 and 11, DL 320, were acquired by the municipality for Georgia Park, now included in the larger Musqueam Park. Bellevue means "beautiful view."

BELLEVUE DRIVE. Surveyed in 1927, Plan 5755, for Westmount Lands Limited, it had been named earlier by Point Grey By-law 483, 1926. Point Grey By-law 763, 1927, Plan 5825, extended it southeast from West 2nd to West 3rd Avenues. The provincial government developed Westmount Park and commissioned J. Alexander Walker to prepare plans, but the government designated the street names. Bellevue Drive, the only new name in the two-block development, was probably named after Bellevue Avenue in Westmount, Quebec.

BELMONT AVENUE. Lies in DL 140 and DL 540. DL 540, surveyed in 1887, Plan 229, showed *Salisbury Avenue*, between present Blanca and Discovery Streets. Named after the Marquis of Salisbury (1830-1903), prime minister of Great Britain, 1885-6. When the part of Langara subdivision in DL 140 was surveyed in 1911, Plan 6583, Salisbury Avenue was extended west from Blanca Street to the eastern boundary of the University Endowment Lands. Point Grey By-law 17, 1912, changed Salisbury Avenue in DL 540 to Belmont Avenue, probably after Belmont Street in Montreal and Westmount. Point Grey

By-law 232, 1924, changed Salisbury Avenue in DL 140 to Belmont.

In 1941, By-law 2699 closed the portion of Belmont Street east of Trimble Street for the RCAF Jericho military station. It is now part of Jericho Park.

BELMONT CRESCENT (Proposed). See Fannin Avenue.

BENNINGTON AVENUE. See Elgin Street.

BENTALL STREET. Named 1954, By-law 3415, after Charles Bentall (1882-1974), prominent contractor, whose firm, Dominion Construction Company, built such buildings as the Sun Tower on Pender Street, the Yorkshire Trust Building, and the Vancouver Block.

BENTLEY STREET. In 1954, By-law 3486 changed Milton Street between West 75th Avenue and the Fraser River to Bentley Street. Leopold Bentley (1905-86), vice-president and managing director of Eburne Sawmills, Canadian Forest Products, had this unused portion of Milton Street opened to gain access to his sawmill. He changed his family name of Block-Bauer to Bentley, after the Bentley automobile.

BERING AVENUE. Named 1978, By-law 5150, after Vitus Bering (1680-1741), a Danish navigator who proved that Asia and North America were separated by the waters of Bering Strait and the Bering Sea. On 26 January and 16 February 1978, the Street Naming Committee decided that Enclave I, Champlain Heights, should have its streets named after explorers.

BERKELEY STREET. First named on Plan 2327 (1909), it lay between the present East 54th and East 59th Avenues. The portion between the present East 41st and East 45th Avenues had been surveyed earlier in 1909, Plan 2208, but had not been named. Plan 3784 (1912) extended the street from East 59th to East 65th Avenues. With the replotting for the Fraserview housing project, the portion between East 57th and East 65th Avenues disappeared. Origin of name unknown.

BEVERLY CRESCENT. Named on Plan 6011 (1921), although not listed in the city directory until 1928. Origin of name given by the CPR not known.

BIDWELL STREET. L.A. Hamilton took the name of Bedwell Bay from the map he used when

assigning street names in DL 185, but the name was incorrectly spelled "Bidwell." Edward Parker Bedwell was second master of the surveying vessel HMS *Plumper*, 1857-60.

BIRCH STREET. Officially registered on Plan 590 (1891) but named on an 1887 map (Map 14160) by L. A. Hamilton, who chose tree names. Point Grey By-law 17, 1914, named the short portion in the Marpole area.

BIRCH WALK. Private thoroughfare in False Creek, lying northwest from Birch Street. Approved by the Street Naming Committee on 15 August 1979.

BISMARK STREET. See Kitchener Street.

BLAIR AVENUE. See Mannering Avenue.

BLAKE STREET. Named after an unidentified person by South Vancouver By-law 251, 1913, it lay between present East 49th and East 54th Avenues. When Champlain Heights area was replotted in 1970, By-law 4470, Plan LF 4530, changed the alignment of Blake Street. In 1978, Plan 3742B amended this alignment, and in 1988 By-law 6376, Plan LF 11231, removed a portion and renamed it Hurst Place.

BLANCA STREET. Named Blanca Avenue by Point Grey By-law 17, 1912, but by 1925, maps show it as Blanca Street. Lieutenant Francisco Eliza, first White man to see Burrard Inlet in 1791, called it Boca de Florida blanca after José Moñino, Conde de Floridablanca (1728-1808), Spanish secretary of state from 1776 until 1792.

BLANCHE STREET. Private thoroughfare shown on Plan LF 11449 (1991). Architects Weber and Associates, building for the Red Door Housing Society, submitted the name (which has no significance).

BLAYDON COURT. Private thoroughfare in Earl Adams Village, Champlain Heights, first listed in 1979 city directory. Streets in this project were named after places in Northumberland County, England. Blaydon is a town on the River Tyne.

BLENHEIM STREET. Named 1907, Vancouver By-law 273, after the Battle of Blenheim, 1704, as suggested by Miss Dora Bulwer (see Alma Street).

Formerly *Cornwall Street* (DL 540) between English Bay and West 16th Avenue on Plan 229

(1887). Named after Clement Francis Cornwall (1836-1910), lieutenant-governor of British Columbia, 1881-7. Renamed to remove duplication with Cornwall Avenue (DL 526).

The adjoining street in Point Grey municipality was called *Johnson Road*

C.F. Cornwall. BCARS, Photo # F-02698.

after Richard Byron Johnson (1867-1957), who owned property in DL 321, where the present Crofton House School stands. South Vancouver Highway By-law, 1903, named Johnson Road and extended it by South Vancouver Highway By-law, 1905. Renamed Blenheim by Point Grey By-law 17, 1912.

Point Grey By-law 284, 1928, diverted Blenheim south of Celtic Avenue to give access to the BC Fishing and Packing Company plant.

BLOOD ALLEY SQUARE. Named 1972, By-law 4636, Plan LF 5892, and created during the renovation of Gastown. It lies just south of Trounce Alley, in early days the scene of many blood-spilling fights among drunken patrons of the nearby hotels and saloons.

BLUE JAY CRESCENT. One of nine private thoroughfares in Enclaves 8, 9, and 10, Champlain Heights, bearing bird names submitted by Matheson Heights Co-operative and approved by the Street Naming Committee on 25 March 1981.

BOATLIFT LANE. Private thoroughfare on Granville Island, Plan LF 11465. Name, approved by the Street Naming Committee in January 1992, indicates the boating activity centred in False Creek.

BOBOLINK AVENUE. Named 1952, By-law 3330, after Bob O' Link Golf Course, Highland Park, Illinois, by J. Alexander Walker, secretary, Vancouver Town Planning Commission. When Bobolink Park was created, the portion between Nanaimo Street and Muirfield Drive was closed. Extended east from Muirfield Drive to Vivian Drive in 1961, By-law 3937.

BODWELL ROAD. Now East and West 33rd Avenue. Named by South Vancouver Highway By-law, 1905, after Ebenezer Vining Bodwell (1827-89), who came to British Columbia in 1879 as accountant for the Dominion government in connection with the construction of the CPR. He moved to Vancouver and is listed in first Vancouver Voters List, 1886.

South Vancouver By-law 141, 1910, changed Bodwell Road between Cambie Street and Victoria Drive to East and West 34th Avenues and between Victoria Drive and Wales Road to East 35th Avenue. Point Grey By-law 17, 1912, changed its portion of Bodwell Road to West 33rd Avenue.

Although not mentioned in By-law 2028, East 34th Avenue between Victoria Drive and present Slocan Street also became East 33rd Avenue. Not until 1929 did By-law 2028 change 34th Avenue in South Vancouver to 33rd Avenue.

BONACCORD DRIVE. Named 1952, By-law 3330, after Bonaccord Golf Course, an eighteen-hole seaside course near Aberdeen, Scotland.

BOND ROAD. See Gladstone Street.

BONNYVALE AVENUE. Named 1952, By-law 3330, after an as-yet-unidentified golf course, Bonnyvale.

BORDEN AVENUE. See Foster Avenue.

BORDEN STREET (DL 328). Named 1913, South Vancouver By-law 251, probably after Sir Robert Laird Borden (1854-1937), then prime minister of Canada.

BORHAM CRESCENT. Private thoroughfare in Champlain Heights, shown on Plan LE 5032. First listed in 1979 city directory. Origin of name unknown.

BOULEVARD, EAST AND WEST. First listed in 1914 city directory with no residents shown. East Boulevard, on the east side of Vancouver and Lulu Island Railway, lies between West 16th and King Edward Avenues, between West 35th and West 57th Avenues, and between West 69th and West 70th Avenues. The part between West King Edward and West 33rd Avenues was changed to Maple Crescent in 1973, By-law 4688. West Boulevard lies between West 37th and West 49th Avenues, and between West 51st and West 61st Avenues.

Although no official by-law named East and West Boulevard, the name, appearing on a 1910 map of Point Grey municipality (Map 13875), describes the wide street, or boulevard, formed by the road on either side of and parallel to the interurban railway.

BOUNDARY AVENUE (DL 181). See Glen Drive.

BOUNDARY AVENUE. Now East 15th Avenue between Knight Street and Commercial Drive. Shown on Plate 91, *Goad's Atlas*, 1913, as 15th Avenue (late Boundary Avenue). An unofficial name that refers to its being the boundary between the City of Vancouver and the Municipality of South Vancouver.

BOUNDARY DRIVE. See Nanaimo Street.

BOUNDARY ROAD. Named from its position as the boundary between the Municipality of South Vancouver, the Townsite of Hastings, and the Municipality of Burnaby. South Vancouver By-law 141, 1910, renamed the portion between East 29th Avenue and the Fraser River *Park Street*, after its location adjacent to Central Park. At amalgamation with Vancouver in 1929, By-law 2014 changed it back to Boundary Road.

In 1950, By-law 3195 designated the portion north of Dundas Street as Boundary Road North.

BOUNDARY STREET (DL 540). See Trafalgar Street.

BOWMAN STREET. See Ormidale Street.

BOYD DIVERSION. Named 1947, By-law 3002, Plan LF 582, after Thomas Henry Boyd (1857-1938), a pioneer property owner in the district who came to Vancouver in 1885. A general contractor and partner in the firm Boyd and Clandening, which cleared Granville Street in 1886, Stanley Park Road in 1888, and Brockton Oval in 1891, he served as licence commissioner in 1906.

BRAEBURN STREET. In Fraserview, named on Plan 8393 (1950), continues the theme of golf course names: Brae Burn Country Club, West Newton, Massachusetts, near Boston.

BRAHMS AVENUE. Private thoroughfare in Champlain Heights, named after the German composer Johannes Brahms (1833-97). The name submitted by Community Builders, developers of Ashleigh Heights, was approved by the Street Naming Committee on 25 March 1984.

BRAKENRIDGE STREET. Named 18 February 1954 by a resolution attached to By-law 3415 and confirmed 5 July 1954 by By-law 3457. After Charles Brakenridge (1885-1968), Vancouver city engineer, 1924-46.

BRANDYWINE PLACE. Private thoroughfare in Champlain Heights named after Brandywine Falls Park near Alta Lake and Whistler Mountain by Community Builders, developers of Park Place. Approved by the Street Naming Committee on 21 June 1978.

BRANT STREET. Surveyed 1909, Plan 2240, and named by South Vancouver By-law 251, 1913, probably after Joseph Brant (1742-1807), chief of the Six Nations. By-law 251 commemorated people prominent in Canadian history (e.g., Brock, Tecumseh, and Wolfe).

BRATTLEBORO AVENUE. See Ross Street.

BRIAR AVENUE. Private thoroughfare in Arbutus Village. The name, of unknown origin, was submitted by Narod Developments Limited and approved by the Street Naming Committee on 21 June 1978.

BRIDGE STREET. See Cambie Street.

BRIDGEWAY. Named on Plan 5461 (1924), when part of Hastings Townsite was resurveyed to provide access to the area adjacent to the first Second Narrows Bridge, completed in 1925.

BRIGADOON AVENUE. Named 1952, By-law 3330, after Brigadoon Golf Course, location unknown. J. Alexander Walker, Vancouver Town Planning Commission, suggested that names in the Fraserview development bear the names of well-known golf courses.

BRIGHTWOOD PLACE. Named 1961, By-law 3937, after Brightwood Golf and Country Club, Dartmouth, Nova Scotia, to continue the theme of golf course street names established in 1952 for Fraserview development.

BRISTOL STREET (Deleted). Probably named arbitrarily after Bristol, England, but not verified. In January 1941 the city surveyor, in a report to the special committee on designation of street names, proposed the name "Bristol" for an existing unnamed street west of Tyne, south from East 54th to East 65th Avenues. Shown on a 1948 map (CVA map 956) and on the official street name map, Plan L325 (1963), attached to By-law 4054. Deleted with development of Champlain Heights.

BRITANNIA STREET (Deleted). Unnamed on Plan 4000 (1910) and named 1913, South Vancouver By-law 251, it lay between present Killarney and Kerr Streets from East 54th to East 58th Avenues. Listed in 1917-22 directories with no residents shown. With the replotting of the area north of Fraserview Golf Course the street disappeared. A common name in the days of the British Empire.

BRITTANY STREET. See Spencer Street.

BROADWAY. Changed from 9th Avenue in 1909, By-law 676. During a real estate boom the name was changed in anticipation of the area becoming the centre of a great metropolis à la Broadway, New York. By-law 2014, 1929, changed the designation to Broadway East and West from Ontario Street. By-law 2082, 1930, stated that 9th Avenue from Courtenay to Blanca Streets would continue to be known as West 9th Avenue.

BROCK STREET. Named 1913, South Vancouver By-law 251, after Sir Isaac Brock (1769-1812), defender of Upper Canada in War of 1812; he died at Battle of Queenston Heights. Surveyed on Plan 1388 (1907).

BROOKS STREET. Named by South Vancouver By-law 251, 1913. Origin of name unknown. In 1970, By-law 4770, Plan LF 4530, added a portion between East 60th and East 52nd Avenues. In 1978, By-law 5195, Plan LE 3742B, renamed this portion as part of Sparbrook Crescent.

BROUGHTON STREET. Named after Broughton Strait, shown on the map that L.A. Hamilton used when naming the streets in DL 185, now the West End. In 1792, Captain George Vancouver named the strait after Lieutenant Commander William Robert Broughton (1762-1821).

BRUCE STREET. See Wallace Street.

BRUCE STREET. Named by South Vancouver By-law 141, 1910, which renamed Hargrave Road between present East 45th and East 49th Avenues. By-law 141 assigned many Scottish names to adjacent streets, so it may have been after Robert the Bruce, a Scottish hero. Mrs. Arthur Cheshire, who lived on Bruce Street, told Major J.S. Matthews it was named after Bruce County, Ontario. He comments that it used to be a joke in the early days that if a man came from Ontario there was but one place he could have come from – Bruce County!

Hargrave Road. Named on Plan 3161 (1909), after owner William H. Hargrave, manager of Eastern Townships Bank, 1908-11.

BRUNSWICK STREET. Shown on Plan 197 (1885). Dr. Israel Wood Powell, owner of DL 200A, probably named it after the Province of New Brunswick.

BUCKBERRY ROAD. See Park Drive.

BUCKETWHEEL. Named 1976, By-law 5010, Plan LF 7386. The name is evocative of the industrial activity along False Creek from the 1920s to the 1950s, where bucketwheels were used to raise water (or other liquids) to the top of the wheels and then pour it out.

BUCKLAND ROAD. Now West 29th Avenue between Camosun and Trafalgar Streets. Surveyed 1912, Plan 3827. Owners of the east portion of Lot 6, DL 2027, were Gertrude and Charles Channing Buckland. First listed in 1906 South Vancouver Voters List, C.C. Buckland (1873-1936) was later president of Vancouver Milling and Grain Company. Changed to West 29th Avenue by Point Grey By-law 17, 1912.

Old Buckland Road, looking west from Alma Road. The building on the right is the Convent of the Sacred Heart, 3851 West 29th Avenue, under construction at the time this photo was taken. Wallace and Crown Streets cross in mid-distance, with the forest on the University Endowment Lands in the far-distance. CVA Str. P. 17, N. 323.

BULLER STREET. See Baldwin Street.

BURKHOLDER DRIVE. Private thoroughfare in Champlain Heights named by the Plumbers and Pipefitters Union, who sponsored a cooperative housing project there and named the three thoroughfares – Burkholder, McIntyre, and Werks – after founding members of the union. Francis H. Burkholder, plumber, was listed in Victoria directory, 1898-1901. Name approved by the Street Naming Committee on 12 January 1984.

BURNABY STREET. Named after Burnaby Lake, shown on the map used by L.A. Hamilton when naming streets in DL 185. Burnaby Lake named after Robert Burnaby (1828-78), private secretary to Colonel Moody, and associated with surveys made by the Royal Engineers of land around New Westminster and Burnaby Lake.

BURNS STREET. See Prince Albert Street.

BURQUITLAM DRIVE. Named 1952, By-law 3330, after the Burquitlam Golf Course, popular name for the Vancouver Golf Club, located in Burquitlam (a compound of Burnaby and Coquitlam).

BURRARD STREET. Named after Burrard Inlet by L.A. Hamilton when naming streets in DL 185. Captain George Vancouver had named Burrard Inlet in 1792 after his friend, Sir Harry Burrard, RN (1765-1840). The opening of the Burrard Bridge linked Burrard Street to *Cedar Street*, which was renamed by By-law 2534, 1938.

Officially registered on Plan 590 (1891), Cedar Street was on an 1887 map (Map 14160) used by L.A. Hamilton, who chose tree names.

BURROWS ROAD. Now East 31st Avenue between Fraser and Knight Streets. Shown on "Plan of the Municipality of South Vancouver, BC," compiled by George H. Dawson, 1908 (Map 14083). Changed to East 31st Avenue in 1910, South Vancouver By-law 141.

South Vancouver Voters Lists, 1903-10, show James Burrows, of Burrows Road, as owner of Block 3, DL 391-2.

BURSILL ROAD (DLs 36 and 51). See Moscrop Street.

BURSILL STREET (DL 37). Shown unnamed on Plan 4126 (1909) and Plan 2542 (1910). South Vancouver By-law 251, 1913, named it after John Francis Bursill (1848-1928), who settled in South Vancouver in 1908, where he founded the Bursill Library and Collingwood Institute. He wrote for Vancouver newspapers under the pseudonym of Felix Penne.

BUSCOMBE STREET. Named 1951, By-law 3250, after Frederick Buscombe (1862-1938) and his brother George (1875-1958), who established the wholesale firm of Buscombe and Company. Frederick served as mayor of Vancouver from 1905-6 and George was an alderman from 1940-5.

Bugler George Buscombe. First military bugler in Vancouver, he was enrolled in No. 5 Co., British Columbia Brigade of Garrison Artillery, old Drill Shed, Pender Street, 17 January 1894 (the second night of organization of first volunteer unit in Vancouver). CVA Port. P. 180, N. 295.

BUTE STREET. Named after Bute Inlet, shown on the map that L.A. Hamilton used when naming the streets in DL 185. Bute Inlet was named by Captain George Vancouver in 1792 after John Stuart, 3rd Earl of Bute (1713-92).

BUTLER STREET. Named by South Vancouver By-law 251, 1913, it lay between present East 46th and East 57th Avenues, but most of the street was not surveyed until the 1940s. Origin of name unknown.

BYWELL COURT. Private thoroughfare in Earl Adams Village, Champlain Heights, first listed in 1979 directory. Streets in this project were named after places in Northumberland County, England. Bywell is a hamlet on the north bank of the Tyne River.

C

"C" ROAD. Now West 64th Avenue between Granville and Ash Streets. A survey designation only, shown in *B.C. Gazette*, 25 January 1900, p. 198.

CAMANO STREET. A private thoroughfare in Enclave 2, Champlain Heights, named by the Street Naming Committee in 1979, after Lieutenant Commander Jacinto Caamaño of the Spanish corvette *Aranzaza*, which was on the northwest coast in 1790. Camano is a misspelling of his name.

CAMBIE STREET. Named in 1886 after Henry John Cambie (1836-1908), first divisional engineer of the CPR, in Vancouver.

In July 1891 a bridge built across False Creek from the south end of Cambie Street connected with *Bridge Street*, shown on Plan

Henry J. Cambie, from group photo. CVA Port. P. 450, N. 767.

590 (1891). In 1912, with the opening of the second Cambie Street Bridge (officially called the Connaught Bridge), Bridge Street was renamed by Vancouver By-law 975, 1912; South Vancouver By-law 1216, 1913; and Point Grey By-law 42, 1912.

The last extension to Cambie Street was from West 71st Avenue to Kent Avenue North, By-law 3731, 1958.

CAMBRIDGE STREET. Named after Cambridge University, England. Shown on Plan 100, a resurvey of Hastings Townsite, in 1906, and first listed in the 1908 city directory.

CAMERON AVENUE. Named by By-law 842, 1911, which renamed Front Street. Likely named after William S. Cameron, born 1876 in Ontario. An alderman for Ward 6, Vancouver, in 1911, he had come to Vancouver in 1907 and established a hardware store. From 1910-3 he was managing director of Federal Investments Limited. Last listed in 1914 city directory.

Strathcona Park, 1909, now the site of Vancouver City Hall. Mr. A.M. Forbes, pioneer, who arrived in Vancouver on the 22 April 1888, driving his hourse and cutter up 12th Avenue. The cutter is a short distance east from the intersection of West 12th Avenue and Cambie Street. The house at the horse's nose is on southeast corner of 10th and Yukon Street. The road appears to be planked. Also, notice the two sets of sleigh bells on the horse. CVA Str. P. 240, N. 148.

The obituary for John Angus Cameron (1871-1951) in the *Daily Province*, 30 April 1951, stated that Cameron Avenue was named after him. However, Major J.S. Matthews, former city archivist, believed that this was not so because Cameron's niece, who had given the information to the press, actually did not know.

Front Street. Named after its position fronting on English Bay. Plan 229 (1887).

CAMOSUN STREET. Named by Point Grey By-law 17, 1912, after Camosun, the Lekwammen name for the site of Fort Victoria (later Victoria). According to Akrigg (1997), Camosun means either "the rush of waters" (in reference to a race of the tide) or "place where the camas plant grows." Although Point Grey By-law 17, 1914, extended it from the present South West Marine Drive to the northern boundary of the Musqueam Band Reserve, the street was not opened.

CAMPBELL AVENUE (DL 196). Shown on Plan 196 and named after George Campbell, co-owner with Edward Heatley of the Hastings Sawmill.

CAMPBELL ROAD (DL 258) (Deleted). Unnamed on Plan 2502 (1910) and named by South Vancouver By-law 251, 1913, it lay between the present East 67th Avenue and South East Marine Drive. It disappeared with the replotting of Fraserview.

Origin of the name has not been established, but the 1910 South Vancouver Voters List shows R. Campbell owning property in DL 258.

CAMPBELL ROAD (DL 327). See Crompton Street.

CAMPBELL STREET (DL 540). See Alma Street.

CANADA PLACE. Named 1986, By-law 5959. Canada Harbour Place Corporation, which owned the private road in 1984, suggested the name. Since then it has become a dedicated roadway.

CANTON ALLEY. First listed in 1906 city directory as a short street in the heart of Chinatown, its name commemorates Canton Province, China, from where many of the residents had come. It is shown in *Goad's Atlas*, 1913, Plate 14. By 1938 it had become a private roadway owned by the city and leased to Ming Yip. The alley disappeared in 1954.

CAPRI CRESCENT. Private thoroughfare in Champlain Heights, first listed in 1982 city directory. Henriquez and Partners, architects, chose Mediterranean place names for the enclave.

CAPTAINS COVE. Private thoroughfare in the Angus Lands near the Fraser River. The name, submitted by owner Wayne Hartshorne to the Street Naming Committee, was approved 22 June 1987. It continues the maritime and nautical theme for the area.

CARDERO STREET. Named after Cordero Channel, shown on the map used by L.A. Hamilton when naming the streets in DL 185. Captain John Walbran states that the name of the channel is evidently derived from Josef Cordero, the draughtsman on Galiano's 1792 expedition. The name on the chart was spelled Cardero.

CARIBOO STREET. Named after the Cariboo Mining Division. Now a short street running southwest one block from East 29th Avenue, this is all that remains of the original Cariboo Street, which ran the length of Hastings Townsite and became Skeena Street in 1950, By-law 3195.

Vancouver Sun, 31 May 1960, reported that Cariboo Street between Moscrop Street and East 29th Avenue would be renamed Gavin Street, but the change did not occur. John Joseph Gavin (1850-1924) was an alderman for Ward 5, Vancouver, in 1892 and 1893. Later a bridge tender for the BCER, he died 1 June 1924.

CARL AVENUE. See Princess Avenue.

CARLISLE STREET. Named 1930, By-law 2082, after John Howe Carlisle (1857-1941), appointed fire chief of the City of Vancouver in 1889 when a professional fire department was established. Previously he had been the third chief of the volunteer fire department.

Originally named as *Park Avenue* on Plan 2398 (1909), probably after its proximity to Hastings Park. Renamed to remove duplication with Park Drive in Point Grey.

CARLTON STREET. See Killarney Street.

CARNARVON STREET. Named on Plan 1003 (1905), after Henry Herbert, 4th Earl of Carnarvon (1831-90). As secretary of state for the colonies he supervised the drafting of the British North

America Act and steered it through the British Parliament.

The adjoining street in Point Grey, known as *York Road* (probably after York, England), was changed to Carnarvon Street by Point Grey By-law 17, 1912. Shown in *Goad's Atlas*, Plates 24, 30-2, and 37, lying between West 16th and West 51st Avenues. Named on Plan 2213 (1909).

CAROLINA STREET. lies in three district lots – DLs 264A, 301, and 313. When DL 264A was re-surveyed in 1905, Carolina Street was so named on Plan 1771, although shown on a 1902 map (Map 14171). Origin of name unknown.

Frederick Street (DL 301). Shown on Plan 187 (1885), was named by the owner, H.V. Edmonds, after Frederick Edmonds. It was changed to part of Carolina Street between East 15th and East King Edward Avenues in 1911, By-law 842, when DL 301 was absorbed into Vancouver. However, the name continues in the present Frederick Street (DL 650), lying directly south, although separated by the Mountain View Cemetery.

In DL 313 South Vancouver By-law 141, 1910, changed *McGeer Avenue* to Carolina Street between South East Marine Drive and the CPR line from Marpole to New Westminster. However, the change never occurred, as Plan 3207 (1910), deposited in the Land Registry Office in 1911 by James McGeer and Jacob Grauer, was cancelled by an Order of Court.

James McGeer (1855-1913), an Irishman and reporter for the *Manchester Guardian* before coming to Vancouver in 1887, established a dairy and later became a milk and dairy inspector. His son, Gerald, became mayor of Vancouver in 1935.

James McGeer, as portrayed in *British Columbians as We See 'Em, 1910 and 1911,* (Vancouver: Newspaper Cartoonist Association of British Columbia, 1911).

CARR ROAD (Deleted). Named by Point Grey By-law 1, 1910, which allocated $3,000 to it. No trace of this road has been found on any surveys or maps. Point Grey Assessment Roll, 1910, shows Stanley Carr and Thomas Carr owning properties in DL 2027.

CARRALL STREET. Named after Dr. Robert William Weir Carrall (1837-79), doctor, politician, and delegate to Ottawa in 1870 to discuss the terms of British Columbia's union with Canada.

Water Street. Named arbitrarily on a fire insurance plan of Granville, British Columbia, August 1885, and published by Sanborn Map and Publishing Company Limited (Map 14258), it lay where the present Carrall Street is, north of Hastings Street.

CARRINGTON STREET. Named 1930, By-law 2082, when Collingwood Street between West 49th Avenue and the Fraser River was renamed. Origin of name unknown.

CARTIER PLACE. So named in 1952, By-law 3325, because it is adjacent to Cartier Street.

CARTIER STREET. Named by Point Grey By-Law 17, 1912, after Jacques Cartier, French navigator and discoverer of the St. Lawrence River. Named on Plan 4502 (1913), a survey of Shaughnessy Heights, as Cartier Avenue; changed by Point Grey By-law 232, 1924, to Cartier Street.

Second Street, Eburne Townsite, shown an Plan 1749 (1908), lay between present West 73rd and West 70th Avenues, later extended to Park Drive. Point Grey By-law 17, 1914, changed it to Cartier Street.

CARTWRIGHT STREET. Private thoroughfare on Granville Island, which was under the jurisdiction of the Vancouver Harbour Commission. Probably named after Conway Edward Cartwright (1864-1938), a consulting engineer (with the engineering firm Cartwright, Matheson, and Company) for the Vancouver Harbour Board.

CASPER CRESCENT (Proposed). See Semana Crescent.

CASSIAR STREET. Named by the provincial government after the Cassiar Mining District in 1906, Plan 100. In 1950, By-law 3195 designated the portion north of Dundas Street as Cassiar Street North.

CASSIAR-RUPERT DIVERSION. Named 1956, By-law 3558, when Cassiar Street was diverted southwest from Charles Street to join Rupert Street at East 1st Avenue.

THE CASTINGS. Named 1976, By-law 5010, Plan LF 7386. The name is evocative of the ironworks located in the former industrial basin of False Creek, where castings or moulds were produced.

CASTLE STREET. Now East 27th Avenue between Windermere and Skeena Streets. A survey name of unknown origin, shown on Plan 1705 (1906) and Plan 1932 (1908).

CAVERSHAM COURT. Private thoroughfare in the Angus Lands. Named by D.L. Helliwell and Associates and approved by the Street Naming Committee on 15 June 1988. In conversation with the compiler, Elizabeth Walker, D.L. Helliwell stated that his firm wanted an English name to go with the English style of architecture in the neighbourhood. As he knew of Caversham Properties on the Thames River, England, whose location resembled that of his property on the Fraser River, this is the name he chose.

CECIL ROAD. Now West 35th Avenue between Blenheim and Collingwood Streets. Name stamped over on Plan 3685 (1909) and West 35th Avenue substituted. Origin of name unknown.

CECIL STREET. Named by South Vancouver By-law 251, 1913, probably after Cecil Rhodes (1835-1902), South African businessman who established the Rhodes scholarships. Surveyed but not named on Plans 2053 (1908), 3205 (1911), and 3941 (1912). Rhodes Street named in same by-law.

CEDAR CRESCENT. Named on Plan 4502 (1913), plan of Shaughnessy Heights, after the adjoining Cedar Street (now Burrard Street). Point Grey By-law 585, 1925, renamed a part of West 17th Avenue (between the present Burrard Street east to the intersection of Fir Street and West 16th Avenue) Cedar Crescent.

CEDAR LANE (DL 50). See Wales Street.

CEDAR STREET (DL 526). See Burrard Street.

CEDAR STREET (THSL). See Atlin Street.

CEDAR COTTAGE ROAD. See Commercial Street.

CEDARHURST STREET. Named by Point Grey By-law 294, 1928, to indicate the many cedar trees in the area. Hurst is an Old English word for a grove of trees, or copse.

CELISTA DRIVE. Private thoroughfare in Champlain Heights named after Celista Provincial Park, as indicated in Vancouver City Council Minutes (v. 132, p. 26) and approved by council on 29 May 1979. Celista Creek was probably named after Celesta, paramount chief of the Okanagan people.

CELTIC AVENUE. Named by Point Grey By-law 32, 1919, after the Celtic Cannery, built in 1897 and in operation until the end of 1917.

Fraser Avenue. Named by Point Grey By-law 17, 1914, after its location parallel to the North Arm of the Fraser River. Renamed Celtic in 1919.

Hutchison Street. Origin of name of this unofficial street unknown. First listed in 1927 city directory at foot of Blenheim Street (with Celtic Cannery) at 9074 Hutchison. Last listed in 1945 directory. The city surveyor has no record of this name. It lay at an angle from the south foot of Blenheim Street to the intersection of Celtic Avenue and Balaclava Street, as shown on 1945 "Dial Map of Greater Vancouver and Suburbs" (CVA map 822).

CEMETERY ROAD. See Fraser Street.

CENTENNIAL ROAD. Private thoroughfare on Port of Vancouver property from north foot of Heatley Street onto Centennial Pier. Named to commemorate the 1958 centennial of the establishment of the Colony of British Columbia in 1858. First listed in 1972 city directory.

CENTRAL STREET. First listed in 1927 city directory and named after its position in Parcel A, DL 2037 (Plan 5703 [1926]). Created when the eastern part of False Creek was filled in and the Canadian Northern Pacific Railway (later Canadian National Railways) built its station and railway yards there. It originally lay between Station and Main Streets (By-law 1556, 1922) but was shortened to its present length between Station and Western Streets by By-law 1803, 1926 (City Engineer Plan Mc10).

CENTRAL ARTERIAL HIGHWAY. See Lougheed Highway.

CENTRE ROAD. Now West 36th Avenue between East Boulevard and Marguerite Street. Named after its position as the centre road in Plan 2975 (1909), when the CPR opened Block 21,

DL 526, for sale once the nearby Vancouver and Lulu Island railway was built. The name is shown in a real estate advertisement in *Vancouver Daily Province*, 16 May 1912, which shows lots of 50 by 120 feet advertised for $1,350 and up.

CENTRE STREET. See Granville Street.

CENTRE STREET (DL 323). See Alberta Street.

CHALDECOTT ROAD (DL 2027, Blocks 79-88). See King Edward Avenue.

CHALDECOTT STREET (DL 2027, Block 77). Named by resolution of council on 18 June 1945 and confirmed by By-law 3250, 1951, after its proximity to Chaldecott Park. Former Point Grey reeve W.H Lembke, in a conversation with Major J.S. Matthews in 1941, stated that F.M. Chaldecott ceded twelve acres for non-payment of taxes, which the municipality set aside for a park (afterwards named Chaldecott Park). Francis Miller Chaldecott (1863-1949), born in England and admitted to the BC bar in 1891, had extensive property holdings in the west part of South Vancouver (later Point Grey).

CHAMBERS STREET. Surveyed in 1910, Plan 2911, and named by South Vancouver By-law 251, 1913, after Albert Chambers (1873-1941), who came to the Collingwood district in 1913. A graduate of the Ontario College of Pharmacy, he was proprietor of Chambers Drug Company on Joyce Street. He served as postmaster for Collingwood East Post Office (later Vancouver Sub Office 26) from 1921 until his death on 11 January 1941.

CHAMBORD PLACE. Private thoroughfare in Champlain Heights named after Chambord, France. Graham Crockart, architect, stated that he chose a French name just because the road was located in Champlain Heights. Name approved by the Street Naming Committee on 16 January 1989.

CHAMPLAIN AVENUE (Deleted). Named by South Vancouver By-law 141, 1910, after Samuel de Champlain (1570?-1635), French explorer who founded the City of Quebec and helped colonize New France. It lay between Kerr and Tyne Streets. By 1929 it extended to Boundary Road, when By-law 2028 changed it to a portion of East 58th Avenue. The street disappeared with the replotting of Champlain Heights.

CHAMPLAIN CRESCENT. Named 1978, By-law 5195, Plan LE 3742B, after Samuel de Champlain (1570?-1635), French explorer. The portion of Tyne Street south of East 54th Avenue was changed with the replotting of Champlain Heights. Dissatisfaction with this change is mentioned in the entry for Tyne Street.

CHANDLERY PLACE. Private thoroughfare shown on Plan LF 11587 (1994). The developer, PCI Realty, Vancouver, chose a name in keeping with the nautical and marine theme already established. A chandlery is a place where commodities (such as those made by a ship's chandler) are sold.

CHAPLIN ROAD. Now East 38th Avenue between Fraser and Ross Streets. South Vancouver By-law 141, 1910, changed it to East 39th Avenue (now East 38th Avenue). On Plan 1797 (1908), W.J. Chaplin and J.D. Chaplin are shown as executors of the will of William Chaplin, deceased, who owned property in DL 667, 1895-1907.

CHARLES STREET. Named on Map 14267, "Plan of the City of Vancouver, western terminus of the Canadian Pacific Railway," complied by H.B. Smith in 1886. It lay east of an arm of False Creek to McLean Drive in DL 182. Gradually extended to Boundary Road and into Burnaby. Origin of name unknown. Plan 2343 (1909) shows *Begbie Street*, between LeRoi and Lillooet Streets, with the words Charles Street in parentheses. A survey name only, likely after Sir Matthew Baillie Begbie (1819-94), chief justice of British Columbia.

CHARLESON ROAD. A dedicated road between Lamey's Mill and Moberly Roads. Named 1976, By-law 5010, after Donald Brims Charleson (1842-1928) who, in March 1889, entered into a contract with Donald A. Smith of the CPR to clear the area from False Creek south to 9th Avenue (now Broadway). He is shown in the first Vancouver Voters List, 1886.

Donald Brims Charleson. CVA Port. P. 369, N. 167.

CHARLOTTE STREET. See St. George Street.

CHATEAU PLACE. Private thoroughfare in the Angus Lands, shown on Plan LF 11569 (1993). Origin of name unknown, but it is not in keeping with the marine theme of other street names in the area.

CHATHAM STREET. Named by South Vancouver By-law 251, 1913, although it had been surveyed on Plans 1911 and 2108 (1909) and Plan 3628 (1911). Origin of name unknown.

CHATHAM STREET (DL 540). See Langara Avenue.

CHATWIN STREET. See Fremlin Street.

CHEAM PLACE. Private thoroughfare named 1972, By-law 4636. United Cooperative Housing Society named its streets after BC geographical features, such as Cheam Peak near Chilliwack.

CHERRY STREET (DL 526). See Pine Street.

CHERRY STREET (DL 37). Named 1913, South Vancouver By-law 251.

CHESS STREET. Named 1951, By-law 3232, after Chess Brothers Limited, a firm of wholesale fruit merchants in the False Creek industrial lands, where the streets were named after companies located there.

CHESTER STREET. Perhaps a contraction of Chesterfield Street or after the city of Chester, England. South Vancouver By-law 141, 1910, renamed Chesterfield Street (between the present East 33rd and East 37th Avenues) and First Street (between the present East 45th and East 49th Avenues). In 1954 By-law 3487 extended Chester Street from South East Marine Drive to North Kent Avenue.

Chesterfield Street. Named on Plan 1209 (1906) and Plan 1369 (1907), it lay within Kensington subdivision, which bore British place names.

First Street. Named on Plans 1390 and 1900

Other streets named after English place names in the Kensington subdivision: Dorchester, Elgin, Kensington, Roslyn, Sherbrooke, Sommerville, Winchester, Windsor. Streets not in the Kensington subdivision, but which also bore British place names: Lancaster, Northumberland, Petersham, Somerset, and Tyne.

(1907), after its location in the plans as the first street east of Fraser Street.

CHESTERFIELD STREET. See Chester Street.

CHESTNUT STREET. Named on Plan 2301 (1909), when the CPR company subdivided its property at Kitsilano Point. First listed in 1913 city directory, the name continues the pattern of "tree" names.

CHEYENNE AVENUE. First shown as a half-road allowance, unnamed, on Plan 1376 (1907). By 1911 it appears as Cheynne Avenue on Plan 3811. *Goad's Atlas*, Plate 96, shows Cheyenne Avenue. From 1914 to 1922 there are various spellings in city directories: Cheyne Walk, Cheynne Walk, and Cheynne Avenue. By 1923 the spelling is established as Cheyenne Avenue. There is no South Vancouver By-law listing Cheyenne, but South Vancouver By-law 251, 1913, assigned names of Native peoples – Cree and Mohawk – to new streets, so the name may have been adopted at the same time, after the Cheyenne people.

CHICKADEE PLACE. One of nine private thoroughfares in Enclaves 8, 9, and 10, Champlain Heights, bearing bird names submitted by Matheson Heights Co-operative and approved by the Street Naming Committee on 25 March 1981.

CHILCO STREET. Named by L.A. Hamilton, after Chilco Lake. "Tsilhqo" is a Tsilhqot'in word meaning "young man's river" (Coull 1996).

CHURCH STREET. Named 1913, South Vancouver By-law 251. A South Vancouver building permit was granted in 1912 for an addition to the Collingwood Methodist Church in Block 39, DL 37, so it is probable that the street was named after that association.

CHURCHILL STREET. This street has a complicated history. The original Churchill Street in DL 325, named by Point Grey By-law 32, 1919, lay between West 68th and West 70th Avenues, east of Adera Street. Point Grey By-law 232, 1924, changed it to Cornish Street, and the name "Churchill" was transferred to another street in DL 526 between West 52nd and West 54th Avenues, east of Adera Street. It was extended to join Connaught Drive in 1926 (Plan 5552).

Named after Samuel Gibbons Churchill (1867-1947), postmaster at Eburne Post Office, 1894-1903, and a director of Greenwood Canning Company. He became a councillor in Point Grey, 1909-11, and reeve in 1913 and 1914.

CHURCHILL STREET (DL 50). See Rupert Street.

S.G. Churchill. From group photo of the Reeves of Point Grey, 1908-1928. CVA Port. P. 188, N. 306 #3.

CITY EDGE PLACE. Private thoroughfare whose name, descriptive of its location at the south-eastern edge of the city, was approved by the Street Naming Committee in January 1992.

CLANCY LORANGER WAY. Private thoroughfare between Hillcrest Park and Capilano Stadium named after Clancy Loranger, a Vancouver sports reporter who retired in 1986. On Plan 6430 (1932) and Plan 6539 (1936) shown as *Melrose Avenue*, one of the names chosen by William B. Young, city engineering staff, who admired the work of Sir Walter Scott. The ruins of Melrose Abbey were close to Scott's home. By 1986 Melrose Avenue had been removed from the city's street system, as it was no longer a dedicated road. Although now on Parks Board property, the Street Naming Committee advised the Parks Board that it had the responsibility to oversee any changes to street names, even though this road was only an access road to a parking lot (Street Naming Committee minutes, 12 November 1986).

CLARENDON STREET. First known as Clarendon Road, it was renamed Clarendon Street by South Vancouver By-law 141, 1910. This by-law also renamed Gilbert Avenue and Gothard Street. Origin of the name "Clarendon" is unknown.

Gilbert Avenue. Named on Reference Plan 274 (1911), it lay between the present East 42nd and East 45th Avenues. Origin of name unknown.

Gothard Street. Between East 29th Avenue and Kingsway, it was named after Ambrose Gothard, a realtor who owned property in the area. He died in Vancouver, 23 June 1914, aged seventy-

three. The portion of Clarendon south of South East Marine Drive was shown on Plan 1653A (1907) and in *Goad's Atlas*, Plate 112, as Philip Road – a survey name of unknown origin. In 1961 this portion was renamed Elliot Street, By-Law 3937.

CLARK DRIVE. Named after Ephraim James Clark (1858-1942), a realtor who donated several acres to the city for a park in 1889. He owned a portion of DL 264A, shown on Plan 222 (1887). The drive originally lay between Powell Street and East 15th Avenue. In 1911, By-law 842 renamed Percival Street, between East 15th and East King Edward Avenues, Clark Drive when DL 301 was absorbed into the city. Shown on Plan 187 (1885), *Percival Street* was named by H.V. Edmonds after Reverend Percival Jenns (1835-1915), rector of St. John's Church, Victoria. His son, Eustace Jenns, married a niece of Edmonds.

CLEADON COURT. A private thoroughfare in Earl Adams Village, Champlain Heights, first listed in the 1979 city directory. Streets in this project were named after places in Northumberland County, England. Cleadon is a location in the south Tyneside district, three miles south of South Shields.

CLERE ROAD. See Dunbar Street.

CLEVELAND ROAD. See Killarney Street.

CLIFFORD STREET (DL 301). Now East 14th Avenue between Main and Prince Edward Streets. Shown on Plan 187 (1885), the owner, H.V. Edmonds, named it after his daughter, Mary Gifford Edmonds, who married C.M. Marpole. It was entered in the Land Registry Office as Clifford rather than Gifford. When DL 301 was absorbed by Vancouver in 1911, it became part of East 14th Avenue.

CLINTON STREET (Hastings Townsite). See Penticton Street.

CLINTON STREET. Now West 76th Avenue from Hudson Street east one block. Named on Plan 3069 (1910). With C.A. Griggs having power of attorney for owners Mary L. and F.T. Griggs, it was changed to West 76th Avenue by Point Grey By-law 17, 1914. Clinton Alonzo Griggs and Forest Truman Griggs (1862-1909) were storekeepers at Eburne. West 75th Avenue was called Griggs Street.

CLIVE AVENUE (DL 37). First listed in 1916 city directory, although surveyed earlier on Plans 1296, 2741, and 3524 (1909-11). Origin of name unknown.

Redmond Avenue. Shown in the 1913 and 1914 city directories as running east from 364 Spencer Street to Joyce Street, with McHardy Street intersecting. Now Clive Avenue. Probably a local name. South Vancouver Voters Lists, 1909 and 1910, show John Redmond as property owner in DL 37. Provincial Voters List, 1908, shows J.N. Redmond, farmer, at Central Park.

CLOUGH AVENUE. Now East 59th Avenue between Ontario and Main Streets. One of the owners on Plan 3065 (1910) was Edward Clough of the real estate firm of Lalande and Clough, 1908-27. Born in England, he died in Richmond, British Columbia, 1 January 1955, aged eighty-six. South Vancouver By-law 141, 1910, changed it to a portion of East 61st Avenue (now East 59th Avenue).

COAL HARBOUR CLOSE. (Deleted). Private thoroughfare on CPR property (Plan LE 5032-3). Marathon Realty proposed the name, descriptive of its location, which was approved by the Street Naming Committee on 9 August 1978.

COAL HARBOUR QUAY. Named by By-law 7474, 1995 (Plan LF 11648), it is a block-long street between Nicola and Cardero Streets. Descriptive name.

COAL HARBOUR ROAD (Deleted). Private thoroughfare on CPR property connecting Cardero Street with north end of Burrard Street. Name submitted by Marathon Realty and approved by the Street Naming Committee in April 1980. Shown on Plan LE 5032 and in city directories 1974-94. Disappeared with redevelopment.

COAL HARBOUR SEAWALK. Descriptive name for public walkway named by By-law 7474, 1995 (Plan LF 11648).

COBBLESTONE AVENUE. Private thoroughfare, shown on Plan LF 11558 (1993) and named arbitrarily by Marine Woods Developments Limited in association with Cornerstone, Fieldstone, Keystone, and Millstone.

COLERIDGE AVENUE. Probably named after the English poet Samuel Taylor Coleridge (1772-1834) in 1929, By-law 2014, which renamed Rice Avenue. In 1970 By-law 4470 extended it west from Raleigh Street into a cul-de-sac. Coleridge falls between East 47th and East 48th Avenues. See page 135.

Formerly *Rice Avenue*, named 1913, South Vancouver By-law 251, after George W. Rice (1856-1937), one of the property owners shown on Plan 3221 (1911) and in South Vancouver Voters Lists, 1910-4.

COLFAX CRESCENT. Private thoroughfare in Champlain Heights, whose name was proposed by the Three Links Care Society, sponsors of a residential complex funded by the Oddfellows and Rebekah Orders, and approved by the Street Naming Committee on 7 March 1983.

Schuyler Colfax (1823-85) wrote most of the ritual for the Rebekah Order, which was adopted by the Grand Lodge of the Independent Order of Oddfellows in 1851. He was vice-president of the United States, 1869-73.

COLK CRESCENT (Proposed). See Kullahun Crescent.

COLLEGE STREET. Probably named in association with the nearby School Avenue. Partially surveyed but not named on Plan 3224 (1910). South Vancouver By-law 6, 1911, allocated $550 for a road (now College Street) in Block 12-13, DL 50. It was first listed in 1917 city directory.

COLLINGWOOD PLACE. Named by By-law 3486, 1954. At the Board of Administration meeting 14 January 1957 (Vancouver City Council Minutes, v. 66, p. 359), the Street Naming Committee reported that the postmaster drew attention to the confusion caused by there being a 6000 block in both Collingwood Place and Collingwood Street. The committee advised the property owners that a name change was possible if they were concerned about any confusion. Evidently the owners were not, as the name is still in use.

COLLINGWOOD ROAD. See Rupert Street.

COLLINGWOOD STREET. Named on "Plan of Provincial Government Property to Be Sold at Victoria by Public Auction, Monday, January 18,

1886" (CVA map 743). This paper survey was superseded by Plan 229 (1887), which showed Collingwood Street between West 16th Avenue and Point Grey Road.

Origin of the name "Collingwood" is unknown. Major J.S. Matthews speculates that several of the men associated with the CPR and the development of Vancouver – L. Hamilton, Sanford Fleming, Henry Beatty – had connections to Collingwood, Ontario.

In the adjoining municipality Point Grey By-law 17, 1912, named Collingwood Street. Point Grey By-law 17, 1914, extended it south from West 49th Avenue to the Fraser River. Part of this extension has been absorbed by the Point Grey Golf and Country Club. In 1930 Vancouver By-law 2082 changed the portion below West 53rd Avenue to Carrington Street.

COLUMBIA STREET (DL 196). Named Columbia Avenue, after the Province of British Columbia on "Plan of the City of Vancouver, British Columbia," compiled by H.B. Smith, 1886 (Map 14267), it lay between Alexander and the present Pender Street. By 1924 it extended to Keefer Street. Changed to Columbia Street in 1950, By-law 3195, to conform with the existing Columbia Street across False Creek (although not in alignment with it).

COLUMBIA STREET (DL 200A, DL 302). Named by Dr. I.W. Powell, owner of DL 200A, after the Province of British Columbia. Shown on an 1887 map surveyed by L.A. Hamilton (Map 14160) and on an 1893 map of Vancouver drawn by Allan Stuart (Map. 14270).

In 1910 South Vancouver By-law 141 changed *Eburne Street* (DL 322) to Columbia Street between West 59th Avenue and South West Marine Drive. Eburne Street probably named after Henry Eburne, who owned property in DL 322, according to South Vancouver Voters List, 1906. Surveyed but not named on Plan 1765 (1908).

COMMERCIAL DRIVE. Named after adjoining Commercial Street in 1911, By-law 651, which renamed *Park Drive*, so called because it led to Clark Park at the southern boundary of the City of Vancouver. Park Drive was named on a 1902 map (Map 14276) and on Plan 1771, 1905, a resurvey of DL 264A.

In 1930-1 the engineering department improved the traffic flow on Commercial Drive by creating linkages between various jogs. By-law 2181, 1931, named the diversion between Adanac and Venables Streets Commercial Drive Diversion North, and the one between East 16th and East 18th Avenues Commercial Drive Diversion South.

In 1954, after the former Central Park line of the BCER interurban railway ceased operation, By-law 3487 abolished Commercial Drive Diversion South and renamed it Commercial Drive.

In June 1982, the Garibaldi Centennial Celebration Committee asked that Commercial Drive, where many Italian immigrants had settled, be changed to Via Garibaldi in honour of the Italian patriot Giuseppe Garibaldi (1807-82). Merchants on the "Drive" were against the change because of the expense. The Street Naming Committee pointed out that there was already a Garibaldi Drive in Champlain Heights, so no change was made.

COMMERCIAL STREET. Lies entirely within the former municipality of South Vancouver, slightly to the east of Commercial Drive. In 1910, South Vancouver By-law 141 changed Cedar Cottage Road, Edmund Street, and Norfolk Road to Commercial Street, probably named in expectation of commercial growth due to a real estate boom.

Cedar Cottage Road. Named by South Vancouver Highway By-law, 1903, it lay between the present East 18th and East 20th Avenues. South Vancouver Highway By-law, 1905, extended it south from East 20th Avenue to present Kingsway.

According to an article in *BC Electric Employees Magazine*, v. 7, June 1924, a wealthy Englishman named Wilson bought considerable acreage south of Kingsway in 1887, started a floral nursery, and built a bungalow that he called Cedar Cottage. The interurban railway to New Westminster, built in 1891, named a station after his nearby home.

Edmund Street. Named on Plan 2900 (1910) as "Edmond" Street and on Plan 4025 (1910) as Edmund Street. *Goad's Atlas*, Plates 95 and 99, shows that Edmund Street lay between East 40th and East 41st Avenues, and East 33rd and East 35th Avenues. Origin of name unknown.

Norfolk Road. Shown on Plan 2199 (1909), between East 48th and East 49th Avenues. Probably named after Norfolk, England, as the adjacent street in the same plan is Suffolk.

COMMISSIONER STREET. Named after the commissioners of the Vancouver Harbour Commission, in existence between 1920-9. A private thoroughfare along Burrard Inlet now under the jurisdiction of the Vancouver Port Corporation, its construction began in 1928 under the Vancouver Harbour Commission. First listed in 1937 city directory, it now extends from Victoria Drive to Renfrew Street.

COMMODORE ROAD. Named 1984, By-law 5756, Plan LF 10627. Imperial Ventures Limited chose a nautical theme for its condominium development at False Creek. Other names in the complex are Spyglass Place, Starboard Square, and Wheelhouse Square.

COMOX STREET. Named after Comox, shown on the map that L.A. Hamilton used when assigning street names in DL 185. Comox, "abundance" in Kwakwala, has long been treasured for its wealth of resources (Coull 1996).

CONNAUGHT DRIVE. Named on Plan 6011 (1921) by the CPR after the Duke of Connaught and Strathearn (1850-1942), third son of Queen Victoria and Governor-General of Canada, 1911-6.

Extended southeast from West 37th Avenue to Granville Street by Point Grey By-law 483, 1926 (Plan 5552, [1926]). The portion of Connaught Drive lying east of Oak Street between West 32nd and West 41st Avenues was changed in 1951 to a portion of Willow Street by By-law 3232.

COOK STREET. Surveyed and named on Plan 5832 (1925), a special survey of part of DL 302. Previously it had been considered as part of Columbia Street. First listed in 1931 city directory with no occupants. Three of the streets in this special survey were named after early Vancouver aldermen.

Edward Beaton Cook (1853-1940) served as an alderman from 1901 through 1905. Born in Ontario, he came to Vancouver in 1886 and was shown in the first Vancouver Voters List. A contractor and stonemason, he built Engelsea Lodge, now gone, and Douglas Lodge, at 1507 West 12th Avenue.

COOPERATIVE WAY. A private thoroughfare, the name chosen by Still Creek Housing Cooperative, Plan LF 11473, and approved by City Engineering Department in 1991.

COPELAND AVENUE. Private thoroughfare in Champlain Heights, named after Copeland Islands Marine Park and approved by the Street Naming Committee on 17 April 1979.

The Manager's Report to City Council, 27 April 1979, regarding street names (Vancouver City Council Minutes, v. 132, p. 26), stated that Abacus Cities, developers of Enclave 15, chose names of provincial parks. Copeland Islands were named in 1945 after Joe Copeland, a hand logger and trapper in Theodosia Arm circa 1900. He is mentioned in *Spilsbury's Coast* as "old Joe Copeland who used to meet the steamboat dressed in a full Confederate Army uniform, complete with the little cap" (White 1987, 51).

COPLEY STREET. Changed from Copley Drive by South Vancouver By-law 141, 1910. Probably named after Richard Theophilus Copley (1851-1917), who came to Vancouver in 1903 from England, where he had been a leather merchant. He owned property in DL 195.

In 1954 By-law 3415 changed the angled arm of Copley Street to part of East 15th Avenue. Kamloops Street between Grandview Highway and East 15th Avenue was renamed Copley.

COQUIHALLA DRIVE. Private thoroughfare named 1972, By-law 4636, after the Coquihalla River by the United Cooperative Housing Society, which named its streets after BC geographical features. According to Akrigg (1997), Coquihalla means "greedy or hungry waters."

CORAL REEF PLACE. Private thoroughfare, name approved by the Street Naming Committee on 3 June 1985. Riverside Landing Housing Cooperative suggested names based on marine features.

CORDIALE DRIVE. Private thoroughfare in Champlain Heights, named by the Le Coeur Housing Cooperative after the French adjective meaning "cordial," or "sincere." Approved by the Street Naming Committee on 25 March 1981.

CORDOVA STREET. Shown on "Plan of the City of Vancouver, British Columbia" compiled by H.B. Smith, 1886 (Map 14267). Named by L.A. Hamilton, CPR land commissioner, who took the name of Cordova Channel from a map. In 1790, Sub-Lieutenant Manuel Quimper of the Spanish navy called the present Esquimalt Harbour

Puerto de Cordova after Don Antonio Bucareli y Cordova, 46th Viceroy of Mexico.

Willow Street. Named arbitrarily on a fire insurance plan of Granville, British Columbia, August 1885, and published by the Sanborn Map and Publishing Company Limited (Map 14258), it lay where the present Cordova Street is, between the present Carrall and Cambie Streets.

In 1897 By-law 187 changed Oppenheimer Street to East Cordova Street east from Carrall Street. The Cordova Diversion was created in 1970 (Plan 14042) to link Cordova Street with Powell Street at Campbell Avenue.

Oppenheimer Street. Shown on "Plan of the City of Vancouver, British Columbia," compiled by H.B. Smith, 1886 (Map 14267). Named after David Oppenheimer (1834-97), one of the shareholders in the Vancouver Improvement Company, which owned most of DL 196. He became second mayor of Vancouver. In 1897 By-law 187 changed Oppenheimer Street to East Cordova Street, then transferred the name "Oppenheimer" to Carl Avenue, which ran north

and south. Evidently the mistake was realized because in 1898 By-law 314 changed Oppenheimer back to Carl Avenue and the name "Oppenheimer" disappeared.

CORNERSTONE STREET. Private thoroughfare shown on Plan LF 11558 (1993) and named arbitrarily by Marine Woods Developments Limited in association with Cobblestone, Fieldstone, Keystone, and Millstone.

CORNETT ROAD. Named 1954, By-law 3486, after Jonathan Webster Cornett (1882-1973), mayor of Vancouver 1941-6. He also served as a councillor and reeve in South Vancouver prior to its amalgamation with Vancouver in 1929.

CORNISH STREET. Formerly Churchill Street. Named by Point Grey By-law 232, 1924, after the Cornish family, who owned property in DL 325. The 1916 Provincial Voters List shows Charles Cornish, DL 325, Point Grey, blacksmith, and Charles Wallace Cornish, DL 325, Point Grey, teamster. Charles Cornish, born in England, died 16 March 1939, aged seventy-six.

Mr. and Mrs. Cornish and their eight sons and two daughters. In the back row are Royal, Frederick, Wilfred, Albert (or "Robin"), Gordon, and George. In the front row are Charles, Muriel, Mr. Cornish, Mrs. Cornish, Eva, and Hebert. CVA Port P. 645.

Cordova Street, looking west, July 1886, five weeks after the great fire. CVA Str. P. 7, N. 31.

Water and Cordova Street (on the right), looking east, June 1932. CVA Str. P. 9, N. 14.

Visit of the Duke and Dutchess of Cornwall and York, 30 September 1901. This is not an actual photo, but was painstakingly built-up by John White, photographer, Carrall Street. In the front row are C.M. Beecher, one of the owners and managers; T.R.H. The Duke and Duchess of Cornwall and York (later George V and Queen Mary); John Hendry, general manager, B.C. Mills, T. & T. Co.; lady in waiting; R.H. Alexander, local manager, Hastings Sawmill; Mrs. John Hendry; Miss Hendry (later Mrs. Eric W. Hamber); and Henry Chambers, mill employee. In the second row are Lt. Col. His Worship T.O. Townley, mayor of Vancouver; Mrs. R.H. Alexander; F.L. Beecher, mill office staff; Geo. R. Maxwell, MP for Vancouver; Sir Wilfrid Laurier, prime minister of Canada; Arthur J. Hendry, Supt. of Hastings Sawmill; E.C. Mahoney, local sales and yards; and Campbell Sweeny, manager, Bank of Montreal. The axeman is Jim McDonald; the sawmen Asa Dunning and Jim Andrews; and the constable is Donald D. McIntosh. cva Duke of C & Y, P 1 Port. N. 18.

CORONATION STREET (Proposed). See Discovery Street.

CORNWALL AVENUE (DL 526). Named to commemorate the visit of the Duke and Duchess of Cornwall and York to Vancouver on 30 September 1901. Shown as Cornwall Street on Plan 848 (1902). Extended by Plan 2301 (1909), from Yew Street to Chestnut Street. In 1958, By-law 3731

belatedly confirmed the name and changed the designation to Cornwall Avenue to conform to the pattern of avenues running east and west.

CORNWALL STREET (DL 540). See Blenheim Street.

CORSICA WAY. Private thoroughfare in Champlain Heights first listed in 1982 city 1941), directory. Henriquez and Partners, architects, chose Mediterranean names for the enclave.

COTTON DRIVE. Named after Francis Lovett Carter Cotton (1874-1919), founder and owner of the *Daily News Advertiser*. He was an MLA (1890-1903), minister of finance (1893-1900), and first chancellor of the University of British Columbia. He died 20 November 1919. Shown on a 1902 map surveyed by Hermon and Burwell (Map 14171) and on Plan 1771 (1905), a resurvey of DL 264A.

COTTRELL STREET. Named Cottrell Avenue in 1947, By-law 3002, Plan LF 579, after the Cottrell Forwarding Company, which leased property in DL 2037, Parcel G. In 1901, George Henry Cottrell (1856-1951) opened Vancouver's first storage warehouses on Water Street. Elected an alderman in 1912, he served on the Parks Board, 1921-5.

Cottrell Forwarding Company moved its operations east to Thornton Avenue and requested the city to exchange street names. By-law 5267, 1979, changed Cottrell Avenue to Thornton Avenue and Thornton Avenue to Cottrell Avenue. Later that year Cottrell Avenue became Cottrell Street (By-law 5299) to conform to the pattern of streets running north and south.

COURTENAY STREET. Named by Point Grey By-law 17, 1912, probably after the town of Courtenay, British Columbia. It lay between West 10th and West 16th Avenues. Extended to West 8th Avenue in 1927 (Plans 5817 and 5867), when Jericho Heights Estates was developed.

COY STREET (Deleted). Named on Plan 1358 (1907) and first listed in 1915 city directory. In 1945, when a road was built between East 14th and East 15th Avenues to connect Clark Drive and Knight Street, Coy Street disappeared and the name was cancelled by a resolution attached to By-law 3415, 1945. Origin of name has not been verified, but the city directory listed several Coys from 1907 on.

CRABTREE LANE (Deleted). A descriptive name, shown on "Plan of the City of Vancouver, British Columbia," compiled by H.B. Smith, 1886 (Plan 14267). It lay at a southeasterly angle from the south end of Raymur Street. When False Creek was filled, and the nearby streets replotted, the lane disappeared.

CRADDOCK STREET. See Duchess Street.

CREE STREET. Named 1913, South Vancouver By-law 251, probably after the Cree people; another street in the same by-law is called Mohawk. Surveyed in 1908, Plan 1777.

Previously known as *Peacey Road*, after John Peacey (1853-1936), who owned property nearby. Born in England, he spent thirty years in Vancouver.

CREEKSIDE DRIVE. A descriptive name for a street near False Creek named 1978, By-law 5199. When the area was developed, the BC Central Credit Union – whose new building would be in the vicinity – asked the Street Naming Committee on 15 January 1978 to call the road Credit Union Way. The 9 August meeting of the committee, however, confirmed the name "Creekside" because the planning department advised that the road could be continued farther along False Creek.

CREELMAN AVENUE. Named after Adam Rutherford Creelman (1849-1916), general counsel for the CPR. Shown on Plan 2301 (1909) and first listed in the 1913 city directory. The city belatedly confirmed the name in 1958, By-law 3731.

CREERY ROAD. Now East 58th Avenue between Prince Edward and Fraser Streets. South Vancouver assessment roll, 1895, shows Alexander McCreight Creery (1863-1942) owning Block 3-7 inclusive, DL 657. Irish born manager of the insurance department of H. Bell-Irving Company, he became an MLA for the Provincial Party in 1924. The property, subdivided in 1908, Plan 1790, shows owners Leslie and Bernard Tate Creery. Shown in *Goad's Atlas*, Plate 106, as 60th Avenue East (late Discovery Road and Creery Road). Changed to East 60th Avenue (now East 58th Avenue) by South Vancouver By-law 141, 1910. See also Discovery Road.

THE CRESCENT. Descriptive name for a "circle" street in Shaughnessy Heights, developed by the CPR and shown on Plan 4502 (1913).

CRESSWELL COURT. Private thoroughfare in Earl Adams Village, Champlain Heights, and first listed in 1979 city directory. Streets in this project were named after places in Northumberland County, England. Cresswell is a village on the North Sea coast.

CROMPTON STREET. Named 1929, By-law 2014, probably after Arthur Crompton (1864-

1941), councillor in South Vancouver, 1922. He was a printer for the *Vancouver Sun* until 1924 and a member of the Typographical Union, Local 226. Formerly *Campbell Road*, unofficially named after Charles Stuart Campbell (1870-1969), property owner in DL 327, who came to British Columbia in 1889 as an import lacrosse player for the New Westminster Salmonbellies. A *Vancouver Daily Province* printer until his retirement in 1952, he served as president of the Typographical Union, Local 226, in 1901, 1902, and 1925-33. Served as a South Vancouver councillor in 1910 and 1911.

Although South Vancouver By-law 141, 1910, renamed it Inverness Street, it continued to be known as Campbell Road until Vancouver By-law 2014, 1929, renamed it Crompton.

CROMWELL STREET. Named by South Vancouver By-law 251, 1913, it lay between the Fraser River and present East 54th Avenue. In 1921, South Vancouver By-law 558 renamed it Battison Street, but this change did not occur; maps of the 1930s still show "Cromwell." With the Champlain Heights development in the 1970s and the construction of Marine Way in the 1980s, only a small portion of Cromwell Street between Marine Way and Kent Street South remains.

Origin of name unknown, but possibly after Oliver Cromwell (1599-1658), English soldier and statesman.

CROWE STREET. Named on Plan 5832 (1925), a special survey of part of DL 302. Previously considered part of Alberta Street, first listed in 1929 city directory. Three of the streets in this special survey were named after early Vancouver aldermen.

Sanford Johnston Crowe (1868-1931) came to Vancouver in 1888 and founded the firm Crowe and Wilson, contractors. An alderman from 1909 to 1915, he was

Senator S.J. Crowe. CVA Port P. 141, N. 328.

elected to the House of Commons in 1917 and appointed to the Senate in 1921.

CROWLEY DRIVE. Named 1994, By-law 7282, after Everett Crowley (1909-84), South Vancouver pioneer who operated the Avalon Dairy, founded by his father in 1906. On 24 October 1995, the Street Naming Committee extended the street to include the 3500 block between Aberdeen and Tyne Streets.

CROWN ROAD (Hastings Townsite). See Glendale Street.

CROWN CRESCENT. Named on Plan 5817 (1927), surveyed by J. Alexander Walker. The plan covered the area between West 10th and West 8th Avenues from Discovery to Crown. An article in *Journal of the Town Planning Institute*, Volume 4, December 1925, stated that the municipal authorities of Point Grey requested the provincial government, in its survey, to contour the streets to this sloping ground rather than to continue the rectangular grid. Other streets so contoured were the north end of Courtenay Street and Wallace Crescent. Plan 5867 (1927) further subdivided part of the area for Jericho Heights Estates.

CROWN STREET. Named by Point Grey By-law 17, 1912, probably, according to Arthur G. Smith (former land registrar for Vancouver), because of its proximity to the nearby naval reserve, DL 176, a Crown reserve. It lay between present West 10th and West 37th Avenues. Point Grey By-law 17, 1914, extended it from South West Marine Drive to the north boundary of the Musqueam Band Reserve.

Moncton Road. Shown on Plan 2439 (1909) and Plan 3720 (1911) between West 35th and West 37th Avenues and on Plan 3720 (1911) between South West Marine Drive and the north boundary of the Musqueam Band Reserve. Probably named after Moncton, New Brunswick, as an adjacent street in Plan 2439 shows St. John's. Changed to Crown Street by Point Grey By-law 17, 1914.

By-law 5010, 1976, plan LF 7356, extended Crown Street into the Musqueam Band Reserve.

CULLODEN STREET. Named by South Vancouver By-law 141, 1910, which renamed Culloden Avenue. Shown on Plan 1645 (1908) and probably named after Culloden Moor,

Scotland. This same by-law also changed Montana and O'Connor Streets.

Montana Street. Named after the state of Montana, on Plan 1522 (1907), it lay between East 33rd and East 37th Avenues. Dr. S.E. Fleming, care of Panton and Hutchison, owned property in DL 700 in 1907. Samuel Panton was connected with the Montana Company, a real estate firm, hence the street name.

O'Connor Street. Named on Plan 1383 (1907), it lay between the present East 37th and East 41st Avenues. Origin of name unknown.

CURATE WYND. Private thoroughfare in Champlain Heights named by the Kinross Creek

Housing Cooperative, which took the name from a street in the Scottish town of Kinross. Approved by the Street Naming Committee on 8 July 1982.

CYPRESS CRESCENT. Named on Plan 6032 (1928), it abuts Cypress Street.

CYPRESS STREET. Officially registered on Plan 590 (1891) but named on an 1887 map (Map 14160) by L.A. Hamilton, who chose tree names. Extended by Point Grey By-laws 17, 1912; 232, 1924; and 483, 1926.

CYPRESS LANE. See Killarney Street.

D

"D" ROAD (DL 319/DL 526). See Park Drive.

DALY ROAD. See Dumfries Street.

DARTMOOR PLACE. Private thoroughfare in Champlain Heights, named by Intrawest Properties Limited, whose development, Moorpark, bears names of moors – Dartmoor, Lynmoor, and Weymoor. Approved by the Street Naming Committee on 25 March 1981.

DAVID ROAD. Now part of East 60th Avenue. Changed to a portion of East 62nd Avenue by South Vancouver By-law 141, 1910. Its location has not been ascertained, nor has any information about its name.

DAVID STREET. See McKinnon Street.

DAVIE STREET. Named by L.A. Hamilton after Alexander Edmund Davie (1847-89), attorney general of British Columbia, 1883-7, and premier, 1887-9.

DAVIES ROAD (Deleted). Shown on Plans 2202 and 2327 (1909), it lay between Victoria Drive and Elliott Street. South Vancouver By-law 141, 1910, changed it to East 61st Avenue, later East 59th Avenue, which disappeared with the replotting for Fraserview.

South Vancouver Voters List, 1910, shows the owner of DL 727 as the estate of T.W. Duff, care

of Maddison, Stirling and Company, Old Drury, London, England. The 1910 edition of Kelly's Post Office Directory for London, England, shows the firm Maddison, Stirling, Humm and Davies, Solicitors, 33 Old Jewry, London. Frederick Farley Davies, admitted to practise as a solicitor in June 1905, joined the firm around 1909.

DAWSON ROAD (DL 195). Now East 17th Avenue from east boundary of John Hendry Park to Nanaimo Street. Shown unnamed on Plan 1224 (1906), surveyed by George Herbert Dawson (1866-1940), who was assistant city engineer, 1889-90. In private practice in Vancouver, 1890-1911, he became surveyor general for British Columbia from 1911-7. An unofficial name, South Vancouver By-law 141, 1910, changed it to East 17th Avenue.

DAWSON STREET (DL 337). First listed in the 1917 city directory but partially surveyed (though not named) on Plan 2347 (1909). The name appears on Plan 4189 (1912). Although this plan was cancelled in 1916, the name, whose origin is not known, was retained.

DEAL AVENUE (Deleted). Shown on Plan Ga 49, attached to By-law 3330, 1952, this part of Fraserview was replotted, and Deal Avenue, named after Royal Cinque Ports Golf Club at Deal, England, disappeared.

DEASE LANE. Private thoroughfare, named 1972, By-law 4636, after Dease Lake, which was named after fur trader Peter Warren Dease (1788-1863).

DEERING ISLAND PLACE. Named 1991, By-law 6808, Plan LF 11267, from its location on Deering Island, which was named on Plan L145 (May 1930). Origin of name unknown.

DENMAN STREET. Named after Denman Island, shown on the map that L.A. Hamilton used when naming the streets in DL 185. Denman Island commemorates Rear Admiral, the Honourable Joseph Denman (1810-74), commander-in-chief, Pacific Station, 1864-6.

DEVON ROAD. Now West 31st Avenue between Blenheim and Balaclava Streets. A survey name only, shown on Plan 2213 (1909), it probably was named after Devon, England.

DEVONSHIRE CRESCENT. Surveyed 1921, Plan 6011, and named by the CPR, developers of Shaughnessy Heights, after the Duke of Devonshire (1868-1938), Governor-General of Canada, 1916-21.

Point Grey By-law 232, 1924, confirmed the name between Cartier and Selkirk Streets and extended the Crescent from Granville to Oak Streets by Point Grey By-law 483, 1926.

DIEPPE DRIVE AND DIEPPE PLACE. In Renfrew Heights subdivision, developed by Central Mortgage and Housing Corporation as low-rental housing for Second World War veterans and named after the Dieppe raid of 19 August 1942, in which nearly 5,000 Canadian soldiers participated. Name approved by Vancouver City Council on 23 March 1948.

DINMONT AVENUE. Shown on Plan 6430 (1932) and Plan 6539 (1936), and first listed in 1942 city directory. According to S.J. Montgomery, secretary of board of works, William B. Young, City Engineering Department, chose the name from Sir Walter Scott's novel, *Guy Mannering*, in which Dandie Dinmont owned a special breed of terrier.

DISCOVERY ROAD (DL 657). Now East 58th Avenue between Prince Edward and Fraser Streets. Shown on a 1910 map of South Vancouver (Map 14272) as Discovery Road (60th Avenue). Changed to East 60th Avenue by South Vancouver

By-Law 141, 1910. Shown in *Goad's Atlas*, Plate 106, as 60th Avenue East (late Discovery and Creery Roads). See also Creery Road.

DISCOVERY STREET (DL 540). Named 1951, By-law 3250, after Captain George Vancouver's ship *Discovery*, when Imperial Street was renamed to remove duplication with Imperial Street in Burnaby. Residents turned down the suggestion that Imperial Street become Coronation Street to commemorate the impending coronation of Elizabeth II (*News Herald*, 8 May 1951).

Imperial Street. Named on Plan 229 (1887), after Imperial Naval Reserve, DL 176, according to E.B. Hermon, pioneer surveyor. It lay between present Belmont and West 6th Avenues. Point Grey By-law 17, 1912, extended it to West 16th Avenue, and Point Grey By-law 232, 1924, further extended it to West 25th Avenue. In 1925 this latter portion became part of the University Endowment Lands. So Imperial Road still exists in Pacific Spirit Regional Park outside the city limits. By-law 2698, 1941, closed Imperial Street between West 2nd and Belmont Avenues to all but the military traffic of RCAF Jericho station.

DOCK STREET. See Windsor Street.

DOGWOOD AVENUE. Named after the dogwood tree in 1930, By-law 2082, which renamed 52nd Avenue South to remove confusion with 52nd Avenue. Surveyed in 1912, Plan 4268. The dogwood tree became the floral emblem of British Columbia in 1956. See page 135.

DOMAN STREET. First listed in *B.C. Gazette*, 24 February 1898, as Doman Road. Named after the Doman family, who had owned property in DL 338 since 1893. South Vancouver By-law 65, 1903, described it as lying between the present East 45th and East 54th Avenues. South Vancouver Highway By-law, 1905, extended it south to what was later Asquith Avenue. In 1970, when Champlain Heights was replotted, By-law 4770, Plan LF 4530, deleted the portion south of East 54th and named a new part, between East 60th and East 62 Avenues, Doman. In 1975 By-law 5195, Plan LE 3742, renamed this short section Sparbrook Crescent.

DOMINION ROAD. Now East 51st Avenue between Prince Edward and Fraser Streets. A survey name only, shown on Plan 727 (1894), and probably an arbitrary choice, as the other name on the plan was Government Road.

DONARD STREET. Now East 40th Avenue between St. Catherines and Ross Streets. Named on Plan 1378 (1907). Changed to East 41st Avenue (now East 40th Avenue) in 1910, South Vancouver By-law 141. Origin of name unknown.

DONCASTER WAY. An arbitrary choice of name, first listed in the 1971 directory. In 1969 University Endowment Lands administration created a subdivision. In 1970 an amendment to the Vancouver Charter transferred this land to the city. In 1974 the Street Naming Committee approved the name, which was already in use.

DONNELLY STREET. Now East 24th Avenue between Rupert and Cassiar Streets. Named on Plan 1769 (1907) after the owner of the property, Patrick Donnelly, born 1875, a real estate agent and financial broker with Canadian Financiers Limited.

DORCHESTER STREET. See Inverness Street.

DOUGLAS CRESCENT. Named as Douglas Avenue on Plan 4502 (1913), when the CPR developed Shaughnessy Heights subdivision. Changed to Douglas Crescent in 1930, By-law 2082, after Thomas Douglas, fifth Earl of Selkirk (1771-1820), who founded the Red River settlement in 1812.

DOUGLAS ROAD. One of the earliest roads in the Lower Mainland, Douglas Road ran from Douglas Street (now 8th Street) in New Westminster through dense forest along Burnaby Lake to Burrard Inlet, where it ended at the New Brighton Hotel. Completed in 1865, the road was named after Sir James Douglas (1803-77), then governor of the mainland colony of British Columbia. Only a small remnant of this historic road exists in Vancouver (within New Brighton Park).

DOVER STREET. See Duff Street.

DRAKE STREET. Named by L.A. Hamilton, CPR land commissioner, after Montague William Tyrwhitt-Drake (1830-1908), an MPP for Victoria, 1883-6. A lawyer and QC, be became a member of the BC Supreme Court in 1889. Shown on Plan 210 (1886).

DRUMMOND DRIVE. Named by Point Grey By-law 17, 1912, probably after Drummond Street in Montreal, where George Stephen, first president of the CPR, had a mansion. Formerly *Dufferin Avenue*, after the Marquess of Dufferin (1826-1902), Canada's third Governor-General. Named on Plan 6583 (1911), a survey of part of Langara subdivision in DL 140. Point Grey By-law 483, 1926, extended Drummond southeast from Blanca Street to West 2nd Avenue.

DUBLIN ROAD. Now East 48th Avenue between Elliott and Vivian Streets. Named on Plan 2484 (1910), probably after Dublin, Ireland.

DUBLIN STREET (DL 301). Now East 13th Avenue between Main and Prince Edward Streets. Shown on Plan 187 (1885) and named by the owner, H.V. Edmonds, after his birthplace of Dublin, Ireland. It became part of East 13th Avenue when Vancouver absorbed DL 301 in 1911.

DUBOIS AVENUE (Deleted). Named after Dubois Street, Burnaby, which it adjoined, and indirectly after Peter Dubois, a stonecutter from Quebec, who owned 7.9 acres in Burnaby Small Holdings (DL 36-49) in 1900. Shown on Plan LF 4530, By-law 4770, 1970 and deleted on plan LE 3742, By-law 5195, 1978.

DUCHESS STREET. Unnamed on Plan 2380 (1909). First listed in the 1917 city directory and likely named in association with nearby Earles and Princess Streets. By-law 3045, 1948, extended it when Craddock Street was renamed (Vancouver City Council Minutes, v. 54, p. 259).

Craddock Street. Unnamed on Plan 2970 (1909) and named on a City Engineer's map, 1930, as Haddock Street [sic] (Map 14317). Craddock Street only listed as such in 1930 and 1931 city directories. The 1932 directory shows "now called Duchess Street," but it was not changed officially until 1948, By-law 3045. In a 1948 letter to J.S. Matthews, John Tyrrwhit Cradock (spelled with one "d") states: "I was engaged by the Municipality of South Vancouver and became assistant engineer 1912-1914." He is listed in 1913 city directory.

DUDLEY STREET. Shown as Dudley Road on Plan 1477 (1907) and renamed Dudley Street in

1910, South Vancouver By-law 141. Origin of name unknown.

DUFF STREET. Named as Duff Road on Plan 2202 (1909), it became Duff Street by South Vancouver By-law 141, 1910. Ellen Harriet Duff is shown as co-owner, with H.J. Humm, of DL 727 on Plan 2202 (1909). However, South Vancouver assessment rolls of 1893 and 1895 show T.W. Duff as owner of 53.5 acres, DL 727. South Vancouver Voters List, 1910, shows "Duff, T.W., Estate of, care of Madison, Stirling and Co., London, England." In 1913, South Vancouver By-law 252 changed Duff Street between the present East 66th Avenue and South East Marine Drive to Elm Street (later Ivy Street).

In 1950 By-law 3195 changed *Dover Street* between South East Marine Drive and Kent Street North to Duff Street. Probably named after Dover, England, by South Vancouver By-law 251, 1913, although surveyed earlier on Plan 2917 (1910) and Plan 3470 (1911).

DUFFERIN AVENUE (DL 140). See Drummond Drive.

DUFFERIN STREET. Now 2nd Avenue between Cambie and Prince Edward Streets. Named on Plan 197 (1885), after the Marquess of Dufferin (1826-1902), Governor-General of Canada, 1872-8, by Dr. Israel W. Powell, owner of DL 200A. Renamed by By-law 1803, 1926.

Painting of His Excellency, the Earl of Dufferin. CVA Port. P. 304, N. 152 #1.

DUKE STREET. Named in association with the existing aristocratic names of adjoining Duchess and Earles Streets when By-law 2014, 1929, renamed Princess Street (DL 37) because of duplication of the name in DL 196. *Princess Street*, unnamed on Plan 2421 (1909), and first listed in the 1914 city directory, probably named in association with nearby Earles Street.

DUMFRIES STREET. Named by South Vancouver By-law 141, 1910, probably after Dumfries, Scotland, as many of the streets named in this by-law had Scottish place names. This by-law also renamed the following streets: Waters Road between East 15th and East 20th Avenues; Thynne Road between East 27th and East 31st Avenues; Daly Street between East 31st and East 33rd Avenues; and Ferrisdale Boulevard between East 45th and East 49th Avenues.

Henderson's Vancouver Directory, 1909. p. 40.

Daly Road. Unnamed on Plan 2318 (1909). The owner, E.A.C. Studd, was in the investment firm Studd and Daly. Harold Mayne Daly, previously in the law firm of Burns and Daly, was last listed in the 1914 city directory. However, South Vancouver By-law 141 was incorrect in renaming Daly Street as part of Dumfries because Daly paralleled Dumfries and

Several Vancouver streets were named after Governors-General: Marquess of Dufferin (1872-8), Marquess of Lorne (1878-83), Marquess of Lansdowne (1883-8), Baron Stanley of Preston (1888-93), Earl of Aberdeen (1893-8), Earl of Minto (1898-04), Duke of Connaught (1911-6), Duke of Devonshire (1916-21), Viscount Willingdon (1926-31), Earl of Athlone (1940-6).

Waters Road. Named on Plan 3142 (1910). Jno., or J.R., Waters, shown in South Vancouver Voters Lists, 1908-15, owned property in DL 755 and DL 756, which abutted the property shown in Plan 3142, so the road was probably named after him.

DUNBAR STREET. Named on "Plan of Provincial Government Property to Be Sold at Victoria by Public Auction, Monday, January 18, 1886" (CVA Map 743). This paper survey was superseded by Plan 229 (1887), which showed Dunbar Street between the present Cameron and West 16th Avenues. Origin of the name is unknown, but it is not named after Charles Trott Dunbar, realtor, who came to Vancouver in 1889.

In the adjoining municipality, Point Grey By-law 17, 1912, changed Clere Road to Dunbar Street between West 16th Avenue and South West Marine Drive. Point Grey By-law 17, 1914, further extended it to the Fraser River. The portion of the street south of West 51st Avenue has been absorbed by Point Grey Golf Club.

Clere Road. Named on Plans 3151, 3268, 3284, and many others, 1910-1. Probably after James E. St. Clere – of the real estate firm St. Clere, Norris and Company – who served as a Point Grey councillor in 1908 and 1909. Listed in Vancouver city directory, 1904-10.

DUNBAR DIVERSION. Named 1928, By-law 1932. Surveyed in 1924, Plan 5534, owner the BCER. A notation on Plan 5534 reads: "to be designated as a public highway." The BCER built a street car line up the side of the Dunbar hill and started service on 3 November 1923 from Alma and 10th Avenue directly to Dunbar Street and 16th Avenue.

DUNDAS STREET. Origin of name unknown. Surveyed but unnamed on Plan 178 (1884) for DL 184. Named on a 1905 map (CVA map 59-B) between Semlin and Nanaimo Streets. Named on Plan 100 (1906), a resurvey of Hastings Townsite. Changed to Powell Street in 1911, By-Law 842, but changed back to Dundas in 1918, By-law 1337.

DUNDEE STREET. Probably named after Dundee, Scotland, when South Vancouver By-law 252, 1913, renamed part of Maple Street (DL-50) south of Kingsway to East 41st Avenue. The other portion of Maple became Moss Street in 1929.

DUNELM AVENUE. A private thoroughfare in Champlain Heights, first listed in the 1979 city directory. Named by the Greater Vancouver Housing Corporation in association with nearby Tyne Street and the Tyne River in England, which bisects the counties of Durham and Northumberland. As there is a Durham Street in Burnaby, the name "Dunelm" was chosen – a former name for Durham.

DUNKIRK STREET. Named by Point Grey By-law 17, 1914, although it had been surveyed in 1907, Plan 1384. Origin of name unknown. There is a Dunkirk in Kent and one in Gloucester, England. Not listed in the city directory until 1949, when many assumed it had been named after Dunkirk, France, where a dramatic evacuation of Allied troops took place in May-June 1940.

DUNLEVY AVENUE. Named after Peter Curran Dunlevy (1834-1904), who owned a ranch and hotel at Soda Creek in the Cariboo. One of the original stockholders of the Coal Harbour Land Syndicate (*Port Moody Gazette*, 16 May 1885).

DUNSMUIR STREET. Named after Robert Dunsmuir (1825-89), prominent colliery owner at Nanaimo, who built the Esquimalt and Nanaimo Railway in 1884-6. He owned property in DL 540, as shown in Vancouver Voters List, 1886.

On 24 May 1973, the Dunsmuir-Melville Connector opened to extend the one-way flow of traffic from Dunsmuir Street to Pender Street.

DUNSMUIR VIADUCT. Named as a dedicated street in 1993, By-law 7237 (Plan LF 11554), so that police, firefighters, and ambulance drivers could give a location in emergencies.

DUPONT STREET. See Pender Street.

DURANLEAU STREET. A private thoroughfare on Granville Island, probably named after the Honourable Alfred Duranleau (1871-1951), minister of marine and fisheries, 1930-5, under whose jurisdiction Granville Island fell. First listed as a street in 1951 city directory.

DURWARD AVENUE. Named after the title character in Sir Walter Scott's novel *Quentin Durward* when By-law 2028, 1929, renamed East 33rd Avenue between Fraser and Windsor Streets because it falls between East 32nd and East 33rd

38

DUNSMUIR VIADUCT. Named as a dedicated street in 1993, By-law 7237 (Plan LF 11554), so that police, firefighters, and ambulance drivers could give a location in emergencies.

DUPONT STREET. See Pender Street.

DURANLEAU STREET. A private thoroughfare on Granville Island, probably named after the Honourable Alfred Duranleau (1871-1951), minister of marine and fisheries, 1930-5, under whose jurisdiction Granville Island fell. First listed as a street in 1951 city directory.

DURWARD AVENUE. Named after the title character in Sir Walter Scott's novel *Quentin Durward* when By-law 2028, 1929, renamed East 33rd Avenue between Fraser and Windsor Streets because it falls between East 32nd and East 33rd Avenues. See page 135.

Formerly *Stretch Road*. Unnamed on Plan 344 (1889), 436 (1890), and 1985 (1909). Mrs. Catherine D. Stretch, shown in 1903 South Vancouver Voters List, owned property in DL 391-2. BC Provincial Voters Lists 1903 and 1907 show Thomas Pinnington Stretch, farmer, on North Arm Road (now Fraser Street) across from the cemetery. He is also listed in the 1901 Canada Census along with his wife, Cathrine D. Changed to East 33rd Avenue in 1910, South Vancouver By-law 141.

E

'E' ROAD. Now West 76th Avenue between Hudson and Selkirk Streets. A survey designation only, described in *B.C. Gazette*, 15 January 1900, p. 198.

EARL STREET. See Argyle Street.

EARLES STREET. Named Earles Road by South Vancouver By-law 65, 1903, after English-born Henry Earle (1842-1929), who came to British Columbia in 1889 and bought land in South Vancouver, where he is shown in South Vancouver Voters Lists, 1893-4. The 1908 Provincial Voters List shows him as a carpenter at Central Park. The road lay between the present Kingsway to the BCER tramline. South Vancouver Highway By-law, 1905, extended it north to the present East 29th Avenue. It eventually extended as far south as East 45th Avenue. A portion of Earles Street between East 67th Avenue and South East Marine Drive was absorbed by the Fraserview Golf Course. In 1910 South Vancouver By-law 141 changed Earles Road and Winters Road to Earles Street.

Winters Road (DL 50). Not shown on any plans or maps, a local name for the road on which lived Thomas Francis Winters (1867-1954). He was born in Ireland and came to the Vancouver area in 1899, where served on the South Vancouver police force and, later, with the National Harbours Board police.

EAST STREET. See Edinburgh Street.

EBURNE AVENUE (DL 318). See South West Marine Drive.

EBURNE STREET (DL 322). See Columbia Street.

ECHO PLACE. Private thoroughfare in Champlain Heights, the name was approved by the Street Naming Committee on 21 June 1978. Community Builders called its project in Enclave 16 Park Place and named its thoroughfares after parks. Echo Lake Park is near Lumby, British Columbia.

EDDINGTON DRIVE. First listed in 1954 city directory. William B. Young, then assistant city engineer, suggested the name after the famous British astronomer Sir Arthur Eddington (1882-1944). According to J.S. Matthews, the CPR proposed to subdivide the vacant lands adjoining the Quilchena Golf Course. A sewer for drainage was necessary, and, as a street for it to pass along was lacking, one was created. A map produced by the City Engineers Office in December 1930 (Map 14317) shows a dotted line where Eddington Drive now lies.

EDGAR CRESCENT. Named 1954, By-law 3457, after Robert McBeth Edgar (1876-1953), who served twenty-seven years on the zoning board for the City of Vancouver. Shown on Plan LC 132.

EDINBURGH ROAD. See Waverly Avenue.

EDINBURGH STREET. Named after the adjacent Edinburgh Street in Burnaby. Changed from East Street on 15 October 1962, when the Street Naming Committee received a petition from all of the property owners requesting that the name be changed to Scenic Highway or Edinburgh Street, as there was confusion arising through incorrect mail delivery.

> Other streets named after Scottish place names: Dumphries, Elgin, Lanark, Tolbooth, Kinross, Glencoe, Montrose, and Swansacre.

East Street (THSL). Named on Plan 4537 (1913). A note on this plan states: "Official plan of lots sold at auction 20 May, 1913." It lay north of Yale Street from Boundary Road to just west of Kootenay Street. When Bridgeway was surveyed in 1924, Plan 5461, a portion of East Street disappeared. Listed in Vancouver city directories from 1924 to 1963, its name indicated its position on the eastern edge of the city.

EDMONDS STREET (DL 301). Now East 24th Avenue between Main and Knight Streets. Named by the owner, Henry Valentine Edmonds, who acquired DL 301 in 1870 and subdivided it in 1885, Plan 187, to form part of the suburb later known as Mount Pleasant. The name disappeared when DL 301 was absorbed into Vancouver in 1911.

EDMUND STREET. See Commercial Street.

EDWARD ROAD. See Elliott Street.

ELECTRIC AVENUE. (DL 264A, Block 146). Now East 4th Avenue between Commercial Drive and Bauer Street. Shown on Plan 722 (1894) and probably named after its proximity to the new electric tram line, the Westminster and Vancouver Tramway, which ran from Vancouver south on Park Drive (now Commercial Drive) to the city limits and on to New Westminster.

ELGIN STREET. Named on Plan 1369 (1907), probably after the city and shire of Elgin, Scotland. It lay between the present East 33rd and East 37th Avenues. Its name was in use when, on 1 December 1909, South Vancouver Council decided that Elgin Street should be completed by day labour (not municiple staff). In 1910 South Vancouver By-law 141 changed Bennington Avenue (between East 31st and East 32nd Avenues) and 5th Street in DL 662-663 (between East 45th and East 49th Avenues) to Elgin Street.

Bennington Avenue. Named on Plan 1635 (1907), likely after Bennington, Vermont, near the birthplace of Simon Fraser, discoverer of the Fraser River.

Fifth Street was the fifth street east of the present Fraser Street on Plans 1390 and 1900 (1907).

ELIZABETH STREET. Named after its proximity to Queen Elizabeth Park. In 1948, By-law 3081 renamed Alberta Street between West 37th and West 41st Avenues.

ELK VALLEY PLACE. Named for Elk Valley Park, near Fernie. Private thoroughfare in Champlain Heights, the name was approved by the Street Naming Committee on 21 June 1978. Community Builders called its project Park Place and named the thoroughfares after BC parks.

ELLERSLIE STREET (Deleted). Named on Plan 3049 (1910). Origin of name unknown. Shown on Plate 108, *Goad's Atlas*, as 61st Avenue East (late Ellerslie Street), it lay between Elliott and Dawson Streets. Upon amalgamation in 1929, East 61st Avenue became East 59th Avenue. With the replotting of Fraserview the street disappeared.

ELLIOTT STREET. Named by South Vancouver By-law 141, 1910, when *Edward Road*, in broken lengths between East 45th and East 65th Avenues, was renamed. Named on Plan 2327 (1909) and Plans 2484, 2580, and 3505 (all 1910). Origin of the name Edward is unknown, as is that of Elliot

The replotting of Fraserview in 1952 changed the street pattern south of East 56th Avenue. In 1961 By-law 3937 gave the name "Elliott" to the street between East 56th Avenue and South East Marine Drive. This by-law also changed the portion of Clarendon Street south of South East Marine Drive to Elliott.

ELLIS AVENUE (Deleted). Named on Plan 1477 (1907), it lay south of and parallel to South East

Marine Drive between Cromwell Street and Boundary Road. Origin of name unknown. South Vancouver By-law 141, 1910, renamed it East 71st Avenue, but various maps between 1919 and 1930 showed it as Ellis Avenue or East 71st Avenue.

The Street Naming Committee, at its meeting of 6 February 1951, stated that the correct designation was Ellis Avenue. When Marine Way was developed south of South East Marine Drive in the 1980s, Ellis Avenue disappeared. Last listed in 1991 city directory as Ellis Avenue, with no residents shown.

ELM STREET (DL 328). See Ivy Street and Duff Street.

ELM STREET. Named by Point Grey By-law 17, 1912, and gradually extended to its present length between West 41st and West 45th Avenues. The name continues the pattern of "tree" names, as it lies west of Larch Street.

ELMHURST DRIVE. First listed in the 1964 city directory; named after the Elmhurst Golf and Country Club, near Winnipeg, to maintain the golf course theme for street names in Fraserview.

ELTHAM ROAD. See Queens Avenue.

ENDACOTT ROAD (Proposed). See Point Grey Road.

ENGLEWOOD DRIVE (Proposed). Named after the Englewood Golf Club, Englewood, New Jersey. According to an article in the *Vancouver Sun*, 5 March 1949, one of the streets to be in the new Fraserview development. However, the name was not in By-law 3330, 1952, nor was it shown on Plan Ga 49.

EPWORTH STREET. See Hull Street.

ESSEX STREET. Now West 59th Avenue between Fremlin and Heather Streets. Unnamed on Plan 2081 (1909). Named in *Goad's Atlas*, 1913, Plate 46, and in an advertisement in the *Daily News Advertiser*, 1 May 1912. Origin of name unknown.

ETON STREET. Named on Plan 100, a resurvey of

> Other streets named after universities: Cambridge, McGill, Oxford, Trinity, Yale.

Hastings Townsite, 1906, after Eton College, largest and most famous of English public schools.

EUCLID AVENUE. Named on Plan 630A (1892), probably in association with the already established School Avenue. Euclid was a geometer of Alexandria, circa 300 BC, whose works and axioms, *Elements,* were taught in schools in the 1890s. It lay between the present Duchess and Tyne Streets. South Vancouver Highway By-law 3, 1903, confirmed the name. By-Law 3937 (1961) extended it east from Tyne Street to Aberdeen Street .

EVANS AVENUE. Named 1948, By-law 3081, which renamed Johnson Avenue to remove duplication with Johnston Street on Granville Island. Probably named after Evans, Coleman and Evans, a building supplies firm, which had its yards in the locality.
Johnson Street. Named 1947, By-law 3002, Plan LF 579, when Canadian National Railways suggested the name for a new street created in the subdivision of its property in DL 2037, Parcel G. Probably named after John V. Johnson, joint manager of Evans, Coleman and Johnson in Victoria, which had a warehouse and dock adjacent to the Canadian National Steamship dock.

EVELEIGH STREET. Shown on the first official map of Vancouver, 1886 (Map 14267), it lay between Burrard and Thurlow Streets. Most of the street has been absorbed by the Bentall Centre (Explanatory Plan 10888 [1971]). Writing to Major J.S. Matthews on 27 April 1936, L.A. Hamilton said he could not remember the reason for adopting the name "Eveleigh."

EXPLORERS WALK. Private thoroughfare in Champlain Heights, the name was approved by the Street Naming Committee on 8 November 1979. It is adjacent to Marquette and Champlain Crescents, named after explorers.

EXPO BOULEVARD. Changed from Pacific Boulevard North in 1994, By-law 7334, to commemorate the world fair, Expo '86, held nearby on the north shore of False Creek.

F

FAIRCHILD ROAD. Private thoroughfare named by developer Fairchild Developments Limited, Plan LF 11456, approved 5 March 1991.

FAIRMONT STREET. First listed in 1914 city directory. Unnamed on Plans 2376, 4126, and 2793, 1909 and 1910. Its name likely came from Fairmont Park, a subdivision advertised in the *Vancouver Daily Province*, 3 August 1912, which Major J.S. Matthews fortunately copied, as it is not available on microfilm. The advertisement states that *Fairmont Park*, an attractive residential section of South Vancouver, is a subdivision of Blocks 8, 9, and 10, DL 37, only 3 blocks from the city boundary.

FALAISE AVENUE AND FALAISE PLACE. On 23 March 1948, Vancouver City Council approved the recommendation of the Vancouver Town Planning Commission that the streets in Renfrew Heights be named after personalities, battles, and events of the two world wars.

> Other Renfrew streets named after WWI and WWII personalities and battles: Anzio, Dieppe, Haida, Malta, Matapan, Mons, Normandy, Seaforth, Vimy, and Worthington.

In the battle of the "Falaise pocket," northwestern France, 12-22 August 1944, Canadian troops participated in the encirclement of German troops.

FALCONER ROAD. Now 48th Avenue between Alberta and Prince Edward Streets. Named on Plans 1748 (1907) and 2063 (1909), it was a survey name only. Who Falconer was has not been ascertained. Also known as Taylor Road.

FALSE CREEK ROAD. See Taylor Street.

FALSE CREEK TRAIL. See Kingsway.

FANNIN AVENUE. Named on Plan 6583 (1911), after John Fannin (1837-1904). One of the "Overlanders" of 1862, he later became first curator of the provincial museum. Shown in 1882 Provincial Voters List as a shoemaker at Hastings, Burrard Inlet.

On 17 May 1946, council considered a request from several property owners on Fannin Avenue that the name be changed to Belmont Crescent, but no change was made (Vancouver City Council Minutes, v. 50, p. 805).

FELLOWES STREET. Named 1961, By-law 3937, after Frederick Lyon Fellowes (1860-1941), city engineer, 1911-24.

F.L. Fellows, from group photo of Board of Works Committee, Vancouver, 1915. CVA C.I. Dept. P. 34, N. 24.

FERGUSON ROAD. See Slocan Street.

FERNDALE AVENUE (Shaughnessy Heights). See Marpole Avenue.

FERNDALE STREET (DL 184). A descriptive name. This short street, which jogs a half-block south of Pender Street, is the southern boundary of DL 184. Named 1929, By-law 2014, when Keefer Street between Victoria Drive and Nanaimo Street was renamed.

FERRIS ROAD. Now East and West 49th Avenue, east of Granville Street. Named by South Vancouver Highway By-law, 1905, after William Douglas Ferris Junior, a farmer on the North Arm of the Fraser River. The road extended from Ontario Street west to Granville Street. When Point Grey Municipality was established in 1908, the name was kept and so designated by Point Grey By-law 22, 1910. Ferris Road, lying east of Cambie Street in the municipality of South Vancouver, was renamed 51st Avenue by South Vancouver By-law 141, 1910. Point Grey By-law 17, 1912, changed Ferris Road to 49th Avenue.

From 1912 to 1929 the same road had two numbers – 49th Avenue west of Cambie Street and 51st Avenue east of Cambie Street. By-law 2028, 1929, changed 51st Avenue to 49th Avenue.

FERRISDALE BOULEVARD. See Dumfries Street.

FERRY ROW. Named 1976, By-law 5010, Plan LF 7386, it evokes the marine activity in False Creek.

FIELDSTONE AVENUE. Private thoroughfare shown on Plan LF 11558 (1993) and named arbitrarily by Marine Woods Developments Limited in association with Cornerstone, Cobblestone, Keystone, and Millstone.

FINCH PLACE. One of nine private thoroughfares in enclaves 8, 9, and 10 in Champlain Heights bearing bird names, submitted by the Matheson Heights Cooperative and approved by the Street Naming Committee on 25 March 1981.

FINDLAY STREET. Named 1932, By-law 2209, when it was changed from a portion of Commercial Drive and so named to differentiate it from the adjacent Commercial Street to the south. George Preston Findlay owned Lot 41, Block 169, DL 264A between East 15th and East 16th Avenues. A retired building contractor, he died 29 May 1964, aged eighty-two.

In *South Vancouver Past and Present*, Alfred Lewis (1920, 43), states: "No man has done more for the district than Mr. George P. Findlay. Before Main Street was widened and paved, and before the cars ran further than 16th and Main the Findlay Bros. were there in business conducting a grocery and post office. He was elected president of the Main Street Improvement Association."

FIR STREET. Named by L.A. Hamilton on an 1887 map (Map 14160) and officially named on plan 590 (1891). From 1913 to 1987 inclusive, city directories showed Fir Crescent (an unofficial name) from West 16th to Marpole Avenues.

FISHER ROAD. See Monmouth Avenue.

FLAGSTAFF PLACE. Private thoroughfare in Champlain Heights named by United Properties. Its project, Compass Point, used nautical terms such as Flagstaff Place. Approved by the Street Naming Committee on 27 May 1983.

FLEMING STREET. Named by South Vancouver Highway By-law, 1905, as Fleming Road, after John Fleming (1865-1931), a plasterer and contractor whose family first owned property in DL 754 in 1904.

South Vancouver By-law 141, 1910, changed Fleming Road between East 15th and East 18th Avenues to Fleming Street and also renamed the following streets: Maxwell Road (between East 20th and East 22nd Avenues), Stewart Street (between East 18th and East 20th Avenues), and Selkirk Street (between East 49th and East 54th Avenues). Short Street between East 55th and East 57th Avenues was renamed Fleming in 1952, By-law 3294.

Maxwell Road. Named on Plan 1990 (1909), probably after the Maxwell family, who lived on that part of Fleming Street.

Selkirk Avenue (DL 737). Named on Plan 2373 (1908), with owners Christian Albertsen and John H. Selkirk. The latter, in real estate, was listed in Vancouver city directories, 1909-14 inclusive.

Stewart Street. Named on Plan 1292 (1906) and Plan 3142 (1910). Person not identified.

Short Street (DL 200). Named by South Vancouver By-law 251, 1913. Origin of name unknown but perhaps descriptive of its length.

FLETT ROAD. Now East 18th Avenue between Knight and Commercial Streets. Unnamed on Plan 832 (1900), with one of the owners shown as John Arthur Flett. Named by South Vancouver Highway By-law, 1905. Changed to East 18th Avenue in 1910, South Vancouver By-law 141. John Arthur Flett (1856-1921) was first listed in 1893 Vancouver directory as a contractor. By 1901 he had established a stove and house furnishings business (later known as J.A. Flett Limited).

FORBES AVENUE. See Lanark Street.

FORBES STREET (DL 182) (Deleted). Named on Plan 786 (1899), between Rogers Street and present Glen Drive north of Powell Street, although shown unnamed on Plan 176 (1884). Named after Forbes George Vernon (1843-1911), chief commissioner of lands and works, who, in 1883, was one of the original owners of DL 182. George Street and Vernon Drive were also named after him. Vancouver By-law 328, 1899, closed Forbes Street when the BC Sugar Refinery built its plant.

FORESHORE WALK. Private thoroughfare on Granville Island, developed by Foreshore Projects Limited. Name approved by the Street Naming Committee in January 1992 (Plan LF 11465 [1991]).

FORGE WALK. Named 1976, By-law 5010, Plan LF 7386, to commemorate the former ironworks located in False Creek.

FORTUNE STREET (DL 301). Now East 16th Avenue between Main and Knight Streets. Shown on Plan 187 (1885) and named by the owner, H.V. Edmonds, after his wife, Jane Fortune (née Kemp) (ca. 1840-1906). When Vancouver absorbed DL 301 in 1911, Fortune Street became part of East 16th Avenue.

FOSTER AVENUE. Named by South Vancouver By-law 251, 1913, and on Plans 1678 (1907), 2587 (1909), and 3442 (1911). Likely after James Foster, who subdivided DL 37, known as Collingwood district, in 1892, Plan 630A.

Borden Avenue. Survey name on Plan 4317 (1912), now part of Foster Avenue from Aberdeen Street east to the first lane. Probably named after Sir Robert Laird Borden, prime minister of Canada, 1911-20.

FOUNDRY QUAY. Named 1976, By-law 5010, Plan LF 7386, to commemorate the former ironworks located on False Creek.

FOUNTAIN WAY AND FOUNTAIN WAY COURT. Private thoroughfares in False Creek area, so named because of a nearby fountain. Name approved by Street Naming Committee on 15 August 1979.

FOXHOUND MEWS. Private thoroughfare in Champlain Heights, named by United Properties Limited, who chose the name to fit the theme of hunting with the hounds for its project "Huntingwood." Name approved by the Street Naming Committee on 17 May 1983.

FRANCES STREET. Named 1929, By-law 2014, when Keefer Street between Vernon and Victoria Drives was renamed in honour of Sister Frances, Fanny Dalrymple Redmond (1851?-1932), Vancouver's first public health nurse. In 1888 she and the Reverend H.G. Fienness Clinton, rector of St. James Church, established one of the city's first hospitals, St. Luke's, on Cordova Street. Here she directed British Columbia's original training school for nurses and Vancouver's first social service centre.

FRANKLIN STREET. Named 1929, By-law 2014, when Albert Street was renamed to remove confusion with Alberta Street. According to J. Alexander Walker, secretary of the Vancouver Town Planning Commission, it was named after the nearby Franklin School, which had been named after the Arctic explorer Sir John Franklin (1786-1847).

Albert Street. Shown on "Plan of the City of Vancouver, British Columbia," compiled by H.B. Smith, 1886 (Map 14267). Origin of name unknown.

FRASER AVENUE (DL 194). See Celtic Avenue.

FRASER STREET. Named after the Fraser River and, indirectly, after Simon Fraser (1776-1862), fur trader, who reached the mouth of the river in 1808, by South Vancouver By-law 141, 1910, which renamed North Arm Road. Vancouver By-law 3081, 1948, standardized the variants of Fraser Street and Fraser Avenue to Fraser Street.

North Arm Road. Named from its location as "the road from North Arm or rather Richmond, to Granville," as mentioned in the *Mainland Guardian*, 9 June 1875. Named on map of Granville-Burrard Peninsula drawn by F.G. Richards in 1876 (Map 13905) and mentioned in annual reports of BC Department of Public Works, 1892-1901.

Cemetery Road. A colloquial name for the North Arm Road, between present Kingsway and East 31st Avenue, leading to Mountain View Cemetery (established in 1886). Frank W. Hart

Sister Frances. CVA Port. P. 128, N. 125.

A number of Vancouver streets have been named after women, although many of them are no longer in use: Agnes, Alexandra, Alice, Ann, Carolina, Elizabeth, Frances, Gaston, Guelph, Harriet, Helena, Juanita, Kathleen, Kemp, Lee, Marguerite, Martha, Marshall, Mary, St. Margaret, Sophia, Wenonah, Winnifred, and Victoria.

recounted an incident when one of his horses fell between the corduroy, and the front wheel of the hearse went down into the mud (Matthews 1931).

Scott Street. Probably after the novelist, Sir Walter Scott, in association with the poet, Robert Burns. Shown on a 1902 map (Map 14171) and on Plan 1771 (1905). By-Law 3195, 1950, renamed it when Scott was joined to Fraser for improved traffic flow.

FRASERVIEW DRIVE. Named 1952, By-law 3330, after the adjacent Fraserview Golf Course. A descriptive name.

FREDERICK STREET (DL 301). See Carolina Street.

FREDERICK STREET. (DL 650). Unnamed on Plan 2742 (1909) and Plan 3116 (1910). Named on a map of South Vancouver, circa 1910, published by Coast Map and Blueprint Company (Map 14066). First listed in 1917 city directory. Probably so named because it lies directly south of the present Cardina Street, formerly Frederick Street (after Frederick Edmonds), until 1911.

FREDERICK STREET (Deleted). Named on Plan 1377 (1907), after the co-owner of NE 1/4, section 40, THSL, Frederick Thomas Andrews (1861-1941), financier. Later part of East 15th Avenue between Kootenay Street and Boundary Road, it disappeared in the replotting of Renfrew Heights, 1948. A survey name only.

FREMLIN STREET. Unnamed on Plan 1870 (1909), it lay between South West Marine Drive and present West 70th Avenue, three blocks west of Heather Street. Co-owners on this plan were A.E. Fremlin and Samuel Chatwin. *Goad's Atlas*, 1913, Plates 46 and 48, shows Fremlin Street extending to the present West 59th Avenue.

Point Grey By-law 17, 1914, changed Fremlin to *Chatwin Street*. Evidently this by-law caused confusion because Point Grey By-law 17, 1915, changed it back to Fremlin.

By-laws 3294 (1952), 3731 (1958), and 3937 (1961) have extended the street.

Arthur Edward Fremlin, first listed in 1908 Vancouver directory, later became a salesman at

Spencer's Store until his death on 20 September 1931, aged seventy-three.

Samuel Chatwin (1866-1942), a real estate agent from 1913 to 1925, died 6 May 1942, aged seventy-six.

FRENCH STREET. Named by Point Grey By-law 17, 1914, after Sir John French (1852-1925), commander-in-chief of the British army, First World War. Plan of Eburne Townsite (Plan 1749 [1908]) showed First Street, which became French Street between West 72nd and Park Drive through Point Grey By-Law 17, 1914.

Field Marshal Sir John French. CVA Port. P. 931.

FRETH STREET (DL 301). Now East 12th Avenue between Main and Prince Edward Streets. Shown on Plan 187 (1885) and named by the owner of DL 301, H.V. Edmonds, after his son Walter Freth Edmonds (1877-1951). Became part of East 12th Avenue when Vancouver absorbed DL 301 in 1911.

FRONT STREET (DL 540). See Cameron Avenue.

FRONT STREET (DL 200A, DL 302). Now First Avenue between Cambie and Prince Edward Streets. Unnamed on Plan 177 (1884) and named on Plan 197 (1885). It fronted on the south shore of False Creek, hence its name. It became part of First Avenue in 1926, By-law 1803.

FRONT STREET (OGT). See Water St.

FRONTENAC STREET. Named by South Vancouver By-law 251, 1913, after Louis de Baude, Comte de Frontenac (1620-98), governor of New France. It lay between the present East 49th and East 54th Avenues and, by 1920, extended north to East 46th Avenue. The replotting for Champlain Heights changed the alignment south of East 49th Avenue in 1970, By-law 4470, Plan LF 4530. In 1978, By-law 5195, Plan LE 3742B, shortened it to end at Hurst Avenue.

G

GALIANO STREET. Named by Point Grey By-law 483, 1926, after Dionisio Alcala Galiano, captain of the Spanish vessel *Sutil*, who explored a portion of the northwest coast in 1792. The Native Sons of British Columbia, Post No. 2, suggested this name for one of the six new roads created by the replotting of DL 139.

GALE STREET. (Proposed) see Rupert Street.

GALT STREET. Named after John Galt (1779-1839), commissioner of the Canada Land Company in Upper Canada, who lived in Canada between 1826 and 1829. By-law 2014, 1929, renamed Wolfe Street to remove duplication with Wolfe Avenue in Shaughnessy Heights.

Wolfe Street (DL 393). Named by South Vancouver By-law 251, 1913, after General James Wolfe, commander of the British expedition, who died on the Plains of Abraham while capturing Quebec on 13 September 1759.

GAOLERS MEWS. Private thoroughfare in Old Granville Townsite, named 1972 By-law 4636, Plan LF 5892. The mews are near the site of the original jail, shown on Plan 168 (1885).

GARDEN DRIVE. Named after James Ford Garden (1847-1914), a surveyor who opened an office with partner E.B. Hermon in Vancouver in 1886. The firm surveyed much of the original layout of the city. Garden was Mayor of Vancouver (1898-1900) and MLA (1900-9).

South Vancouver By-law 141, 1910, changed Garden Drive between East 15th and East 19th Avenues to Gladstone Street, but in 1929 it reverted to Garden Drive (By-law 2082). In 1950, By-Law 3195 designated the portion north of Dundas Street as Garden Drive North.

GARIBALDI DRIVE. Private thorougfare in Champlain Heights named by Community Builders, whose project, Park Place, bears the names of BC parks. Named after Mount Garibaldi, which commemorates the Italian patriot Giuseppe Garibaldi (1807-82). Name approved by the Street Naming Committee 21 June 1978.

GARIBALDI, VIA (Proposed). see Commercial Drive.

GARTLEY ROAD. See Welwyn Street.

GASTON STREET. Named 1994, By-law 7282, to honour Sadie Gaston, Collingwood district pioneer and active community leader.

GATINEAU PLACE. Named 1961, By-law 3937, after the Gatineau Golf Club, Aylmer, Quebec, to continue the theme of golf course names.

GAVIN STREET (Proposed). See Cariboo Street.

GEORGE AVENUE(DL 393). Now East 30th Avenue between Nanaimo and Baldwin Streets. Named on Plan 3086 (1910), a survey name only, of unknown origin.

GEORGE ROAD. Now part of East 47th Avenue between Argyle and Bruce Streets and Elliott and Vivian Streets. George Road, between Argyle and Bruce, shown on Plan 3161 (1909), probably named after one of the owners, George Herbert Dawson (1866-1940), a surveyor in Vancouver who became surveyor general of British Columbia in 1911. Plan 2484 (1910) shows George Road between Elliott and Vivian Streets. Origin of name unknown. South Vancouver By-law 141, 1910, changed both parts to East 48th Avenue (now East 47th).

GEORGE STREET. See Saint George Street.

GEORGE STREET (DL 182). Named after Forbes George Vernon (1843-1911), chief commissioner of lands and works who, in 1883, was one of the original owners of DL 182. Forbes Street and Vernon Drive were also named after him.

GEORGE STREET (DL 301). Now East 15th Avenue between Main and Knight Streets. Shown on Plan 187 (1885) and named by the owner, H.V. Edmonds, after an unknown family member. When DL 301 was absorbed into Vancouver in 1911, George Street became part of East 15th Avenue.

GEORGIA DRIVE (DL 320) (Deleted). Named by Point Grey By-law 17, 1914, probably in association with the Strait of Georgia. The map accompanying this by-law showed Georgia Drive curving southeast from Camosun Street below Marine Drive to the northern boundary of the Musqueam Band Reserve. The land was never

Georgia Street at Howe, approximately 1900. Note the old trail to English Bay (on a diagonal in the left mid section of the photo) and the wooden sidewalks. CVA Str. P. 34, Bu. N. 23.

developed, and, in 1922, the municipality acquired blocks 10 and 11, DL 320, for Georgia Park (now part of the larger Musqueam Park).

GEORGIA STREET. Named in 1886 after the Strait of Georgia, shown on the map used by L.A. Hamilton. The street lay between Chilco and Beatty Streets. By-Law 1231, 1915, extended it east to Boundary Road and renamed Harris Street.

Harris Street. Named after Dennis Reginald Harris (1851-1932), a shareholder in the Vancouver Improvement Company and appearing in the first Vancouver Voters List, 1886. A civil engineer for the CPR, he later became city engineer for Victoria, 1884-6, and was involved in real estate. By-law 643, 1908, changed Harris Street, between an arm of False Creek and present Main Street, to Shore Street.

Shore Street. This descriptive name lasted from 1908 to 1915 but was not in general use. Shown in *Goad's Atlas*, 1913, Plate 69. The 1909 city directory still listed the 100 block Harris Street as having several women as residents. Named in response to a petition from residents "praying that the name west of Westminster Avenue be changed so that the evil shade that hangs over the association of the street name with 'restricted district' may not extend to the sections where reputable residents are dwelling" (*Vancouver Province*, 17 November 1906).

GEORGIA VIADUCT. Named as a dedicated street in 1993, By-law 7237, Plan LF 11554, in order that police, firefighters, and ambulance drivers could give the location in emergencies and on reports.

GHENT LANE. Private thoroughfare in Canadian Forces Base near Jericho Park, first listed in 1958 city directory and named after the Belgian city of Ghent, occupied by German forces in both world wars.

GIBSON ROAD. Now East 20th Avenue between Knight and Commercial Streets. Named on Plan 3142 (April 1910) after the owner, Moses Gibson, who came to Vancouver in 1886. He bought property in South Vancouver, where he served as a councillor in 1893, and as a school trustee and secretary for South Vancouver School, 1894-5. He died 23 July 1937, aged eighty-six. Changed to East 20th Avenue by South Vancouver By-law 141, December 1910.

GILBERT AVENUE. See Clarendon Street.

GILFORD STREET. Named after Gilford Island, shown on the map of the Pacific coast that L.A.

Hamilton used to name the streets in DL 185. Gilford Island commemorates Viscount Gilford, captain of *HMS Tribune*, which served on the Pacific coast, 1862-4.

GILLNET PLACE. Private thoroughfare in the Angus Lands, named by the developers, Riverfront Properties Limited, who chose a name evocative of the fishing industry along the Fraser River. Name approved by the Street Naming Committee on 17 February 1987.

GLADSTONE STREET. Originally called Gladstone Road by South Vancouver Highway By-law 65, 1903. This by-law stated that the road commenced "west of Lot 1, Block 8, DL 393, known as the Gladstone Hotel, and due north to the tramway line." The Gladstone Hotel, or Inn, probably named after William Ewart Gladstone (1809-98), British prime minister, was one of a number of stagecoach roadhouses along the road between Granville and New Westminster. In 1891 settlers first met there to discuss organizing the surrounding area into a municipality (MacDonald 1992, 17).

South Vancouver By-law 141, 1910, changed Gladstone Road to Gladstone Street and also renamed the following streets: Garden Drive, Maddison Road, Upland Street, and Bond Road.

Garden Drive. Named after James Ford Garden (1847-1914), it extended as far south as the present East 19th Avenue. However, South Vancouver By-law 141, 1910, renamed it Gladstone Street because the portion between East 15th and East 19th Avenues actually lay in South Vancouver.

Maddison Road (DL 727). Named on Plan 2202 (1909) between present East 54th and East 59th Avenues. The owner of DL 727 in 1910 South Vancouver Voters List was estate of T.W. Duff, care of Maddison, Stirling and Company, Old Drury, London, England. Frederick Brunning Maddison matriculated from Brasenose College, Oxford, in 1869, aged nineteen. He gained his BA in 1874 and was called to the bar at Lincoln's Inn in 1876. He was debarred at his own request in 1884 in order to become a solicitor. His active involvement with the company appears to have ended around 1904, although the name "Maddison" continued to appear in the company's name until the 1950s.

Upland Drive (DL 329). A descriptive name shown on Plan 1826 (1908) between present East

59th and East 65th Avenues, in Rowling Heights addition, and on Plan 2330 (1909). Absorbed by Fraserview development.

Bond Road. Named on Plan 2564 (1910), between present East 65th Avenue and South East Marine Drive, after the owner, Lambert John Blair Bond (1864-1915) of the law firm Bond and Sweet. Born in Ireland and educated as a lawyer, he came to Vancouver in 1901, where he died 13 October 1915. Director of Burrard Inlet Tunnel and Bridge Company.

Ross Road (DL 741). Shown on Plan 1295 (1907), it lay south from Vanness Avenue to halfway between East 24th and East 25th Avenues. Origin of this survey name unknown.

With the development of Fraserview in the 1950s, the portion of Gladstone below East 61st Avenue disappeared.

GLEN DRIVE. Named on Plan 1771 (1905), after a deep glen in the vicinity, since filled. In 1911, when Boundary Avenue was renamed, By-law 820 extended Glen Drive from Powell Street south to the north shore of False Creek. By-law 842, 1911, further extended it when James Street in DL 301 was renamed. When the eastern part of False Creek was filled in, the two parts of Glen Drive were joined.

Boundary Avenue (DL 181). Formed the boundary between DL 181 and DL 182 and was so named on "Plan of the City of Vancouver, British Columbia," compiled by H.B. Smith, 1886 (Map 14267). It lay between Burrard Inlet and the north shore of False Creek. In 1899 By-law 328 closed the section north of Powell Street when the BC Sugar Refinery built its plant. In 1911 certain property owners and residents of the city requested that council change the name to Glen Drive, which was effected by By-law 820.

James Street (DL 301). Shown on Plan 187 (1885) and named by the owner, H.V. Edmonds, after his cousin, James A. Webster. When Vancouver absorbed DL 301 in 1911, James Street became Glen Drive from East 15th Avenue to East King Edward Street, By-law 842.

GLENCOE AVENUE (DL 300 and 331) (Deleted). Unnamed on Plan 3091 (1910) and named by South Vancouver By-law 251, 1913, probably after Glencoe, Scotland. Parallel to and south of the present South East Marine Drive between

Kinross and Hartley Streets, it disappeared with the replotting for Marine Way in the 1980s.

GLENCOE STREET (DL 333 and 334). Now East 56th Avenue between Elliott and Vivian Streets. Named on Plan 3049 (1910), likely after Glencoe, Scotland, and renamed by South Vancouver By-law 141 to East 58th Avenue (now East 56th Avenue) between Elliott and Dawson Streets. Since shortened with the replotting of Fraserview.

GLENDALE STREET. Named 1929, By-law 2014, when Crown Road was renamed to remove duplication with Crown Street in the former Point Grey municipality. By-law 3558, 1956, extended it into a cul-de-sac. A descriptive name.

Crown Road (THSL). Unnamed on Plan 1722 (1907) and first listed in Vancouver city directory, 1922. Origin of name unknown.

GLENDALOUGH PLACE. Named 1956, By-law 3558, after "Glendalough," the former home of prominent businesswoman and alderwoman, Anna Sprott, located on this site prior to its subdivision. Anna Sprott (1879-1961), of Irish ancestry, probably named the house after Glendalough, a valley in County Wicklow, Eire.

GLENGYLE STREET. Originally called Smith Street, then renamed Glengyle Street in 1929, By-law 2014. Mentioned in Sir Walter Scott's poem *Lady of the Lake*, Canto II, verse 16, line 5: "And, bearing downwards from Glengyle," which is near Loch Katrine, Scotland.

Smith Street. Unnamed on Plan 1496 (1907) and named on Plan 4281 (1912). Origin unknown, but Plan 1344 (1907) shows a James A. Smith owning property in the adjoining DL 352, Block 16, which lies south of the present East 22nd Avenue and near Alice Street.

GODFREY ROAD. See Saint George Street.

GOLDEN LINK CRESCENT. Private thoroughfare in Champlain Heights, named by Three Links Care Society, sponsors of a residential complex funded by the Oddfellows and Rebekah Orders. Three golden links, the symbol of the Independent Order of Oddfellows, represent friendship, love, and truth. Name approved by the Street Naming Committee on 7 March 1983.

GOODMURPHY ROAD. Now West 77th Avenue between Hudson and Oak Streets. Named by South Vancouver Highway By-law, 1905, after William Davis Goodmurphy (1830-1916), cannery proprietor, who owned part of DL 318. Point Grey By-law 39, 1912, closed Goodmurphy Road east of Oak Street, and Point Grey By-law 17, 1914, renamed the remaining part West 77th Avenue.

GORE AVENUE. Named by L.A. Hamilton after William Sinclair Gore (1842-1919), surveyor general of British Columbia in 1878. Henry S. Rowling in a letter to Major J.S. Matthews, 16 May 1932, mentions that there was a skid road from False Creek to Burrard Inlet near the present Gore Avenue. The existence of this road probably influenced the surveyor to run Gore Avenue at an angle in relation to the other north-south roads in DL 196.

GOTHARD STREET. After Ambrose Gothard, who was born in England, owned property in DL 52, and was in real estate. He died in Vancouver on 23 June 1914, aged seventy-three. The street has had a varied history because DL 52 has had several surveys. Originally there was a Gothard Road, which became Clarendon Street between Kingsway and East 29th Avenue by South Vancouver By-law 141, 1910. When DL 52 was further subdivided by Plan 1752 (1908), the name "Gothard" was transferred to the short street between Clarendon and Slocan Streets.

GOVERNMENT ROAD. Now East 29th Avenue between Nanaimo Street and Boundary Road. It was the southern boundary of the government reserve, called Hastings Townsite, established circa 1860 or 1861. South Vancouver By-law 141, 1910, named it East 29th Avenue, and By-law 2014, 1929, confirmed the name.

GOVERNMENT ROAD (DL 650). Now East 49th Avenue between Prince Edward and Fraser Streets. A survey name on Plan 727 (1894), named arbitrarily in association with Dominion Road.

GOWAN STREET. See Lanark Street.

GRAHAM AVENUE. See Nanaimo Street.

GRANDVIEW AVENUE (Deleted). Descriptive name for a street shown in Plans 1826 (1908), 2894 (1910), and 3505 (1910). A survey name only, it became East 65th Avenue and later East 63rd Avenue between Victoria Drive and Vivian Street.

Disappeared in the replotting for Fraserview Golf Course and Fraserview development.

GRANDVIEW HIGHWAY. Named after the Grandview district through which it passed, when the city engineer, in his report to the board of works, 1 November 1921, presented the list of suggested names for the new road, which lay along the north side of the Great Northern Railway from Clark Drive to a point just east of Nanaimo Street.

In 1928, By-law 1932, Plan L 103, named the Grandview Diversion, a road along the south side of the same railway from Lakewood Drive to east of Slocan Street, where it entered 13th Avenue.

There was confusion between 12th Avenue, 13th Avenue, the Grandview Diversion, and Grandview Highway. Consequently, in 1946, By-law 2961, Plan LD 197, named the following streets: Grandview Highway from Slocan Street to Boundary Road (formerly part of East 13th Avenue); Grandview Highway South from Lakewood Drive to Slocan Street (i.e., the former Grandview Diversion); and Grandview Highway North (from Slocan Street northwest to Clark Drive near East 5th Avenue). This same by-law changed East 13th Avenue between Nanaimo and Slocan Streets to part of Grandview Highway North.

GRANT ROAD. See Tyne Street.

GRANT STREET. Named on Plan 1771 (1905), after John Grant (1842?-1919), mayor of Victoria for four terms in the 1890s and also MPP for Victoria for two.

GRANVILLE ROAD. See Kingsway.

GRANVILLE STREET. Named by L.A. Hamilton after Granville Townsite, which was established in 1870 and named in honour of the second Earl of Granville, then British secretary of state for

North Arm Rd., now Granville St., circa 1895, near the "Summit," now 37th Ave. (North Arm was probably a colloquial name, as there is no legal record of Granville being called North Arm.) The road passed through the CPR clearing, now Fairview, and entered the forest at Sixteenth Ave., the boundary between the City of Vancouver and the Municipality of South Vancouver. The first habitation reached was William Shannon's farm, now 57th Ave., where the CPR land grant ended. Shannon's had the only telephone between False Creek and Eburne's. The construction of this road in 1889 by the CPR saved farmers of Sea Island, Lulu Island, and the lower North Arm driving horse-drawn vehicles eastwards along River Rd., now Marine Dr., to old North Arm Rd., now Fraser St. This forest was famed for the excellence of the spars for sailing ships it produced. It was logged off with oxen. CVA Str. P. 238, N 396.

Earl of Granville. cva Port. P. 644, N 261 #3.

the colonies. The street lay between Burrard Inlet and the north shore of False Creek.

From the south shore of False Creek to the city limits at West 16th Avenue lay *Centre Street*, named on an 1887 map (Map 14150) by L.A. Hamilton, perhaps after its position in the centre of the CPR land grant, DL 526. Centre Street was first listed in the 1900 Vancouver directory as "continuation of Granville over False Creek." Plans 590 (1891) and 991 (1905) show Granville Street. In 1907, By-law 598 changed the name to South Granville Street as far as the city limits at 16th Avenue. South Vancouver Highway by-laws in 1893 and 1905, respectively, mention Centre Street or Lulu Island Road (Centre Road) in connection with the legal description of other roads. When Point Grey Municipality was established in 1908, Centre Street fell within its jurisdiction. Point Grey By-law 31, 1911, defined Granville Street South through the municipality.

In 1996 By-law 7590, Plan LF 11681, changed the portion of Granville Street under the Granville Street Bridge north of West 3rd Avenue to Anderson Street.

GRANVILLE SEAWALK NORTH. Named 1989, By-law 6541, Plan LF 11324, after its location between the north end of the Granville Street Bridge to the Burrard Street Bridge and north of Granville Island.

GRAUER ROAD (Deleted). Shown on Plan 3207, deposited in the Land Registry Office by James McGeer on behalf of himself and Jacob Grauer in 1911, although surveyed in 1910. South Vancouver By-law 141, 1910, changed it to East 68th Avenue (presently East 69th Avenue) between St. George and Fraser Streets. But the change never occurred, as Plan 3207 was cancelled by Court Order.

Jacob Grauer and his wife, Marie, came to Sea Island in 1886 from Germany.

GRAVELEY STREET. Named after Walter Edward Graveley (1854-1939), who came to Vancouver in 1885 and was in real estate, insurance, and loan businesses. First commodore of the Royal Vancouver Yacht Club. Shown on

Same location as photo on page 49 (Granville St. at 37th Ave.), April 1919, just fourteen years later. cva Str. P. 373, N 332.

a 1902 map by Hermon and Burwell (Map 14171) and on Plan 1771 (1905), a resurvey of DL 264A.

GRAY ROAD. See Windsor Street.

GREAT NORTHERN WAY. Named after the Great Northern Railway Company, which provided most of the land for a new street from Prince Edward Street to Glen Drive, north of East 5th Avenue, as reported in the *Vancouver Sun*, 31 May 1960. It now extends to Clark Drive.

GREEN ROAD. See Killarney Street.

GREENCHAIN. Named 1976, By-law 5010, Plan LF 7386, to commemorate the former lumber industry along False Creek. A green chain is a moving chain from which green lumber is sorted (Sorden and Vallier 1986).

GREENSBORO PLACE. Private thoroughfare in Langara Estates, adjacent to Langara Golf Course. Named by Daon Development Company after the Greater Greensboro Open golf tournament held annually at Greensboro, North Carolina. Approved by the Street Naming Committee on 16 February 1978.

GREER AVENUE. Named 1929, By-law 2014, as Greer Street, after Samuel Greer, (1844-1925), who claimed property at Greer's Beach (later Kitsilano Beach). The CPR disputed his claim, Greer refused to be evicted, and a confrontation resulted (see Matthews 1931). In 1958, By-law 3731 changed it to Greer Avenue to conform to the pattern of avenues running east and west.

Formerly *Short Street*, a descriptive name for the one-block-long street named by the CPR in 1909, Plan 2301, a survey of Kitsilano Point.

GRIFFITHS WAY. Formerly Stadium Road East, renamed September 1994, By-law 7334, to honour Frank Armathwaite Griffiths, owner of the Vancouver Canucks hockey team from 1974 until his death on 7 April 1994.

Stadium Road East. Named 1991, By-law 6781, as part of the ring road system around BC Place Stadium.

GRIGGS STREET. Now West 75th Avenue from Hudson Street east to the Canadian Pacific Railway terminal. Named on Plan 3069 (1910), with owners Mary L. and F.T. Griggs, and changed to West 75th Avenue by Point Grey By-law 17, 1914. Forest Truman Griggs (1862-1909) and Clinton Alonzo Griggs were storekeepers at Eburne. West 76th Avenue was called Clinton Street.

GRIMMETT AVENUE. See Sophia Street.

GROUSE WALK. Private thoroughfare in the Little Mountain housing project. Named by Vancouver Housing Authority in 1954, without approval of city council. Street Naming Committee minutes, 15 November 1954, recorded that the deputy director of planning stated that these walks (i.e., Grouse, James, and Oriole) should not be given official street names, as they were not public streets. Named after the bird or after Grouse Mountain, which is in view.

GROVE AVENUE and **CRESCENT.** See Atlantic Street.

GUELPH STREET. Named 1912, By-law 980, after the family name of Queen Victoria. First named as Victoria Street on Plan 830 (1901), probably after the late Queen Victoria. Changed to Laurier Street in 1911, By-law 842, after Sir Wilfred Laurier (1841-1919), prime minister of Canada, 1896-1911. Renamed Guelph in 1912 to remove duplication with Laurier Avenue in Shaughnessy Heights.

GWILLIM CRESCENT. Private thoroughfare in Champlain Heights, named after Gwillim Lake Provincial Park, as indicated in city manager's report to council, 27 April 1979 (Vancouver City Council Minutes, v. 132, p. 26). Council approved the name 29 May 1979.

Gwillim Lake named in 1921 after John Cole Gwillim (1868-1921?), professor of mining at Queen's University, Kingston, Ontario. He did field work for the BC government in 1919 in the Peace River country and wrote *Report of Oil Survey in Peace River District, 1919*.

H

HADDEN AVENUE. See Marine Drive.

HADDOCK STREET. Now East 46th Avenue between Ontario and Prince Edward Streets. The western half of DL 647, surveyed but not named on Plan 1504 (1907), owned by William John Haddock (1878-1928), who came to Vancouver in 1903 and formed a partnership with John R. Parsons in the wholesale produce firm of Parsons-Haddock Company Limited.

South Vancouver By-law 141, 1910, changed Haddock Street to East 48th Avenue, now East 46th Avenue.

HAGGART STREET. Named 1954, By-law 3457, and extended southeast to West 32nd Avenue in 1957, By-law 3618. Andrew Weemys Haggart entered Vancouver's civil service as assistant building inspector in 1920 and rose to be chief building inspector when he retired in 1952.

HAIDA DRIVE. In Renfrew Heights subdivision, was named after HMCS *Haida*, a "tribal class" destroyer named after the Haida people. The destroyer was present at the Normandy invasion, 6 June 1944.

HAIG STREET. Named 1929, By-law 2014, after Field Marshal Earl Haig (1861-1928), commander-in-chief of the British forces on the Western Front in the First World War. Renamed to remove duplication with Kitchener Street in East Vancouver.

Kitchener Street. Point Grey Municipality, first listed in 1917 Vancouver city directory and probably named after Horatio Herbert Kitchener, Lord Kitchener (1850-1916), distinguished British soldier.

HALTON ROAD. See Ross Street.

HALSS CRESCENT. In Musqueam Park subdivision, leased from the Musqueam Band, was named by By-law 4266, 1966. Halss, meaning "magic people," was the name of an old settlement (City Clerks Correspondence Outgoing, 13 October 1966, p. 502). The city originally suggested the name "Demaret Crescent," after well-known American golfer James Newton "Jimmy"

Demaret (1910-83), because Musqueam Park subdivision abuts Shaughnessy Golf Course.

HAMILTON STREET. Named by Lauchlan Alexander Hamilton (1852-1944), land commissioner for the CPR, after himself, when he laid out the streets in DL 541.

L.A. Hamilton. cva Port. P. 147, N. 80 #2.

Lachlan Hamilton had probably the most individual influence over the naming of Vancouver streets. In 1885, he named the following streets in District Lot 541: Abbott, Beatty, Cambie, Hamilton, Homer, Richards, Seymour, Granville, Howe, Hornby, Burrard, Cordova, Hastings, Pender, Dunsmuir, Georgia, Robson, Smithe, Nelson, Helmcken, Davie, Drake, and Pacific. In the same year, he also decided to use Pacific Coast place names for streets in District Lot 185 (the "West End"): Alberni, Bidwell, Broughton, Burnaby, Bute, Cardero, Gilford, Haro, Harwood, Hornby, Howe, Jervis, Pacific, Pender, Pendrell, and Thurlow. He also decided to name a group of streets in District Lot 526 after trees (Alder, Arbutus, Balsam, Cedar, Cypress Fir, Hemlock, Maple, Oak, Pine, Spruce, Vine, Willow, and Yew). According to Major J.S. Matthews, former city archivist, Hamilton, who was going out of town, instructed his draftsman to alphabetize his list of trees before they were added to the new drawing laying out Vancouver street names. To his dismay, he discovered upon his return that the draftsman had failed to alphabetize the tree names, and it was too late to change the drawing.

HANBURY AVENUE. An unofficial name for East 24th Avenue between Gladstone and Brant Streets. Unnamed on Plan 1295 (1907) but named in South Vancouver Road Loan By-law 6, 1911, as receiving an appropriation of $650. Mrs. Mary Hanbury is shown in South Vancouver Voters 1908-10 and 1916-8 as a property owner in DL 741. Also known as Ambrey Road.

HANCE ROAD. Now East 63rd Avenue between Prince Edward and Prince Albert Streets. Unnamed on Plan 2212 (1909). The owner of part of DL 326, Block A, was T.A.W. Hance, shown in South Vancouver Voters Lists, 1907–16. Plan 3986 (1912) shows Hance Road between Fraser and Prince Albert Streets.

HANDEL AVENUE. Private thoroughfare in Champlain Heights, named by Community Builders, developers of Ashley Heights, after the composer George Frederic Handel (1685-1759). Approved by the Street Naming Committee on 25 March 1981.

HANLEY STREET. Now East 25th Avenue between Rupert and Cassiar Streets. Named on Plan 1769 (1907). When Hastings Townsite was absorbed by Vancouver in 1911, Hanley Street became part of East 25th Avenue. Origin of name unknown.

HARCOURT ROAD. Now West 43rd Avenue between Balaclava and Macdonald Streets. Origin of name unknown. Unnamed on Plan 1987 (1909) and named on Plans 2493 and 2521 (1909). Shown in *Goad's Atlas*, Plates 37 and 38, between Balaclava and Macdonald Streets. Point Grey By-law 17, 1912, changed Harcourt Road to West 43rd Avenue.

HARGRAVE ROAD. See Bruce Street.

HARO STREET. Takes its name from Haro Strait, shown on the map that L.A. Hamilton used when naming the streets in DL 185. Haro Strait was named in 1790 by Sub-Lieutenant Manuel Quimper of the Spanish navy, after his first mate, Gonzales Lopez de Haro.

HAROLD STREET. Named after Harold II (1022?-1066), last Anglo-Saxon king of England, killed at the Battle of Hastings. Named by South Vancouver By-law 251, 1913. Adjoining streets are called Senlac and Wessex. Unnamed on Plan 1820 (1908) and Plan 2426 (1909).

HARRIET STREET. Named by South Vancouver By-law 251, 1913, but origin of name unknown. Unnamed on Plan 1738 (1908), and named as *Heath Street* on Plan 1750 (1908). A survey name only, probably after a "Heath" (initials indecipherable), one of three owners shown on Plan 1750.

HARRIS STREET. See Georgia Street.

HARRISON DRIVE. Located in the Fraserview development and named by J. Alexander Walker, Vancouver Town Planning Commission, after Harrison Lake Hotel Golf Course, By-law 3330, 1952. Harrison Lake was named after Benjamin Harrison, a director and, later (1838-9), deputy governor of the Hudson's Bay Company.

HARTLEY STREET. Probably named after Francis William Hartley (1866-1940), who owned fifty-six acres in DL 330-331, according to South Vancouver Assessment rolls, 1893 and 1895. From 1895 to 1901 he was a clerk in the Land Registry Office, Vancouver. Later associated with the Royal Trust Company, he died in Victoria on 10 August 1940. Unnamed on Plan 3091 (1910), and first listed in the 1917 city directory, the street lay between East 65th Avenue and the Fraser River, one street east of Kerr Street. With the development of Champlain Heights, By-law 4470, Plan LF 4530 (1970), deleted the portion between East 65th Avenue and South East Marine Drive, and named a section between East 61st and East 62nd Avenues. In 1978, By-law 5195, Plan LE 3742, renamed this latter section Munroe Crescent. The portion between South East Marine Drive and East Kent Avenue North disappeared with the resurvey for Marine Way in 1984. Only a short portion still exists in 1998 south of East Kent Avenue South.

HARVIE STREET (Deleted). Named by South Vancouver By-law 251, 1913, after Eben N. Harvie, municipal engineer for South Vancouver in 1910. Associated with Harvie and Simmonds, general contractors, from 1936-41, he was last shown in 1974 Vancouver directory as retired.

Harvie Street lay between present East 49th and East 56th Avenues. Extended northward to present East 46th Avenue by South Vancouver By-law 557, 1921, which changed Kirkland to Harvey [sic].

For the next decade considerable confusion existed on maps and in directories between "Harvey," "Harvie," and "Kirkland." By 1931 the block of land between East 47th and East 49th Avenues remained unopened, so the two streets – Harvie and Kirkland – remained distinct.

The initial plotting of Champlain Heights in 1970, By-law 4470, Plan LF 4530, showed a portion of Harvie between Watling and Irmin Streets west of Boundary Road, but this portion was deleted in 1978, By-law 5195, Plan LE 3742B. A short portion existed south of East 49th Avenue until 1997.

HARWOOD STREET. Named after Harwood Island, shown on the map that L.A. Hamilton used when naming the streets in DL 185. Captain George Vancouver named Harwood Island in 1792 after Dr. Edward Harwood, naval surgeon.

HASTINGS STREET. Perpetuates the name of Hastings Townsite, named by the provincial government in the 1860s after Rear-Admiral, the Honourable George Fowler Hastings (1814-76), commander-in-chief, Pacific Station, 1866-9.

By the time L.A. Hamilton named the street in 1886, Hastings was a well-developed road between Granville and Hastings Townsites.

Rear-Admiral George F. Hastings. CVA Port. P. 35, N. 72.

In 1914, By-law 1169 changed Seaton Street to Hastings Street between Burrard and Jervis Streets.

Seaton Street. Appeared on the first official map of Vancouver, compiled by H.B. Smith, 1886 (Map 14267). L.A. Hamilton, in a letter to Major J.S. Matthews, former city archivist, 27 April 1936, stated he did not remember why the name was chosen but that he might have wandered off the map he was using and chosen names of lakes. Seaton Lake (now spelled Seton) was named after Colonel Alexander Seton, who commanded the soldiers on the ship *Birkenhead*, which sank in 1853.

HAWKS AVENUE. Named by L.A. Hamilton after John Francis Hawks of Soda Creek, shown in *Port Moody Gazette*, 16 May 1885, as one of the original stockholders of the Coal Harbour land syndicate.

HAY ROAD. See Quebec Street.

HAYWOOD TERRACE. See Marshall Street.

HAZELTON STREET. After Hazelton to continue the pattern of streets in Hastings Townsite being named after BC towns. Named 1927, By-law 1832, although surveyed in 1911, Plan 3191.

Granville at Hastings Street, September 1921. Note the left hand "rule of the road," changed 1 January 1922. CVA Str. P. 106, N. 351.

HEATHER STREET. Named on Plan 228 (1887), a subdivision of DL 472, it lay between present West 15th and West King Edward Avenues. DL 472 was pre-empted in 1874 by William Mackie, who was believed to have named the street used by him as access to his isolated tract of land. He sold the land to G.E. Corbould, who subdivided it in 1887. L.A. Hamilton adopted the name when he surveyed part of DL 526 in 1887 (Map 14160). Registered on Plan 590 (1891).

South Vancouver Highway By-law 1, 1893, gave the legal description of the road between West King Edward and West 16th Avenues but did not name it. Point Grey By-law 1, 1910, allocated $5,500 for the improvement of Heather Street. Point Grey By-law 17, 1912, extended it from the present West King Edward Avenue to present West 37th Avenue. Point Grey By-law 232, 1924, changed Dixon Street to Heather Street from West 59th Avenue south to the Fraser River.

Dixon Road. Described in South Vancouver Highway By-law, 1905, was named after Alfred Black Dixon, a fisher and farmer at Terra Nova, Lulu Island. In 1894 he became a clerk and assessor for Richmond for eleven years. He moved to Eburne, where he died 17 June 1936, aged eighty-four.

HEATLEY AVENUE. Shown on Plan 196 and named after Edward Davis Heatley, co-owner, with George Campbell, of the Hastings Sawmill.

E.D. Heatley. CVA Port. P. 205, N. 1109.

HEBB AVENUE. After Alfred Howard Hebb (1886-1971), general agent for the Great Northern Railway from 1932 to 1956. Named 1951, By-law 3232, as Hebb Street and renamed Hebb Avenue in 1954, By-law 3415.

HECATE PLACE. Private thoroughfare in Champlain Heights, first listed in 1981 city directory, commemorates the surveying vessel *HMS Hecate* which, under Captain George Richards, surveyed the coast of British Columbia in 1861-2.

HELENA AVENUE. Now East 34th Avenue between Culloden and Commercial Streets. Named on Plan 1522 (1907), after Helena, Montana. Dr. S.E. Fleming, care of Panton and Hutchison, owned property in DL 700 in 1907. Samuel Panton was connected with the Montana Company, a real estate firm, hence the street name. Changed to East 35th Avenue by South Vancouver By-law 141, 1910, and then to East 34th Avenue in 1929, By-law 2028.

HELMCKEN STREET. Named by L.A. Hamilton after Dr. John Sebastian Helmcken (1825-1920), surgeon for the Hudson's Bay Company, son-in-law of Sir James Douglas, and member of the first Legislative Assembly of Vancouver Island in 1855.

HEMLOCK COURT. Private thoroughfare in False Creek, adjacent to the northern end of Hemlock Street, whose name was approved by the Street Naming Committee on 15 August 1979.

HEMLOCK STREET. Officially registered on Plan 590 (1891) but named on an 1887 map (Map 14160) by L.A. Hamilton, who chose tree names for the large block of land between Cambie and Yew Streets.

HENNEPIN AVENUE. Named 1978, By-law 5150, after Louis Hennepin (1626?-1705?), who was with the La Salle expedition on the upper Mississippi River in 1680. The Street Naming Committee, at its meetings of 26 January and 16 February 1978, decided that the streets in Enclave 1, Champlain Heights, were to be named after explorers.

HENRY ROAD (DL 329) (Deleted). Named on Plan 2664 (1910). One block long, it lay immediately east of the present Elliott Street and was the second street north of South East Marine Drive. Survey name only, it became part of East 66th Avenue and disappeared when Fraserview Golf Course developed. Origin of name unknown.

HENRY STREET (DL 391-392). Unnamed on Plan 2534 (1910) and named in 1913 by South Vancouver By-law 251, after the owner, M.J. Henry, who had a nursery on the Westminster Road (now Kingsway) in 1895.

HENRY STREET (DL 301). Now East 22nd Avenue between Main Street and Clark Drive. Shown on Plan 187 (1885) and named by Henry V. Edmonds after his son Henry Lovekin Edmonds (1871-1952). When Vancouver absorbed DL 301 in 1911, Henry Street became part of East 22nd Avenue.

Hogan's Alley, April 1958. CVA BU. P. 508-53.

HERBERT ROAD. See Argyle Street.

HERMON DRIVE. Named 1962, By-law 3977, after Ernest Bolton Hermon (1863-1937), pioneer surveyor whose firm, Hermon and Burwell, surveyed much of early Vancouver. See Cotton (1995) for a depiction of the firm's history.

HERON PLACE. One of nine private thoroughfares in Enclaves 8, 9, and 10, Champlain Heights, bearing bird names submitted by Matheson Heights Co-operative and approved by the Street Naming Committee on 25 March 1981.

HIGH ROAD. Dedicated but unopened road east of Kootenay Street and north of Edinburgh Street, on Plan 5461 (1924). Probably named after its location high above the 1958 Second Narrows Bridge and the CPR

HIGHBURY STREET. Named by Point Grey By-law 17, 1912, probably after the Highbury Park subdivision in DL 320, Plan 1847 (1908), and advertised in *Vancouver Daily Province*, 28 April 1910. There is a Highbury Park and Highbury Place in London, England. Point Grey By-law 17, 1914, extended it from West 8th Avenue to English Bay and south from West 55th Avenue to the Fraser River.

HIGHGATE STREET. Unnamed on Plan 2911 (1910) and named by South Vancouver By-law 251, 1913, probably after Highgate Hill, London, England.

HIGHLAND AVENUE (Deleted). Descriptive name. Unnamed on Plan 2330 (1909) but named on Plan 2894 (1910). Became East 64th Avenue (later East 62nd Avenue) between Victoria Drive and Nanaimo Street. Disappeared with the replotting of Fraserview.

HILL STREET. See Victoria Drive.

HINKLY STREET. Now East 47th Avenue between Fleming and Argyle Streets. Shown on Plan 1966 (1909) and in *Goad's Atlas*, Plate 103, as East 49th Avenue (Hinkly). Origin of name unknown.

HOBSON STREET. See Yew Street.

HOGAN'S ALLEY. Origin of this unofficial name not ascertained. The 1921 city directory lists Harry Hogan, singer, at 406 Union Street – the only listing for him. The alley "started right at Park Lane (later Station Street) and ran right straight up between Park and Union, ended around Jackson Avenue – that's when you

A century ago, some downtown alleys (more like private streets) were named: Blood Alley, Canton Alley, False Creek Alley, Hogan's Alley, Lafonde's Alley, Market Alley, Shanghai Alley, and Trounce Alley. Recently named alleys are Ackery, Blood Alley Square, and Railspur.

were out of Hogan's Alley," according to Austin Phillips, who came to the area in 1925 (Marlatt and Itter 1979, 140).

The unofficial name appeared frequently in newspaper reports. However, reports of the Environmental Health Inspection Division of the city's Health Department made no mention of the name in its detailed reports of conditions in the Union Street area. The *Vancouver Daily Province*, 21 April 1939, stated that "to the average citizen Hogan's Alley stands for squalor, immorality and crime" and asked: "Is Hogan's Alley the blemish or just the focal point of the area around it?"

The alley disappeared with the building of the present Georgia Viaduct in 1972.

HOLLAND STREET. After William Sowden Holland (1863-1939), who established a real estate and insurance business in the early 1900s in Vancouver, was managing director of the Vancouver Horse Show, and one of the original directors of the Exhibition Association. Unnamed on Plan 2442 (1909) but named on Plan 3720 (1911). Point Grey By-law 17, 1912, named Holland Drive between South West Marine Drive and West 39th Avenue. Point Grey By-law 17, 1914, extended it south to the northern boundary of the Musqueam Band Reserve.

HOLLYHOCK LANE. Private thoroughfare in Champlain Heights, named by the Kinross Creek Housing Cooperative after Hollyhock Lane in Kinross, Scotland. Name approved by the Street Naming Committee on 8 July 1982.

HOMER STREET. Named by L.A. Hamilton after Joshua Attwood Reynolds Homer (1827-86), a New Westminster merchant and MP for New Westminster, 1882-6.

J.A.R. Homer. cva Port. P. 228, N. 483.

HORLEY STREET. South Vancouver Road Loan By-law 6, 1911, allocated $1,300 to Horley Street, DL 37, between Rupert and Earles Streets. Origin of name unknown.

HORNBY STREET. Named after Hornby Island by L.A. Hamilton. The island named for Rear-Admiral Phipps Hornby, commander-in-chief of the Pacific Station, 1847-51.

HORNE ROAD. Named after James Welton Horne (1854-1922), a pioneer Vancouver realtor who served on Vancouver City Council 1888-90, chaired the Parks Board 1888-94, and was an MLA, 1890-4. Welton (now Sophia) and James Streets also named after him. Changed to East 28th Avenue between Main and Knight Streets by South Vancouver By-law 141, 1910. First named on Plan 960 (1904).

HOSMER AVENUE. Shown on Plan 4502 (1913), Shaughnessy Heights, and named by the CPR after Charles Rudolph Hosmer (1851-1927), a director of the company and at one time manager of the CPR telegraph system.

HOWARD STREET (DL 37). See Ward Street.

HOWARD STREET (DL 302). See Watson Street.

HOWE STREET. Named after Howe Sound by L.A. Hamilton when naming the streets in DL 541. Captain George Vancouver named Howe Sound in 1792 after Earl Howe, First Lord of the Admiralty, 1783-8.

HOWE STREET (DL 325). See Adera Street.

HOY STREET. Probably named after Charles Hoy (1874-1936). South Vancouver Voters Lists, 1907 and 1908, show Eliza L. Hoy and Charles Hoy owning property in DL 51-36. The 1908 Provincial Voters List shows Charles Hoy, baker, Collingwood.

Unnamed on Plans 2537 and 2393 (1909). South Vancouver By-law 151, 1911, allocated $400 to Hoy Street from Wellington Avenue to BCER right-of-way.

Plan 1918 (1909), showed Hoy Street between Moscrop Street and East 29th Avenue as *Weeks Road*. Origin of this survey name unknown.

HOYLAKE AVENUE. Named by By-law 3330, 1952, after the Royal Liverpool Golf Club's course at Hoylake, Cheshire, as suggested by J. Alexander Walker. In 1961, By-law 3937 extended the avenue to Muirfield Drive.

HUDSON STREET. Named Hudson Avenue, between present West 37th and West 57th Avenues, after the explorer Henry Hudson, by Point Grey By-law 32, 1911. Point Grey By-law 17, 1912, named Hudson Street between West 25th and

J.W. Horne, "Real Estate Office in Big Tree." Mr. Horne is the individual in the centre, pointing to a map or city plan. CVA Tr. P. 2, N. 6.

West 27th Avenues to join Hudson Street in Shaughnessy Heights, Plan 4502 (1913). Point Grey By-law 232, 1924, changed Hudson Avenue to Hudson Street.

Plan of Eburne Townsite (Plan 1749 [1908]) showed Fourth Street between present South West Marine Drive and West 70th Avenue, later extended to West 59th Avenue. Became Hudson Street by Point Grey By-law 17, 1914.

HULL STREET. First listed in the 1917 city directory. Not known how or when named. Originally called *Lakeview Road,* and so named by South Vancouver By-law 65, 1903, probably after Lakeview Station on the Vancouver-New Westminster Tramway (later Central Park Line of the BCER).

Goad's Atlas, Plate 92, 1913, shows *Epworth Street* (late Lakeview Avenue [sic]). In an in-terview with William Fleming in 1935, Major J.S. Matthews recorded that "Epworth was named by Frank L. Vosper whose home was nearby at Bella Vista Street. He wanted the district called Epworth after Epworth, Kent, where the Epworth League started."

HUMBLECROFT ROAD. Now East 29th Avenue between Fraser and Prince Albert Streets. Plan 1727 (1908) showed the owner as G.A. Humblecroft.

Granville Alfred Humble-Croft (hyphenated form) was first listed in 1907 city directory with the real estate and business brokerage firm of Keller and Humble-Croft. Shown in South Vancouver Voters List, 1908, owning property in DL 391-2 and living on the North Arm Road (now Fraser Street).

Humblecroft Road changed to East 29th Avenue in 1910, South Vancouver By-law 141.

HUM-LU-SUM DRIVE. Named on Plan LF 10811 (1985). This street name on land leased from the Musqueam Band means "fresh water splash in the face."

Musqueam Elder Dominic Point tells the story about the Traveller, Haals, coming across the continent to teach people what to eat, what not to eat, and what herbs were safe. People warned that he was a jealous god and not to hurt his feelings. A man at Hum-lu-sum, although so warned, said he did not believe it. "No one tells me!" One day, while at a stream, he leaned down to splash fresh water on his face. Haals came and turned him into stone. One can see him there, a big rock, and nearby is his pot, which was turned into a small rock. (Letter from Wanona Scott, executive secretary, Musqueam Band, 17 July 1996.)

HUMM STREET. After Henry Josiah Humm, co-owner with Ellen Harriet Duff of DL 727, shown on Plan 2202. He continued to own property in DL 727 until 1940, as shown in Vancouver assessment rolls.

South Vancouver Voters List, 1910, lists the estate of T.W. Duff, care of Maddison, Stirling and Company, Old Drury, London, England, as owners of DL 727. The 1910 edition of Kelly's Post Office Directory for London, England, shows Maddison, Stirling, Humm and Davies,

solicitors, 33 Old Jewry. Humm was admitted to practice in 1899, joined the firm about 1904, and was a partner as late as 1951.

Shown as Humm Road on Plan 2202 (1909) and renamed Humm Street by South Vancouver By-law 141, 1910. It then lay between East 54th and East 59th Avenues but has been shortened by the replotting for the Fraserview development.

HUMMINGBIRD PLACE. One of nine private thoroughfares in Enclaves 8, 9, and 10, Champlain Heights, bearing bird names submitted by Matheson Heights Cooperative and approved by the Street Naming Committee on 25 March 1981.

HURST AVENUE. Named 1970, By-law 4770, Plan LF 4530, after Hurst Street in Burnaby, which lies directly east. In 1978, By-law 5195, Plan LE 3742B, reconfirmed the name.

HURST PLACE. Private thoroughfare in Champlain Heights, named 1988, By-law 6376, Plan LF 11231, which changed part of Blake Street.

HUTCHISON STREET. See Celtic Avenue.

HYACK DRIVE. Private thoroughfare in Champlain Heights named after Hyack, one of the orcas (killer whales) in the Vancouver Aquarium. Alexander Laidlaw Cooperative submitted the name to the Street Naming Committee. Approved on 25 March 1981. See also Skana and Tuaq Drives.

I

IMPERIAL STREET. See Discovery Street.

INDUSTRIAL AVENUE. Named after its location on the industrial land created when the eastern part of False Creek was filled in by 1918. Originally named Industrial Street by By-law 1556, 1922, and repealed by By-law 1803, 1926, which gave a more exact legal description. In 1950, By-law 3195 renamed it Industrial Avenue.

INVERNESS STREET. Named by South Vancouver By-law 141, 1910, probably after Inverness, Scotland, as many adjacent streets bore Scottish names. This same by-law also renamed Thomas Street, Campbell Road, Winnifred Avenue, and Dorchester Street.

Thomas Street (DL 301). Between East 16th and East 25th Avenues. Shown on Plan 187 (1885) and named by H.V. Edmonds, owner of DL 301, after some member of his family. In 1911 DL 301 was absorbed into the City of Vancouver, but the South Vancouver name of Inverness was retained.

Campbell Road (DL 327). Between South East Marine Drive and the Fraser River. Although mentioned in South Vancouver By-law 141, 1910, the road was not changed. See Crompton Street.

Winnifred Avenue (DL 740). Between East 49th and East 57th Avenues. Named Winifred on Plan 3254 (1911). Origin of name unknown.

Dorchester Street. Between East 33rd and East 37th Avenues. Shown on Plan 1369 (1907) as a street in Kensington Place subdivision, which bore English place names.

Morton Road. Described in South Vancouver Highway By-law, 1905, as lying between the present East 28th and East King Edward Avenues. South Vancouver Council minutes, 20 November 1909, authorize the clearing of the boulevard on Morton Road. Although the name is not mentioned in South Vancouver By-law 141, 1910, it became part of Inverness. R.B. Morton is listed in 1894 and 1901 South Vancouver Voters Lists as owning property in DL 391.

IRMIN AVENUE (Deleted). Named by By-law 4470, 1970, Plan LF 4530, it lay directly west of Irmin Street in Burnaby, from whence it took its name. With the replotting of the Champlain Heights area, By-law 5195, 1978, Plan LE 3742B, deleted it.

IRONWORK PASSAGE. Named 1976, By-law 5010, Plan LF 3786, to commemorate the former ironworks located along False Creek.

ISLAND AVENUE. Probably named after its position looking across the Fraser River to Mitchell Island. Unnamed on Plan 2122 (1909) and named by South Vancouver By-law 251, 1913.

ISLAND PARK WALK. Private thoroughfare through a park named by the Street Naming Committee on 15 August 1979 after its location near Granville Island. The extension west from Anderson Street is a dedicated road, named by By-law 5741, 1984, Plan LF 9615.

IVANHOE STREET. Named 1930, By-law 2082, after Ivanhoe, the hero in Sir Walter Scott's novel, *Ivanhoe*. Changed from part of the former East 41st Avenue in South Vancouver. See page 135.

IVY STREET (DL 328) (Deleted). A short street that ran from East 66th Avenue to South East Marine Drive, one block east of Victoria Drive. Originally called Duff Street. South Vancouver By-law 252 renamed it Elm Street in 1913. In 1929, Vancouver By-law 2014 renamed it Ivy Street to remove duplication with Elm Street in Kerrisdale. Ivy Street disappeared in the replotting for Fraserview subdivision.

J

JACKSON AVENUE. Named after Robert Edwin Jackson (1826-1909) of the law firm Drake, Jackson and Helmcken in Victoria. In 1950, By-law 3195 changed the part of Jackson Avenue between Prior and Atlantic Streets to Malkin Avenue.

JADE TREE COURT. Private thoroughfare in Champlain Heights first listed in 1980 city directory and named after the jade tree.

JAMES STREET (DL 301). See Glen Drive.

JAMES STREET (DL 337). See Raleigh Street.

JAMES STREET. Originally it lay between East 18th and East 20th Avenues in DL 628. Named after James Welton Horne (1854-1922), a pioneer Vancouver realtor who served on Vancouver City Council 1888-90, was chairman of the Parks Board 1888-94, and an MLA, 1890-4.

South Vancouver Highway By-law, 1905, renamed this street Quebec Street and transferred the name "James" to a short broken street immediately to the west and from just north of East 28th Avenue to the present East 35th Avenue. It was first listed in the 1914 city directory. Now ends at East 33rd Avenue.

JAMES WALK. Private thoroughfare in the Little Mountain housing project in Riley Park, which absorbed James Street south of East 33rd Avenue but perpetuated the name. First listed in the 1954 city directory.

J.W. Horne, as portrayed in *British Columbians as We See 'Em, 1910 and 1911*, (Vancouver: Newspaper Cartoonist Association of British Columbia, 1911).

JANE STREET. Now East 17th Avenue between Main and Knight Streets. Shown on Plan 187 (1885) and named by H.V. Edmonds, after his wife, Jane Fortune (née Kemp, ca. 1840-1906). DL 301 was absorbed into Vancouver in 1911, and Jane Street became part of East 17th Avenue.

JANES ROAD. Now East 41st Avenue between Victoria Drive and Rupert Street. Named by South Vancouver By-law 65, 1903, the road lay between Victoria Drive and Wales Street. By 1910 it extended to Kerr Street, when South Vancouver By-law 141 changed it, incorrectly, to East 43rd Avenue instead of East 42nd Avenue; became East 41st Avenue by Vancouver By-law 2028, 1929.

Named after Thomas John Janes (1855-1926), an early settler in South Vancouver. Born in Cornwall, England, he came to British Columbia in 1883 and worked as a butcher for George Black in Granville. Later, he ran a stage between Vancouver and New Westminster.

JASPER CRESCENT. Named 1952, By-law 3330, after the Jasper Park Lodge Golf Course in Jasper, Alberta, in keeping with the golf course theme suggested by J. Alexander Walker, Vancouver Town Planning Commission.

JELLICOE STREET. Probably named after Sir John Jellicoe (1859-1935), British naval officer who commanded the British Grand Fleet at the Battle of Jutland, May 1916. First listed in 1917 city directory, running from East 65th to East 67th Avenues between Vivan and present Killarney Streets. This portion disappeared with the development of the Fraserview Golf Course. By 1953 Jellicoe Street extended from South East Marine Drive to the Fraser River.

Sir John Jellicoe. CVA Port. P. 21, N. 1131.

Besides the streets in Renfrew named after WWI and WWII personalities and battles (see Falaise Avenue), there are a number of other streets names derived from these two historic wars: French, Haig, Jellicoe, Seaforth, Worthington, Aisne, Alamein, Ghent, and Malta.

JENSEN ROAD. Now East 62nd Avenue between Main and Fraser Streets. Named on Plan 1798 (1908) after owners Soren and Margarethe Jensen. Soren Jensen is shown in South Vancouver Voters Lists, 1903-10 inclusive. South Vancouver By-law 141, 1910, changed the street to East 64th Avenue, now East 62nd Avenue (Vancouver By-law 2028, 1929).

JERICHO CIRCLE. Shown on Plan 5970 (1928) and first listed in 1930 city directory, it was probably named after its proximity to the Jericho Country Club. Jericho, an area of Vancouver, takes its name from the logging camp Jerry Rogers established at Jerry's Cove ("Jericho") in 1865.

JERSEY ROAD. Now East 46th Avenue between Prince Edward and Fraser Streets. Origin of name unknown. In 1910, South Vancouver By-law 141 changed the street to East 48th Avenue. Upon amalgamation in 1929, Vancouver By-law 2028 changed East 48th Avenue to East 46th Avenue between Manitoba and Fraser Streets. The portion between Ontario and Prince Edward had been called Haddock Street. The name is mentioned in South Vancouver council minutes, 18 September 1909, when tenders were called for two-foot-wide sidewalks.

JERVIS STREET. Named after Jervis Inlet, shown on the map used by L.A. Hamilton when naming the streets in DL 185. Captain George Vancouver named the inlet in 1792 after Rear-Admiral John Jervis (1735-1823).

JOHN STREET See Prince Edward Street.

JOHN STREET. Origin of name unknown. Named on Plan 2634 (1910) by owner James W. Horne. Unnamed on Plans 1338 and 1365 (1907).

JOHNS AVENUE. Now East 32nd Avenue east of Victoria Drive to its intersection with East 30th Avenue and Baldwin Street. Origin of name unknown. Named on Plan 1955 (1909). Changed to East 32nd Avenue by South Vancouver By-law 141, 1910.

JOHNSON AVENUE (DL 2037). See Evans Avenue.

JOHNSON ROAD. See Blenheim Street.

JOHNSON ROAD (DL 743). Now East 23rd Avenue between Victoria Drive and Sidney Street. Listed in the index to Volume 2 of *Goad's Atlas*, 1913, as Johnson Road (now East 23rd Avenue), South Vancouver. Also known as Springridge Avenue. Unnamed on Plan 1552 (1907). Johnson has not been identified.

JOHNSON STREET (DL 196) (Deleted). Also spelled Johnston Street. On 15 July 1887 the minutes of Vancouver Board of Works recommended that Park Avenue and Johnston Street be provided with five-foot-wide sidewalks.

The 1887 Vancouver Voters List shows Charles G. Johnson as a tenant of lot 2, Block 23, DL 196, which lies just south of Prior Street and west of Main Street. *Goad's Atlas*, 1897-1903, Plate 12 (Map 14053), shows a roadway, since gone, south of Lot 2, probably the one mentioned in the 1887 minutes. Charles Gardiner Johnson (1857-1926), in his reminiscences of the 1886 fire that destroyed most of Vancouver

C.G. Johnson. From group photo of Commissioners and Pilots of Vancouver Pilotage District, 1879-1916. CVA Port. P. 189, N. 138.

(*Vancouver Sun*, 18 April 18 1936, supplement), stated that he lived in a cottage close to False Creek near the Westminster Bridge. He became managing director of Johnson Wharf and head of C. Gardiner Johnson and Company, shipping.

JOHNSTON STREET. Private thoroughfare on Granville Island, probably named after Alexander Johnston (1867-1951), deputy minister of marine and fisheries, 1910-31. Granville Island was under the jurisdiction of this ministry through the Vancouver Harbour Commission.

JOYCE STREET. Named as Joyce Road by South Vancouver Highway By-law, 1905, it lay between the present East 45th and School Avenues and then northeast to the present East 29th Avenue. South Vancouver By-law 141, 1910, renamed it Joyce Street, and also changed *Balsam Lane*, named on Plan 243 (1888) by owner George Wales, to Joyce between East 45th Avenue and School Avenue.

South Vancouver Assessment Roll, 1893, showed Joyce and Dinmore owning ten acres in DL 338, abutting East 45th Avenue, where they operated a market garden. Abraham Joyce served as a school trustee for East Vancouver (now Carleton) School, 1897-8. He died 21 May 1931, aged eighty-two.

JUANITA DRIVE. An unofficial street name of unknown origin, first listed in 1974 city directory "from 3100 East 45th Avenue North"; that is, between Kerr and Doman Streets, with only two residents shown. In 1978 there was one resident on the street, the last year any were listed. It may have been a postal address. City surveyor has no record of surveys.

K

KAMLOOPS STREET. Named by the provincial government after the Kamloops Mining Division. Shown on Plan 100, a resurvey of Hastings Townsite, 1906, it extended from Princess Street (now East Pender Street) to Barnard Street (now Adanac). A note on this plan states Kamloops Street had not been previously surveyed.

By-law 3195, 1950, renamed the street north of Dundas Street as Kamloops Street North, although the designation was in use in 1916. The portion between Grandview Highway South and East 15th Avenue became part of Copley Street in 1954, By-law 3415.

KASLO STREET. Shown on Plan 100, a resurvey of Hastings Townsite, 1906, and named by the provincial government after the City of Kaslo. According to Akrigg (1997), the city and river were named after John Kasleau, a prospector. By-law 3195 renamed the portion of Kaslo Street north of Dundas as Kaslo Street North in 1950, although the designation had been in use since 1913.

KATHLEEN STREET. See Windsor Street.

KAYE ROAD. See Macdonald Street and Trafalgar Street.

KEEFER STREET. Named after George Alexander Keefer (1836-1912), property owner in DL 196 and shareholder in the Vancouver Improvement Company. He came to British Columbia in 1871 to survey a route for the CPR and to handle its construction from Boston Bar to Lytton, 1876-85. He opened a private engineering practice in Vancouver in 1886.

In 1929, By-law 2014 changed the part between Vernon Drive and Victoria Drive to Frances Street, and that between Victoria Drive and Nanaimo Street to Ferndale Street.

In 1984, By-law 5741, Plan LF 9511, extended Keefer west to Taylor Street; and in 1992, By-law 7001, Plan LF 11491, further extended it to a cul-de-sac beyond Abbott Street and changed the entire section west of Carrall to *Keefer Place.*

KEITH DRIVE. Named after James Cooper Keith (1852-1914), first manager of the Bank of British Columbia in Vancouver, as many of the streets in DL 264A were named after prominent BC businessmen. He became reeve of North Vancouver municipality, which named Keith Road after him. Shown on a 1902 map surveyed by Hermon and Burwell (Map 14171) and on Plan 1771 (1905), a resurvey of DL 264A.

J.W. Horne, as portrayed in *British Columbians as We See 'Em, 1910 and 1911,* (Vancouver: Newspaper Cartoonist Association of British Columbia, 1911).

KE-KAIT PLACE. Private thoroughfare in Musqueam Band Reserve No. 2, shown on Plan LF 10811 (1985). Ke-Kait is just the name of a place (letter from Wanona Scott, executive secretary, Musqueam Band, 17 July 1996).

KELOWNA STREET. After the city of Kelowna, whose name comes from the Okanogan village that elders remember as Skela'-unina, "grizzly bear" (Coull 1996). Unnamed on plans 2048 and 2628, 1909, and named 1915, By-law 1230.

KEMBALL ROAD. Now East 56th Avenue between Main and Fraser Streets. Origin of name unknown. Named on Plan 1751 (1908). On Plan 2980 (1910), shown as Kimby Road. South Vancouver By-law 141, 1910, changed it to East 58th Avenue (now East 56th Avenue).

KEMP ROAD (DL 329) (Deleted). Perhaps named after George Kemp, Cedar Cottage, owning property in DL 329, according to South Vancouver Voters Lists, 1910 and 1914-5. A short road between Victoria Drive and Nanaimo Street, which South Vancouver By-law 141, 1910, changed to East 62nd Avenue (later East 60th Avenue), it has since disappeared in the re-plotting for Fraserview.

KEMP STREET. Now East 11th Avenue between Main and Prince Edward Streets. Shown on Plan 187 (1885) and named by the owner, H.V. Edmonds, after his wife, Jane Fortune (née Kemp, ca. 1840-1906). Became part of East 11th Avenue in 1911, when Vancouver absorbed DL 301.

KEMPTON PLACE. Named 1961, By-law 3937, after an unidentified golf course (Vancouver City Council Minutes, v. 77, p. 606.)

KENSINGTON AVENUE. Now East 35th Avenue between Fraser and Culloden Streets. Kensington Avenue, after the borough of Kensington, London, was the centre street in the subdivision Kensington Place, shown on Plan 1369 (1907). South Vancouver By-law 141, 1910, changed it to East 36th Avenue (now East 35th Avenue).

KENT AVENUE. Named arbitrarily, perhaps after Kent, England. First shown in the 1922 city directory as: "From Main Street east, used by BCER, Eburne-Westminster." It gradually grew, in varying lengths, along with industry on both sides of the tracks (which it paralleled). The only avenue in the city with a North and South designation.

KERR STREET. South Vancouver Highway By-law 1, 1893, established Kerr Road, named after George Kerr (1826-1912), owner of five acres in DL 337, as shown in South Vancouver assessment rolls, 1893. South Vancouver By-law 141, 1910, changed Kerr Road and Spruce Lane to Kerr Street.

Spruce Lane. Named on plan 243, 1888, by George Wales, lay between the present East 45th and School Avenues.

In 1960 the Rupert-Kerr Diversion linked the two streets to create a north-south highway from South East Marine Drive to the Second Narrows Bridge.

The southern part of Kerr Street became an access road to the Kerr Road garbage dump, in existence from the 1940s until 1967.

KERRISDALE AVENUE. See Mackenzie Street.

KERSLAND DRIVE. Named to honour Newton J. Ker (1866-1946), CPR land agent in Vancouver, 1887-1936, after Kersland Barony, Ayrshire, old home of the Ker clan. Named on Plan 8324 (1950) and first listed in the 1951 city directory.

KEVIN PLACE. An arbitrary choice of name, first listed in the 1971 city directory. In 1969 the University Endowment Lands administration created a subdivision. In 1970 an amendment to the Vancouver Charter transferred it to the city. In 1974, the Street Naming Committee approved the name, already in use.

KEYSTONE STREET. Private thoroughfare shown on Plan LF 11558 (1993) and named arbitrarily by Marine Woods Developments Limited in association with Cobblestone, Cornerstone, Fieldstone, and Millstone.

KIELDER COURT. Private thoroughfare in Earl Adams Village, a project of the Greater Vancouver Housing Corporation, which named streets after places in Northumberland County, England. Kielder is a village near Kielder forest. First listed in 1979 city directory.

KILLARNEY STREET. Named 1951, By-law 3255, after nearby Killarney Park. Changed from

Carlton Street to remove duplication with Carlton Street in Burnaby. Because of opposition to the change, the Street Naming Committee held five meetings with residents of the street. Angry letters appeared in the *Vancouver Sun* and *Vancouver Daily Province* on 16, 18, 23, 27, 28, and 31 July 1951, but to no avail.

Carlton Street. Origin of name unknown. Named by South Vancouver By-law 141, 1910. This by-law, in addition to changing Carlton Avenue, renamed Green Street (between East 54th and Vanness Avenues) and Cypress Lane (between East 45th Avenue and the present Kingsway). The spelling of Carlton Street gradually changed unofficially to "Carleton," as it was near Carleton School, which had been named in 1911 after Sir Guy Carleton (1724-1808).

Green Road. Probably named after the Green family. South Vancouver assessment roll, 1893, shows Lila A. Green owning twenty acres in DL 50. South Vancouver Highway By-law, 1905, extended it from East 45th to East 54th Avenues.

Cypress Lane. Named on Plan 243 (1888), by the owner, George Wales.

Cleveland Road. Shown in *Goad's Atlas*, Plate 104, as Carleton Street (late Cleveland Road), between East 45th and East 54th Avenues. An unofficial name after property owners John Ballentorn Cleveland, storekeeper, and Eugene Wyman Cleveland (1857-1934), contractor.

KILLDEER PLACE. One of nine private thoroughfares in Enclaves 8, 9, and 10, Champlain Heights, bearing bird names that were submitted by the Matheson Heights Cooperative and approved by the Street Naming Committee on 25 March 1981.

KILMARNOCK STREET. See Rupert Street.

KIMBY ROAD. See Kemball Road.

KING STREET. See Kings Avenue.

KING EDWARD AVENUE. Named after King Edward VII, who reigned 1901-10, by Point Grey By-law 17, 1912, but first listed in Point Grey By-law 1, 1910, which allocated $10,000 to it for road work. The 1912 by-law also renamed Chaldecott Road between Camosun and Macdonald Streets, named by South Vancouver Highway By-law, 1905. Frederick Miller Chaldecott (1863-1949), solicitor, owned property in Point Grey.

The opening of Kingsway, 30 September 1913, at Boundary Road by the Hon. Thomas Taylor, MLA, Minister of Public Works, Victoria. The open top automobile did not become unfashionable for several years. Speed limits must not exceed 25 miles per hour. A civic holiday in Burnaby, six hundred automobiles made the trip between New Westminister and Vancouver on the day the road was opened. CVA Str. P. 288. N. 338.

In 1929 Vancouver By-law 2014 changed 25th Avenue in South Vancouver municipality to King Edward Avenue. The next year By-law 2082 changed the designation to East and West King Edward, with Ontario Street being the division point, except for West 25th Avenue between Puget Drive and Trafalgar Street, now called Alamein.

In 1950 By-law 3195 renamed East and West King Edward to King Edward Avenue East and West, and King Edward East beyond Kingsway was changed back to East 25th Avenue.

In 1952 By-law 3312 renamed West 23rd Avenue, between Arbutus and Yew Streets, King Edward Avenue West.

A private thoroughfare known as King Edward Avenue exists in the Arbutus Village subdivision.

KINGS AVENUE. Renamed by South Vancouver By-law 251, 1913, to harmonize with the adjacent Queens Avenue, named at the same time. Previously called King Street on Plan 2197 (1909). Origin of name unknown.

KINGS LYNN STREET. Named 1996, By-law 7590, Plan LF 11680, after Kings Lynn, Norfolk, the birthplace of Captain George Vancouver (Administrative report to Vancouver City Council, 30 April 1996).

KINGSWAY (DL 538). Now West 4th Avenue between present Discovery and Alma Streets. Probably named after Kingsway, a thoroughfare in London, England, named in honour of King Edward VII. Not verified. Named on the map accompanying Point Grey By-law 17, 1912, but not used. In a letter to the editor, *Vancouver Daily Province*, 16 May 1910, a reader had proposed that 4th Avenue be renamed Kingsway in memory of the late King and to give "a distinctiveness" to an important thoroughfare.

KINGSWAY. After Kingsway, a thoroughfare in London, England. Completed in 1906 and named in honour of King Edward VII. Vancouver By-law 1114, 1913 (covering the distance between Main and Knight Streets), and South Vancouver By-law 197, 1913 (covering the distance from Knight Street to Boundary Road), changed Westminster Road to Kingsway.

In 1911, Vancouver By-law 842 changed New Westminster Road to Westminster Road. There was no comparable South Vancouver By-law. The Granville and New Westminster Road, shown on Plan 187 (1885), was the popular name for the trail slashed between New Westminster and the Granville Townsite. This trail was also known as the False Creek Trail, constructed in 1860 on the recommendation of Colonel Moody, to link New Westminster with the government reserve on English Bay.

KINROSS STREET. Named, although not verified, after nearby Kinross Creek and, indirectly, after Kinross, Scotland. South Vancouver By-law 141, 1910, changed Doman Road to Kinross Street. Surveyed but unnamed on Plan 3704 (1909) and Plan 2593 (1910), it lay between the present East 54th Avenue and the Fraser River.

Confusion arose between the location of Doman and Kinross, but by 1930 Kinross was established as lying south of East 65th Avenue and slightly to the east of Doman, which ended at East 65th Avenue.

The development of Champlain Heights, By-law 4770, 1970, Plan LF 4530, changed Kinross to a one-block-long street north of East 62nd Avenue. A short portion also exists south of Marine Way.

KIRKLAND STREET. First listed in 1917 Vancouver city directory, between present East 46th and East 47th Avenues, and probably named after William Kirkland, an area resident and secretary of the South Vancouver School Board in 1913.

In 1921 South Vancouver By-law 557 renamed it Harvey [sic], with the intent of connecting it to Harvie Street, which lay immediately south between the present East 49th and East 54th Avenues.

For the next decade there was considerable confusion on maps and in directories between "Harvey," "Harvie," and "Kirkland" Streets. By

1931, the problem had been resolved, as the block of land between East 47th and East 49th Avenues remained unopened and thus separated the two streets.

KITCHENER STREET (DL 319). See Haig Street.

KITCHENER STREET. Named 1915, By-law 1234, after Horatio Herbert Kitchener, Lord Kitchener (1850-1916), secretary of state for war in the British Cabinet, 1914. Changed from Bismark because of anti-German sentiments during the First World War.

Bismark Street. Named after Otto von Bismarck (1815-98), Prussian statesman who united the German states into one country. Named on Plan 1771 (1905), a resurvey of DL 264A, but first listed in the 1904 city directory.

KITSILANO DIVERSION. Named after the Kitsilano district through which it passes. Kitsilano is a modified form of Khahtsahlano, name of a

A portrait of August Jack Khatsahlano unveiled by his wife at Kitsilano High School, 27 October 1943. CVA Port. P. 658, N. 271.

Many street names in Vancouver are derived from Native names: Atlin, Brant, Camosun, Canada, Celista, Cheam, Comox, Coquihalla, Cree, Cheyenne, Haida, Kelowna, Kokanee, Kootenay, Lillooet, Maquinna, Moosomin, Mohawk, Nicola, Nootka, Penticton, Qualicum, Quilchena, Sasamat, Shawnee, Skana, Skeena, Slocan, Stikine, Tecumseh, Toba, Tuam, Tuaq, Qualicum, Quatsino, Quilchena, Waneta, Wenonah, Yuculta, and Yukon. However, the only Native named relevant to this area and its language are: Halss, Hum-lu-sum, Ke-kait, Kitsilano, Kullahum, Musqueam, Salish, Semana, Sennok, Si-lu, Staulo, Tamath, Thellaiwhaltun, and Tytahum.

chief of the Squamish Band. Named 1928, By-law 1932, when the linking of West 10th and West 12th Avenues between Stephens and Mackenzie Streets was completed.

KNIGHT STREET. Originally called Knight Road after Robert Knight (1829-1913), who owned property in South Vancouver, 1893-1904, by South Vancouver Highway By-law 1, 1893. It ran north from the present East 31st Avenue to the present Kingsway. In 1910 South Vancouver By-law 141 renamed it Knight Street, as did Vancouver By-law 842, 1911. In 1954 By-law 3457 extended Knight Street at a north-west angle between East 14th and East 15th Avenues to join Clark Drive. This diversion im-

R. Knight. CVA Port. P. 660, N. 273.

proved traffic flow from the Fraser River north to important east-west connecting roads. The opening of the Knight Street Bridge on 15 January 1974 made the street an arterial highway.

KOKANEE PLACE. Private thoroughfare in Champlain Heights, named by Community Builders, developers of Park Place, after Kokanee Glacier Provincial Park. The Okanagan people called the land-locked salmon "kokanee," meaning "little salmon." Name approved by the Street Naming Committee on 21 June 1978.

KOOTENAY STREET. Named by the provincial government after the Kootenay Mining District and indirectly after the Ktunaxa people, and shown on Plan 100, a resurvey of Hastings Townsite, 1906. It lay between the present Yale and Adanac Streets. Gradually extended, its north-south delineation has been altered by the Trans-Canada Highway angling across the townsite. In 1950, By-law 3195 named the portion north of Dundas Street Kootenay Street North, although the name had been in use since 1918.

KOPERNIK DRIVE (Proposed). See Rosemont Drive.

KULLAHUN DRIVE. In Musqueam Park subdivision, leased from the Musqueam Band and named by By-law 4266, 1966. Kullahun, meaning "fence or barricade," was the name of an old settlement (CVA, Vancouver City Clerk, Series 29, loc. MCR 30-181, p. 502). The city originally suggested Colk Crescent after Benjamin Colk, then professional golfer at Langara golf course, because Musqueam Park subdivision abuts Shaughnessy Golf Course.

L

LABURNUM STREET. Named on Plan 2301 (1909) by the CPR, after the tree. Point Grey By-law 17, 1914, extended it between West 47th and West 49th Avenues and West 57th and West 59th Avenues. Point Grey By-law 232, 1924, further extended it between West 37th and West 41st Avenues and West 60th Avenue to Angus Drive.

LAFONDS ALLEY. An unofficial name, only listed in the 1909 city directory, after Alfred Lafond, proprietor of Lafonds Pool Rooms, 909 Westminster Avenue, who lived in Lafonds Alley, which lay between Prior Street and False Creek on the west side of the present Main Street.

LAGOON DRIVE. Named 1929, By-law 2014, after its location close to Lost Lagoon in Stanley Park. Formerly known as *Park Drive* and shown on an 1887 map surveyed by L.A. Hamilton (Map 14160).

LAKEVIEW AVENUE or **DRIVE.** Now East 19th Avenue between Porter and Copley Streets. Name descriptive of its location near Trout Lake. Unnamed on Plan 745 (1895), the name appears as Lakeview Drive in an advertisement for Lakeview subdivision in the *Vancouver Daily Province*, 24 November 1906.

South Vancouver By-law 141, 1910, changed Lakeview Drive to East 18th Avenue, but the name was not used. *Goad's Atlas*, 1913, Plate 92, shows it as 19th Avenue East (late Lakeview Drive). City directories continued to list it as Lakeview Drive until 1927. In 1930, By-law 2082 changed Lakeview Avenue to East 19th Avenue.

LAKEVIEW ROAD. See Hull Street.

LAKEWOOD DRIVE. A descriptive name for the long street extending south from Oxford Street to what was the city boundary at East 15th Avenue near Trout Lake. Named on Plan 607 (1891) and on a 1902 map compiled by Hermon and Burwell, surveyors (CVA map 133).

Stainsbury Avenue (DL 195, blocks 19-20). Named after Elizabeth Stainsby Frost, spelt incorrectly as "Stainsbury." Changed to Lakewood Drive, south of Trout Lake, by South Vancouver By-law 141, 1910. See also entry under Stainsbury Avenue (DL 195, Blocks 6, 7, and 8).

In 1950 By-law 3195 designated the portion north of Dundas Street as Lakewood Drive North, although the designation had been in use in 1918.

LALANDE AVENUE (DL 652) (Deleted). An unofficial street name shown on a 1910 map of South Vancouver (Map 14272), it became part of East 52nd Avenue between Main and Prince Edwards Streets.

Abraham Lalande (1854-1948), an alderman in Dawson City, Yukon, in 1904-5, came to Vancouver in 1906 where, for many years, he was a real estate agent. In 1910, he owned property in DL 652, which eventually reverted to the municipality of South Vancouver and is now part of Sunset Park.

LAMBERT STREET (DL 331) (Deleted). Named 1913, South Vancouver By-law 251, after Lambert John Blair Bond, property owner in DL 330-331. Born in Ireland and educated as a lawyer, in 1901 he came to Vancouver, where he established the firm of Bond and Sweet. Director of Burrard Inlet Tunnel and Bridge Company, he died 13 October 1915, aged fifty-one. The street, one block west of Boundary Road between East 65th Avenue and South East Marine Drive, disappeared with the replotting of Champlain Heights.

LAMEY'S MILL ROAD. Named 1976, By-law 5010, Plan LF 7386. The False Creek Development

Group, in its report to the Street Naming Committee on 12 March 1976, proposed Lameys Mill Road after Lameys Sawmill, which operated in the 1880s. The name probably was transposed from Leamy, as Leamy and Kyle operated a sawmill on False Creek. Vancouver Voters List, 1887, shows James Leamy owning Lot 1, Block 1, DL 302, just east of the former Connaught (Cambie) Bridge. James Leamy came to New Westminster in 1885. In 1895 he became a Crown timber agent for the Dominion government, a position he held until his death on 8 May 1911, aged sixty-three.

LANARK STREET. Named by South Vancouver By-law 141, 1910, probably after Lanark, Scotland, in association with other Scottish place names in the area. This by-law also renamed Studd Road, Forbes Avenue, Gowan Street, and Sheldrick Street.

Studd Road (DL 705). Between East 31st and East 33rd Avenues. Named on Plan 2571 (1910) after owner, Edward Arthur Chichester Studd. Born in England in 1880 and educated at Eton, he was a partner in Studd and Daly, financial brokers, in 1913 and 1914. By 1920 he was associated with the Foundation Company of British Columbia, Engineering and General Contractors. Last listed in 1957 city directory.

Forbes Avenue. Between East 41st and East 49th Avenues. Probably named after Horace Forbes, property owner in DL 715, from 1911 to 1918, South Vancouver Voters Lists. Unnamed on Plans 2551 and 2780, 1910. South Vancouver Board of Works Report, 9 November 1911, requested that a sidewalk be laid on Forbes Avenue from Wilson Road to Ferris Road (now East 41st to East 49th Avenues).

Gowan Street. The name does not appear on any surveys or in any South Vancouver Voters Lists.

Sheldrick Street. Between East 37th and East 41st Avenues, although not mentioned in By-law 141. Named on Plan 1787 (1907) and shown in *Goad's Atlas*, Plates 99 and 103, as Lanark Street (late Sheldrick). Origin of this survey name unknown.

LANCASTER PLACE. Named in association with Lancaster Street to the north and first listed in the 1964 directory.

LANCASTER STREET. Probably named arbitrarily after Lancaster, England. First listed in

1916 city directory between School Avenue and the present East 54th Avenue, with no residents shown between East 46th and East 54th Avenues.

LANGARA AVENUE. Langara Avenue, named by Point Grey By-law 32, 1919, after the Langara district shown on a map issued by the provincial government in 1909 for an auction of lands in District Lots 139, 140, 540, and 2027. Don Juan de Langara, died 1806, was a Spanish admiral. Formerly *Chatham Avenue*, named by Point Grey By-law 17, 1912, after HMS *Chatham*, one of Captain George Vancouver's ships. With the creation of Locarno Park circa 1930, and the closure of Langara Avenue between Trimble and Discovery Streets for RCAF Jericho Station (By-law 2698, 1941), the avenue is now one block long.

LANGARA STREET. Named by Point Grey By-law 483, 1926, when Langara Avenue between Blanca and Tolmie Streets was resurveyed for the Westmount Park subdivision (Plan 5755). Langara Street runs at a southeasterly angle from Belmont Avenue to Langara Avenue.

LANGFORD AVENUE. Private thoroughfare in Enclave 15, Champlain Heights, after Langford Park, near Langford Lake, Vancouver Island. Named after Captain Edward E. Langford (1809-95), manager of the Esquimalt farm operated by the Hudons's Bay Company's subsidiary, Puget Sound Agricultural Company.

The name, submitted by the developer, Abacus Cities, was approved by the Street Naming Committee on 17 April 1979. The manager's report, 27 April 1979, to city council concerning street names stated that the developers of Enclave 15 had chosen names of provincial parks (Vancouver City Council Minutes, v. 132, p. 26.)

LANSDOWNE STREET. See Waterloo Street.

LANSDOWNE STREET (DL 200A). Now 4th Avenue between Yukon and Scotia Streets. Named on Plan 197 (1885), amended 13 May, 1886, after the Marquess of Lansdowne, Governor-General of Canada, 1883-8, by Dr. Israel W. Powell, owner of DL 200A. Changed to part of 4th Avenue in 1926, By-law 1803.

LARCH STREET. Shown on Plan 848 (1902), its name continues the pattern of tree names established by L.A. Hamilton. Point Grey By-

law 17, 1912, named the portion between West 33rd and West 45th Avenues.

LASALLE STREET. Named 1978, By-law 5150, after the French explorer Rene-Robert Cavelier, Sieur de La Salle (1643-87), in accordance with the Street Naming Committee's decision of 26 January 1978 to name the streets in Enclave 1, Champlain Heights, after explorers.

> Other streets named after French explorers and fur traders are Cartier, Champlain, Hennepin, Marquette, Quesnell, and Radisson. Streets named after important people of the French colonial pariod are Frontenac, Laval, and Talon.

LATIMER STREET. Now East 39th Avenue between Victoria Drive and Clarendon Street. Lawrence Bruce Latimer (1867-1941), active in real estate until the 1930s, owned property in DL 394 in 1910. Unnamed on Plans 1600, 1694, and 2164 (1908-9). South Vancouver By-law 141, 1910, changed Latimer to East 38th Avenue. However, *Goad's Atlas*, 1913, Plate 100, corrected it to East 40th Avenue (later Latimer Road), and it was known as such until Vancouver By-law 2028, 1929, changed it to East 39th Avenue.

LATTA STREET. Probably named in 1913 by South Vancouver By-law 251, after Ralph Latta (1880-1971), who, according to South Vancouver Voters List, 1910, owned property in DL 337. Associated with the Collingwood Land Company, 1910-4 inclusive.

LAUREL STREET. Officially registered on Plan 590 (1891) but named by L.A. Hamilton on an 1887 Map (14160). Some of the by-laws extending the street were Point Grey By-law 17, 1912, and Vancouver By-laws 3250, 3294, 3558, 3731, and 3937, between 1951 and 1961.

LAURIER AVENUE (DL 526). Named on Plan 4502 (1913) by the CPR, developers of Shaughnessy Heights, after Sir Wilfrid Laurier (1841-1919), prime minister of Canada, 1886-1911.

LAURIER STREET (DL 264 A). See Guelph Street.

LAVAL PLACE. Private thoroughfare in Champlain Heights named after Francois Xavier de Laval-Montmorency (1623-1708), first Roman

Catholic bishop of Quebec City and founder of a seminary, now Laval University. Approved by the Street Naming Committee on 8 November 1979.

LAWRENCE STREET. Now part of East and West 62nd Avenue. South Vancouver By-law 141, 1910, made Lawrence Street part of 64th Avenue East and West (now East and West 62nd Avenue). Limits are not known, but it probably straddled Ontario Street. No information about origin of name.

LAWSON ROAD. See St. George Street.

LEASIDE STREET. Named 1952, By-law 3330, after the Leaside Golf Course near Toronto.

LEE ROAD. Changed to East 30th Avenue between Prince Edward and Fraser Streets by South Vancouver By-law 141, 1910. South Vancouver Assessment Roll, 1895, lists Martha Lee, Mount Pleasant, owning blocks 10 to 13 inclusive, DL 391-2.

This unofficial name does not appear on any plans and is not mentioned in any South Vancouver reports.

LEG-IN-BOOT SQUARE. Named 1976, By-law 5010, Plan LF 7386, after the 1887 finding of a leg in a boot, minus the body, in the forest at False Creek. The boot was hung up at the police station for two weeks but no one claimed it. The incident is mentioned in *The Queen's Highway* by Stuart Cumberland (1887).

LEMA CRESCENT (Proposed). See Sennock Crescent.

LEONARD ROAD. Now West 35th Avenue between Crown and Dunbar Streets. Named on Plan 2439 (1909). The map accompanying Point Grey By-law 17, 1912, shows Leonard Road as changed to West 35th Avenue. Origin of name unknown.

LEROI STREET. Named 1915, By-law 1230, after the Le Roi mine at Rossland, where Frank Woodside, first alderman for the Hastings area after its amalgamation with Vancouver in 1911, had worked between 1896 and 1902.

LIARD PLACE. Private thoroughfare in Champlain Heights named after Liard River Hot Springs Park, as indicated in the Vancouver City Council Minutes (v. 132, p. 26). Name approved by council on 29 May 1979. According to Akrigg (1997), the Liard River was earlier known as "Riviere aux Liards," "liard" being a cottonwood tree.

LIGHTHOUSE WAY. Private thoroughfare shown on Plan LF 11623, approved 28 October 1994. The Fraser Lands development uses a maritime theme.

LILLOOET STREET. Shown on Plan 100, a re-survey of Hastings Townsite, 1906, and named by the provincial government after the Lillooet Mining Division. The portion between Broadway and the Great Northern Railway was not named until 1951, By-law 3232.

Lillooet is derived from the name of the Lil'wat people (Coull 1996).

LILY STREET. Probably an arbitrary choice of name, either after the flower or a girl. Unnamed on Plan 725 (1894), and first listed in the 1913 city directory. Shown in *Goad's Atlas*, 1913, Plate 80.

LIME STREET. Named by Point Grey By-law 17, 1914, to continue the pattern of tree names. First listed in 1927 city directory.

LIMEWOOD PLACE. Private thoroughfare in Champlain Heights named after the wood of the lime tree. Name approved by the Street Naming Committee on 8 November 1979. See also Raintree, Marchwood, Teakwood.

LINCOLN STREET. Not known if name is of personal or geographical origin. Shown in *Goad's Atlas*, Plate 101, lying between present East 45th Avenue and Kingsway on the west side of Block 13, DL 36-49. Plate 101 also shows an unnamed street, sometimes called Ormidale, between the present Kingsway and Vanness Avenue on the west side of Block 5, DL 36-49. This section officially named Lincoln Street in 1917, By-law 463.

LINDEN ROAD. Named by Point Gray By-law 483, 1926, to continue the pattern of tree names.

LINDEN STREET. Now East 53rd Avenue between Inverness and Argyle Streets. A tree name first shown on Plan 1645 (1908) and extended by Plans 1673, 1681, 2373, and 3085 from 1909 to 1910. Plan 1673 shows Indian Street – a misprint. South Vancouver By-law 141, 1910, renamed it East 55th Avenue (now East 53rd Avenue).

LITTLE STREET. Named on Plan 1955 (1909) as Little Avenue and changed to Little Street in 1910 by South Vancouver By-law 141. Origin of name unknown, but it may be descriptive of the little street, which is one block long.

LOCARNO CRESCENT. Named on Plan 5970 (1928) and first listed in the 1930 city directory. Probably named after its proximity to Locarno Park, established in 1925 and so named to commemorate the Locarno treaties of 1925, which were designed to guarantee international stability and peace.

LOCKE CRESCENT (Proposed). See Tamath Crescent.

LOCKIN STREET. Now East 10th Avenue between Main and Prince Edward Streets. Shown on Plan 187 (1885) and named by the owner, H.V. Edmonds, after his son, Henry Lovekin Edmonds (1871-1952), and incorrectly entered in Land Registry records as Lockin. When Vancouver absorbed DL 301 in 1911, Lockin Street became part of East 10th Avenue.

LOGAN STREET. Unnamed on Plan 1870 (1909) but named by Point Grey By-law 17, 1914. Origin of name unknown.

LONG LIFE PLACE. Private thoroughfare between Cambie and Ash Streets and south of West 10th Avenue. Plan LF 11550 approved 6 July 1993.

LORD STREET. Named 1952, By-law 3294, after Judge Arthur Edward Lord (1897-1982), who joined the city's legal department in 1923 and rose to be corporation counsel. In 1951 he became a County Court judge and, in 1955, a BC Supreme Court judge.

LORNE ROAD. Changed to East 71st Avenue (later East 69th Avenue) by South Vancouver By-law 141, 1910. The road's location and origin of name unknown.

LORNE STREET (DL 200A). Named on Plan 197 (1885), after the Marquess of Lorne, governor-general of Canada, 1878-83, by owner Dr. I.W. Powell.

Lorne Street between Alberta and Main Streets became 3rd Avenue in 1926, By-law 1803.

LOUGHEED HIGHWAY. Named in 1931 by the provincial government after Nelson Seymour Lougheed (1882-1944), minister of public works for British Columbia in 1928. The section within Vancouver, originally known as the *Central Arterial Highway* from 1941 to 1950, was a continuation of East Broadway between Rupert Street and Boundary Road and ran at a northeast angle into Burnaby. By-law 3195, 1950, renamed it Lougheed Highway.

LYNBROOK DRIVE. Named 1952, By-law 3330, Plan Ga 49, after Lynbrook Golf Course, Moose Jaw. Later extended from the lane east of Muirfield Drive to Vivian Drive in 1961, By-law 3937.

> By-law 3330 named a number of streets after golf courses, and later additions have added to this group. Streets named after golf courses include: Ancaster, Ashburn, Bobolink, Bonaccord, Bonnyvale, Brigadoon, Burquitlam, Deal, Englewood, Fraserview, Greensboro, Harrison, Hoylake, Jasper, Kempton, Leaside, Lynbrook, Muirfield, Newport, Pinehurst, Prestwick, Qualicum, Quinte, Rosedale, Rosemont, Scarboro, Seigniory, Thornhill, and Turnberry.

LYNMOOR PLACE. Private thoroughfare in Champlain Heights, named by Intrawest Properties Limited, whose development, Moorpark, bears names of moors – Dartmoor, Lynmoor, and Weymoor. Approved by the Street Naming Committee on 25 March 1981.

M

MCALPINE ROAD (Proposed). See Point Grey Road.

MCARTHUR ROAD. Now East 38th Avenue between Gladstone and Nanaimo Streets. Unnamed on Plan 1700 (1907) but named on Plan 3350 (1911). Changed to East 39th Avenue (now East 38th) by South Vancouver By-law 141, 1910.

According to William Williamson, ward foreman, Ward 2, South Vancouver, it was named after John C. McArthur, who was born in Ontario and came to British Columbia in 1891 and to South Vancouver in 1908, where he was police magistrate for three years. In August 1913 he became police magistrate for Point Grey. Last shown in the 1917 city directory.

MCBAIN AVENUE. Named 1954, By-law 3457, at the suggestion of the CPR, after Clark W. McBain, land agent for the company, who retired in 1957. McBain Avenue east of Valley Drive is a private thoroughfare in Arbutus Village development.

MCCLEERY STREET. Named by Point Grey By-law 17, 1914, after the pioneer McCleery family, who preempted land in the Point Grey area in 1862. In 1961 By-law 3937 extended the street from Celtic Avenue south to the river.

MACDONALD STREET. Shown on Plan 774 (1898) and named after Sir John Alexander Macdonald (1815-91), first prime minister of Canada.

In the adjoining municipality, Point Grey By-law 17, 1912, extended Macdonald Street, spelled "McDonald," from West 16th to West 37th Avenues. This inconsistency in spelling was not standardized as "Macdonald" until 1938, By-law 2537.

Point Grey By-law 6, 1921, changed Kaye Road from West 49th Avenue to the Fraser River to McDonald Street.

Kaye Road. First mentioned in Point Grey By-law 1, 1910, which allocated $5,500 for road clearing. Point Grey By-law 5, 1910, extended the road to the Fraser River.

Kaye Road between West 16th and West 41st Avenues was changed to Trafalgar Street by Point Grey By-law 17, 1912.

Alexander Kaye (1873-1951) was first listed in the 1905 South Vancouver Voters List as owning property in DL 321. Educated at Repton College and Caius College, Cambridge University, he was an assayer in Atlin, British Columbia, at the Le Roi mine in Rossland, and later with the Canadian government assay office in Vancouver.

MCFARLANE ROAD. See Argyle Street.

McCleery farmhouse, built by Fitzgerald McCleery. The front was built in 1873 and the back in 1882. In 1936, it was the oldest building in Vancouver. CVA Bu. P. 1, N. 25.

MCGARRIGLE STREET. Now East 39th Avenue between Fraser and Commercial Streets. Named on Plans 1383 and 1787 (1907), and 3747 (1910).

Changed to East 40th Avenue (now East 39th Avenue) by South Vancouver By-law 141, 1910. Origin of name unknown.

MCGEER AVENUE. See Carolina Street.

MCGEER STREET. Named 1992, By-Law 7047, after Gerald Grattan McGeer (1888-1947), lawyer, politician, mayor of Vancouver 1935-6, 1947. He was made a senator in 1947, the year of his death.

MCGILL STREET. Named after McGill University, Montreal, on Plan 100, a 1906 resurvey of Hastings Townsite, and first listed in the 1908 city directory.

MCGUIGAN AVENUE. Named 1951, By-law 3250, after William Joseph McGuigan (1853-1908), mayor of Vancouver in 1904. Dr. McGuigan was medical superintendent for the CPR in Vancouver.

W. J. McGuigan. From a group photo of the Capilano Water Works Dam, circa 1903. CVA C.I. Dept. P. 33, N. 5.

MCHARDY STREET. Named after James McHardy (1862-1927), born in Ontario, who owned property in DL 36-51 from 1906 to 1918. Originally McHardy Road, and renamed McHardy Street in 1910 by South Vancouver By-law 141. First named on Plan 3448 (1910).

MCINTYRE DRIVE. Private thoroughfare in Champlain Heights named by the Plumbers and Pipefitters Union, Local 170, which named three streets in its cooperative housing project after founding members of the local.

Samuel James McIntyre (1871-1968) was a charter member of Local 170, established on 18 November 1898. Born in Ontario of Irish parents, he came to British Columbia in 1889 and worked as a plumber until his retirement in 1931. He died in West Vancouver on 24 September 1968.

Name approved by the Street Naming Committee on 12 January 1984.

MCKENDRY ROAD. Now East 27th Avenue between Gladstone and Penticton Streets. Named after Edward McKendry, who was born in Ireland

and died on 23 October 1902, aged seventy-six. Shown in South Vancouver Voters Lists, 1893-1902 inclusive. Named in *B.C. Gazette*, 8 December 1898, the road lay between the present Gladstone Street and the BCER right of way. South Vancouver By-law 141, 1910, changed it to a portion of East 27th Avenue.

MACKENZIE PLACE. Named 1954, By-law 3457, after its proximity to Mackenzie Street.

MACKENZIE STREET. Named on Plan 1003 (1905), after Alexander Mackenzie (1822-92), second prime minister of Canada, 1875-8. Point Grey By-law 17, 1912, changed the adjoining Street, Kerrisdale Avenue, to McKenzie [sic].

Kerrisdale Avenue. Unnamed on Plan 1682, property owner Helen Mackinnon. *Goad's Atlas*, Plates 30, 32, and 38, shows Kerrisdale Avenue lying between West 23rd and West 25th Avenues, and West 27th and West 41st Avenues. The Mackinnon home was called "Kerrisdale" after Mrs. Mackinnon's great-grandfather's home, "Kerrysdale House," near Gairloch, Scotland.

Point Grey By-law 821, 1927, called the McKenzie Street Diversion By-law, improved the traffic flow between West 16th and West 18th Avenues.

By-law 2537, 1938, standardized the spelling as Mackenzie.

MCKINNON STREET. Named by South Vancouver By-law 252, 1913, which renamed a portion of David Street from Kingsway south to School Avenue. The by-law also named *David Street* as running northeast from Kingsway to Euclid Avenue. However, the name "David" seems to have been in popular use for the whole section between School and Euclid Avenues, and is so shown on maps until 1949.

In 1950 By-law 3195 changed David to McKinnon to remove duplication with David Avenue in Burnaby, and McKinnon then lay between Euclid and East 54th Avenue. Origin of the name "David" is unknown. The initial plotting of Champlain Heights in 1970, By-law 4470, Plan LF 4530, showed a new portion of McKinnon between 61st and 63rd Avenues, but in 1978 By-law 5195, Plan LE 3742, renamed it Munroe Crescent.

Spencer Robinson, former South Vancouver councillor, told Major J.S. Matthews that a Mr.

McKinnon owned acreage on McKinnon Street. The 1913 South Vancouver Voters List shows three McKinnons owning property in DL 37.

MCLEAN DRIVE. Named after Malcolm Alexander MacLean (1842-1895), Vancouver's first mayor, 1886-7. Note the difference in spelling.

MCMULLEN AVENUE. Named after James E. McMullen (1872-1955), for forty-eight years a solicitor with the CPR's legal department. Named on Plan 2913 (1910), it lay between the present Ontario and Cambie Streets in the municipality of South Vancouver. Upon amalgamation with Vancouver in 1929, McMullen Avenue, a survey name, became a part of West 26th Avenue, By-law 2028. However, the CPR reused the name when it developed its property west of Arbutus Street and south of West King Edward Avenue in 1954, By-law 3457, Plan 9119. McMullen Avenue east of Valley Drive is a private thoroughfare in Arbutus Village.

MCNICOLL AVENUE. Named after David McNicoll (1852-1916), a vice-president of the CPR and also general manager. Named on Plan 2301 (1909), when the CPR opened a subdivision at Kitsilano Point. First listed in 1913 city directory. The city belatedly confirmed the name in 1958, By-law 3731.

MCRAE AVENUE. Shaughnessy Heights, shown on Plan 4502 (1913), was named by the CPR after Alexander Duncan McRae (1874-1946), prominent in the lumbering and fishing industries and, later, a senator. His mansion, Hycroft, was nearby.

MCRAE ROAD (DL 328). See Argyle Street.

MCSPADDEN AVENUE. Named after Lieutenant Colonel George McSpadden (1865-1920), city building inspector 1900-6 and, later, alderman 1907-9, 1912-3. Commanding Officer of the 11th Irish Fusiliers of Canada. First listed in 1930 city directory. Surveyed in 1894, Plan 722, and called *Tramway Avenue* – shortened to Tram Avenue in *Goad's Atlas,* Plate 83 – after its proximity to the

G. McSpadden. From a group photo of the Capilano Water Works Dam, circa 1903. CVA C.I. Dept. P. 33, N. 5.

newly opened tramline operated by the Westminster and Vancouver Tramway Company.

MACKIE STREET. Named on Plan 6942 (1941), after William Mackie, pioneer logger in the Fairview and Shaughnessy Heights districts, who preempted 160 acres in DL 472 in 1871. C.W. McBain, land agent for the CPR, owners of the property, probably suggested the name. Extended on Plan 7106 (1944). First listed in 1945 city directory.

MADDAMS STREET. Named after Charles Cleaver Maddams (1852-1925), owner of the property. Formerly a steward with Lieutenant-Governor Clement Cornwall, he came to Vancouver in 1887. Shown as Maddams Avenue on Plan 2335 (1909) and first listed as such in 1914 city directory.

MADDISON ROAD. See Gladstone Street.

MADRONA STREET. Now East 51st Avenue between Inverness and Argyle Streets. Named after the madrona, or arbutus, tree. Named on Plan 1645 (1908) and extended by Plans 1673, 1681, 2373, and 3085 between 1908 and 1910. South Vancouver By-law 141, 1910, changed it to part of East 53rd Avenue (now East 51st Avenue).

MAGEE ROAD. Now part of West 49th Avenue. Named after Hugh McGee (1821-1909), one of the pioneers of the Vancouver peninsula, who preempted DL 194 in 1867 and DL 321 in 1873. Named by South Vancouver Highway By-law 1, 1893, Magee Road lay between present Carnarvon and Granville Streets. Renamed 49th Avenue by Point Grey By-law 17, 1912.

MAGEE STREET (Proposed). See Wiltshire Street.

MAGNOLIA STREET. Named after the magnolia tree. Shown on Plan 11644 (1963), first listed in 1965 city directory.

MAIN STREET. Formerly Westminster Avenue, Vancouver By-law 739, 1910, and South Vancouver By-law 141, 1910, renamed it Main Street.

Nelson (1927) says that the Main Street Improvement Association was instrumental in having Westminster Avenue in South Vancouver widened from sixty to eighty feet and in changing the name to Main Street. The belief was that 9th Avenue and Westminster Avenue (now

Broadway and Main) would become the centre of a grand metropolis.

Later came attempts to rename it. On 30 December 1940, city council recommended that the Special Committee on Street Names, when preparing the official street name map, give consideration to the proposal that the name of Main Street be changed to Westminster (Vancouver City Council Minutes, v. 42, p 129). However, because of the exigencies of the war, the map was not prepared.

The Street Naming Committee, on 11 March 1948, requested that the chairman, Alderman Halford Wilson, approach Mount Pleasant Chamber of Commerce and ask it to canvass merchants on that street for a suggestion about a name change. There is no record of any action being taken.

Westminster Avenue. Named on "Plan of the City of Vancouver, British Columbia," compiled by H.B. Smith, 1886 (Map 14267). It extended south from Alexander Street to the city limits and into South Vancouver. Likely so named because it met the New Westminster Road (now Kingsway) at Broadway, and, indirectly, after Westminster, England, the seat of colonial power.

MAINLAND STREET. Lies in the part of DL 541 first owned by the CPR, whose yards were in the vicinity. Between 1911 and 1913 a portion of False Creek (where the Mainland Transfer Company had its dock) was filled in, as shown in *Goad's Atlas*, Plates 13 and 14. The unnamed street on Plan 3469 (1911) was named after the company by the CPR and first listed in the 1913 city directory. The Mainland Transfer Company, first listed in 1904 city directory, merged in 1960 with other companies to form Transco Services Limited.

MALKIN AVENUE. Named after William Harold Malkin (1868-1959), prominent businessman and mayor of Vancouver, 1929-30. In 1950 By-law 3195 renamed Jackson Street between Prior and Atlantic Streets, and the new street, which ran southeast from the intersection of Jackson and Atlantic Streets as far as Glen Drive, became Malkin Avenue.

MALTA AVENUE AND MALTA PLACE. Named to commemorate the bravery of the citizens of the island of Malta, who were bombarded by German and Italian bombers in the Second World War. Named 23 March 1948 by city council.

MANITOBA STREET. Named by Dr. Israel Wood Powell, who owned DL 200A, after the province of Manitoba.

MANNERING AVENUE. Originally *Blair Avenue*, named on Plan 1955 (1909) after an unidentified person. Changed to East 33rd Avenue by South Vancouver By-law 141, 1910. Upon amalgamation with Vancouver in 1929, By-law 2028 changed East 33rd Avenue to Mannering Avenue, after the novel *Guy Mannering*, by Sir Walter Scott, because the avenue falls between East 32nd and East 33rd Avenues. See page 135.

MANOR ROAD. Now West 42nd Avenue from Balaclava Street to east of Mackenzie Street. Manor Road was a short road that led to the MacKinnon home, Kerrisdale, perhaps also called "the manor." Unnamed on Plans 1730 (1908) and 1987 (1909), and named on Plans 2493 and 2521 (1909). By 1913, *Goad's Atlas* shows 42nd Avenue (late Manor Road) in Plates 37 and 38. A survey name only, as it is not shown on the map accompanying Point Grey By-law 17, 1912, which renamed many streets.

MANROSS AVENUE. First listed in the 1970 city directory with two residents. From 1971 to 1990 it was still listed, with no residents shown, as "From 1900 Block E22nd Ave. north." City survey office has no record of the name.

MANSON STREET. Named 1951, By-law 3250, after William Manson, vice-president, CPR, Pacific region, in 1951. Manson lived in Vancouver until 1957.

MAPLE CRESCENT. Named 1973, By-law 4688, which renamed Maple Street from Hosmer Avenue to East Boulevard, and from East Boulevard at its intersection with West King Edward Avenue south to West 32nd Avenue.

MAPLE STREET. Now East 26th Avenue between Windermere and Skeena Streets. A survey name only, shown on Plans 1705 (1906) and 1932 (1908).

MAPLE STREET (DL 37). See Moss Street.

MAPLE STREET (DL 50). See Dundee Street.

MAPLE STREET. Officially named on Plan 590 (1891) but named on an 1887 map (Map 14160) by L.A. Hamilton, who chose tree names.

Plan 2975 (1909) labelled the street between the Vancouver and Lulu Island branch of the CPR and West 37th Avenue *De Banco Road*, after an unidentified person. Changed to Maple Street by Point Grey By-law 17, 1912, and extended from West 37th to West 41st Avenues by Point Grey By-law 232, 1924.

MAQUINNA DRIVE. Named 1984, By-law 5741, after Maquinna, a chief of the "Nootka" (now Nuu-chah-nulth) in 1788.

On 11 April 1980, the Street Naming Committee suggested that this dedicated road be called St. Roch Avenue, but the Champlain Heights Advisory Committee opposed that name. So the Street Naming Committee later proposed Maquinna.

MARCHWOOD PLACE. A private thoroughfare in Champlain Heights whose name, origin unknown, was approved by the Street Naming Committee on 8 November 1979, in association with Limewood, Teakwood, and Raintree.

MARGATE STREET. See St. Margaret's Street.

MARGUERITE STREET. Named 1913, Plan 4502, by the CPR, developers of Shaughnessy Heights, after the Honourable Marguerite Kathleen Shaughnessy (1891-1958), daughter of Lord Shaughnessy.

Marguerite Street originally lay within Shaughnessy Heights and as far south as West 29th Avenue. Point Grey By-law 17, 1914, named the adjoining street between West 29th and West 37th Avenues Markham Street, and Point Grey By-law 232, 1924, extended it between West 52nd and West 57th Avenues.

Point Grey By-law 385, 1925, renamed the portion of Markham between West 29th and West 37th Avenues Marguerite Street.

When the land between West 37th and West 41st Avenues was opened, Point Grey By-law 483, 1926, named the street Markham. However, a group of residents in October 1926 asked that the street be changed to Marguerite because of the confusion of having one street with two names. Accordingly, Point Grey By-law 913, 1926, made the change. Point Grey Council, aware that there was still a Markham Street south of West 41st Avenue, initiated a postcard ballot to determine the residents' preference. The results were thirty-nine for Marguerite and eight for Markham. Point Grey By-law 275, 1927, changed the street south of West 41st to Marguerite.

Among those favouring the retention of *Markham* was Newton Ker, representing the CPR, which had suggested the name after one of its employees, Colonel Alfred Markham (1841-1935). Markham came to Vancouver in 1906 after having been managing director of the *Saint John Sun* from the 1880s until its sale in 1906. He was in charge of clearing Shaughnessy Heights of timber, then became manager of the CPR gardens and, later, of the gardens at Shaughnessy Military Hospital.

"Germany surrenders," 11 November 1918, at 12:42 a.m. Vancouver was awakened by the noise of factory whistles. That afternoon, a jubilant population held a great impromtu procession on downtown streets. These are "returned soldiers" passing up Granville Street at Hudson's Bay corner, Georgia Street. The man in the dark uniform is Col. A. Markham. CVA Mil. P. 90, N. 156.

HERE STOOD
HAMILTON
FIRST LAND COMMISSIONER
CANADIAN PACIFIC RAILWAY
1885
IN THE SILENT SOLITUDE
OF THE PRIMEVAL FOREST
HE DROVE A WOODEN STAKE
IN THE EARTH AND COMMENCED
TO MEASURE AN EMPTY LAND
INTO THE STREETS OF
VANCOUVER

In compliment to all pioneers resident in Vancouver prior to the arrival of the first passenger train on 23 May 1886, the Board of Park Commissioners invited them to be their honored guests at a banquet in the Pavilion, Stanley Park, on Monday, 6 April 1953, the sixty-seventh anniversary of the incorporation of the City of Vancouver. During the course of the evening, the bronze commemorative panel in tribute to Lauchlan Alexander Hamilton was unveiled by his only child, Miss Isobel Ogilvie Hamilton, of Toronto. It was later affixed to the street wall of the former Canadian Bank of Commerce, Victory Square branch, on the south west corner of Hamilton and Hastings Street, directly above the exact place where the historic survey stake was driven in the winter of 1885-1886. The panel was the work of sculptor Sydney March of Farnborough, Kent, and was completed in 1952. Photograph by Carlyn Craig.

"Lauchlan Alexander Hamilton [Hamilton Street, p. 52] was the CPR civil engineer who hiked through dense woods in 1885 marking out Vancouver's future street system and naming the streets. He later became the CPR's land commissioner. As senior councillor on the first city council in 1886, he proposed the creation of Stanley Park. He laid out the path around Stanley Park's perimeter, gave the neighbourhood "Fairview" its name and created the city's coat of arms, which was used until 1903" (Bruce Macdonald, 1992).

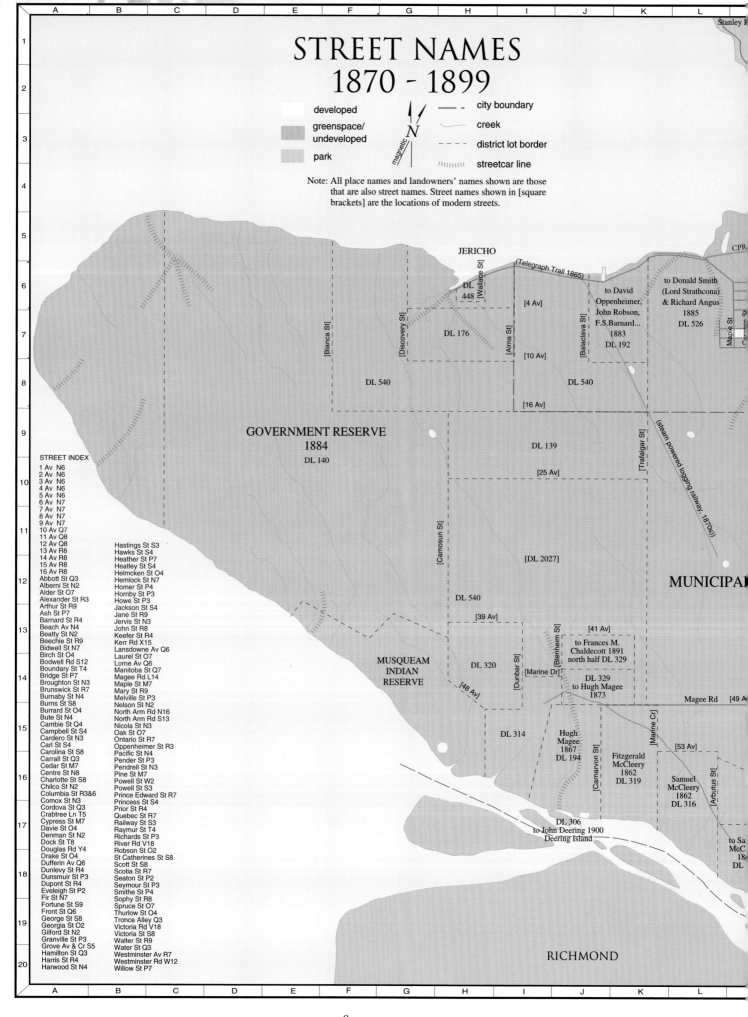

STREET NAMES
1870 - 1899

- developed
- greenspace/ undeveloped
- park

N magnetic

- — · — city boundary
- —— creek
- - - - district lot border
- ∧∧∧∧ streetcar line

Note: All place names and landowners' names shown are those that are also street names. Street names shown in [square brackets] are the locations of modern streets.

JERICHO

(Telegraph Trail 1865)

DL 448

[Wallace St]

[Blanca St]

[Discovery St]

DL 176

[Alma St]

[4 Av]

[10 Av]

[Balaclava St]

to David Oppenheimer, John Robson, F.S.Barnard... 1883 DL 192

to Donald Smith (Lord Strathcona) & Richard Angus 1885 DL 526

[Maple St]

DL 540

DL 540

[16 Av]

GOVERNMENT RESERVE 1884
DL 140

DL 139

[25 Av]

[Trafalgar St]

(steam powered logging railway, 1870s)

[Camosun St]

[DL 2027]

MUNICIPA

DL 540

[39 Av]

[Blenheim St]

[41 Av]

to Frances M. Chaldecott 1891 north half DL 329

MUSQUEAM INDIAN RESERVE

DL 320

[Dunbar St]

[Marine Dr]

DL 329 to Hugh Magee 1873

[48 Av]

Magee Rd

[49 A

DL 314

[Carnarvon St]

[Marine Cr]

Hugh Magee 1867 DL 194

Fitzgerald McCleery 1862 DL 319

[53 Av]

[Arbutus St]

Samuel McCleery 1862 DL 316

DL 306 to John Deering 1900 Deering Island

to Sa McC 18 DL

RICHMOND

Stanley

CPR

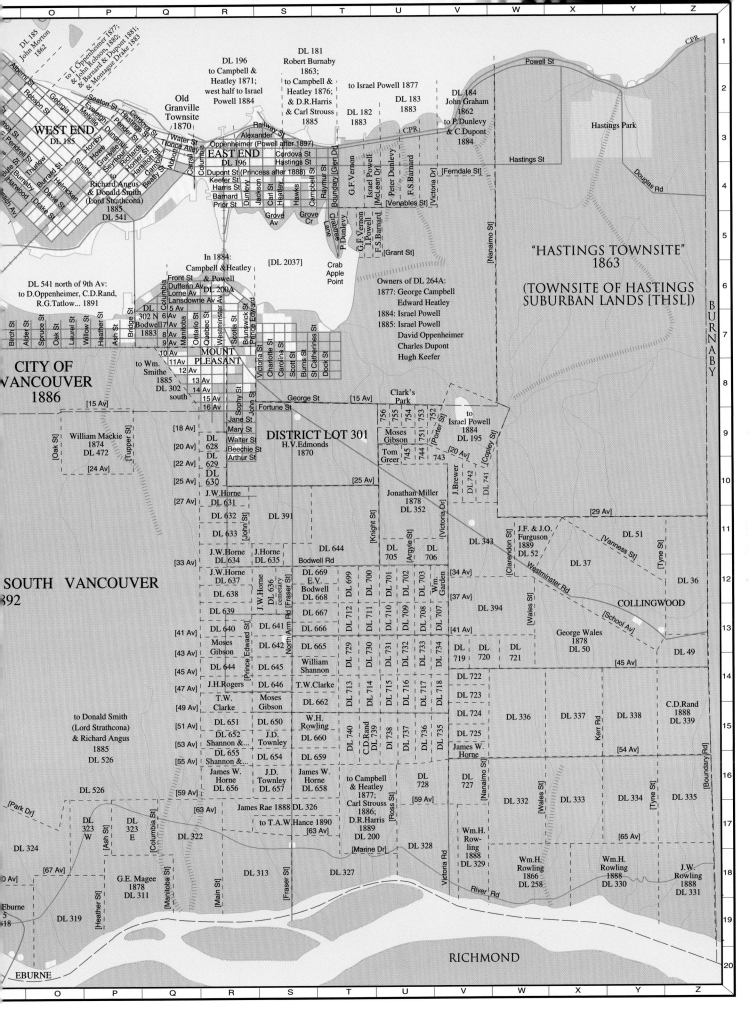

WEST END
DL 185

DL 185
John Morton
1862

to I. Oppenheimer 1877;
& John Robson 1880;
& Barnard & Dupont 1881;
& Montague Drake 1883

DL 196
to Campbell &
Heatley 1871;
west half to Israel
Powell 1884

DL 181
Robert Burnaby
1863;
to Campbell &
Heatley 1876;
& D.R.Harris
& Carl Strouss
1885

to Israel Powell 1877

DL 182
1883

DL 183
1883

DL 184
John Graham
1862
to P. Dunlevy
& C.Dupont
1884

Powell St

CPR

Hastings Park

Hastings St

Old
Granville
Townsite
1870

Railway St
Alexander
Oppenheimer (Powell after 1897)

EAST END
DL 196

Cordova St
Hastings St

Dupont St (Princess after 1888)

Keefer St
Harris St
Barnard St
Prior St

Grove
Av

Grove
Cr

Crab
Apple
Point

In 1884:
Campbell &Heatley
& Powell
DL 200A

[DL 2037]

Owners of DL 264A:
1877: George Campbell
Edward Heatley
1884: Israel Powell
1885: Israel Powell
David Oppenheimer
Charles Dupont
Hugh Keefer

"HASTINGS TOWNSITE"
1863

(TOWNSITE OF HASTINGS
SUBURBAN LANDS [THSL])

BURNABY

to
Richard Angus
& Donald Smith
(Lord Strathcona)
1885
DL 541

DL 541 north of 9th Av:
to D.Oppenheimer, C.D.Rand,
R.G.Tatlow... 1891

DL
302 N
Bodwell
1883

Front St
Dufferin Av
Lorne Av
Lansdowne Av
5 Av
6 Av
7 Av
8 Av
9 Av
10 Av
11 Av
12 Av
13 Av
14 Av

MOUNT
PLEASANT

to Wm.
Smithe
1885
DL 302
south

[15 Av]

15 Av
16 Av

Fortune St

George St

[15 Av]

Clark's
Park

to
Israel Powell
1884
DL 195

CITY OF
VANCOUVER
1886

[18 Av]

William Mackie
1874
DL 472

[24 Av]

[20 Av]

[22 Av]

[25 Av]

DL
628

DL
629

DL
630

Jane St
Mary St
Walter St
Beechie St
Arthur St

DISTRICT LOT 301

H.V.Edmonds
1870

756 755 754 753 752
751 750
749 748 747 746 745
744
743

Moses
Gibson

Tom
Greer

[20 Av]

[25 Av]

[27 Av]

J.W.Horne
DL 631

DL 632

DL 633

DL 391

Jonathan Miller
1878
DL 352

J.Brewer

DL 742

DL 741

[29 Av]

J.F. & J.O.
Furguson
1889
DL 52

DL 51

DL 37

DL 343

[Vanness St]

[Tyne St]

DL 36

SOUTH VANCOUVER
1892

[33 Av]

J.W.Horne
DL 634

J.Horne
DL 635

Bodwell Rd

DL
705

[Argyle St]

DL
706

Westminster Rd

Wales St

DL 394

[Clarendon St]

COLLINGWOOD

J.W.Horne
DL 637

DL 636
cemetery

E.V.
Bodwell
DL 668

DL 669

DL 699

DL 700

DL 701

DL 702

DL 703

Wm.
Garden

[34 Av]

[37 Av]

[School Av]

DL 638

DL 667

DL 712

DL 711

DL 710

DL 709

DL 708

DL 707

George Wales
1878
DL 50

DL 49

DL 639

DL 641

DL 666

DL 729

DL 730

DL 731

DL 732

DL 733

DL 734

[41 Av]

DL
719

DL
720

DL
721

[45 Av]

[41 Av]

DL 640

DL 642

DL 665

William
Shannon

DL 713

DL 714

DL 715

DL 716

DL 717

DL 718

DL 336

DL 337

DL 338

Kerr Rd

C.D.Rand
1888
DL 339

[43 Av]

[45 Av]

DL 644

DL 645

Moses
Gibson

[47 Av]

J.H.Rogers
DL 646

T.W.Clarke

DL 662

T.W.Clarke

DL 722

DL 723

DL 724

DL 725

James W.
Horne

[54 Av]

[Boundary Rd]

[49 Av]

[51 Av]

T.W.
Clarke
DL 651

Moses
Gibson
DL 650

W.H.
Rowling
DL 660

DL 740

C.D.Rand
DL 739

DL 738

DL 737

DL 736

DL 735

[53 Av]

[55 Av]

DL 652
Shannon &...

DL 655
Shannon &...

J.D.
Townley
DL 654

J.D.
Townley
DL 659

DL 332

DL 333

DL 334

DL 335

to Donald Smith
(Lord Strathcona)
& Richard Angus
1885
DL 526

[59 Av]

James W.
Horne
DL 656

J.D.
Townley
DL 657

James W.
Horne
DL 658

to Campbell
& Heatley
1877;
Carl Strouss
1886;
D.R.Harris
1889
DL 200

DL
728

DL
727

[59 Av]

[Ross St]

[Nanaimo St]

DL 526

James Rae 1888 DL 326

to T.A.W. Hance 1890

[63 Av]

[65 Av]

[Park Dr]

DL
323
W

DL
323
E

DL 322

DL 313

DL 327

DL 328

Wm.H.
Rowling
1888
DL 329

[Wales St]

[Tyne St]

DL 324

[67 Av]

[Ash St]

[Columbia St]

[Marine Dr]

Victoria Rd

Wm.H.
Rowling
1866
DL 258

Wm.H.
Rowling
1888
DL 330

J.W.
Rowling
1888
DL 331

Eburne
5
18

DL 319

G.E. Magee
1878
DL 311

[Heather St]

[Manitoba St]

[Main St]

[Fraser St]

River Rd

EBURNE

RICHMOND

CPR

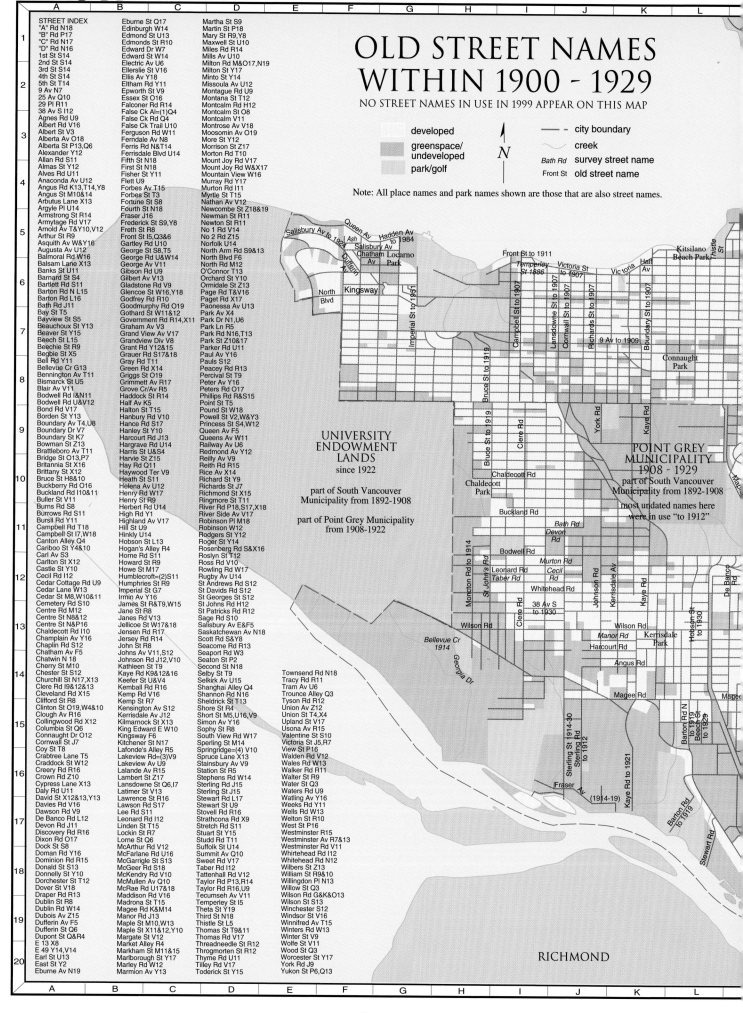

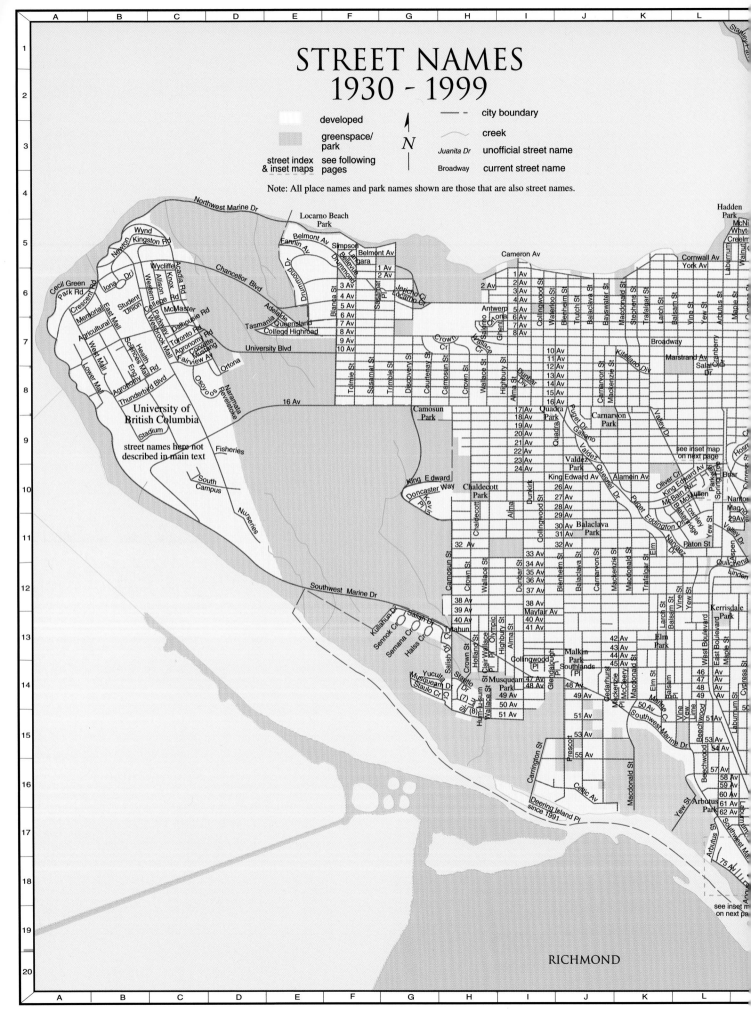

STREET NAMES
1930 - 1999

□ developed

▨ greenspace/ park

street index & inset maps   see following pages

- - - city boundary

〜 creek

Juanita Dr   unofficial street name

Broadway   current street name

N

Note: All place names and park names shown are those that are also street names.

Northwest Marine Dr

Locarno Beach Park

Hadden Park

Cameron Av

Cornwall Av
York Av

Wynd
Newton
Kingston Rd

Belmont Av
Fannin Av
Simpson
Belmont Av
Niagara
1 Av
2 Av

Cecil Green Park Rd
Iona Dr
Wycliffe
Acadia Rd
Crescent Rd
Allison
Knox
Western Parkway
College Rd
McMaster
Dalhousie Rd
Toronto Rd
Agronomy Rd
Fairview Av
Ortona

Memorial
East Mall
Student Union
Agricultural
West Mall
Agronomy
Science Eng
Health Sciences Mall Rd
Thunderbird Blvd
Lower Mall

Chancellor Blvd

Adelaide
Tasmania
Queensland
College Highroad
University Blvd

Blanca St
Sasamat
Drummond
Jericho Ci
Locarno

3 Av
4 Av
5 Av
6 Av
7 Av
8 Av
9 Av
10 Av

1 Av
2 Av
3 Av
4 Av
5 Av
6 Av
7 Av
8 Av

Collingwood St
Waterloo St
Blenheim St
Trutch St
Balaclava St
Bayswater St
Macdonald St
Stephens St
Trafalgar St
Larch St
Balsam St
Vine St
Yew St
Arbutus St
Maple St

Cameron Av

2 Av

Antwerp
Iona
Ghent
Crowt Cr
Wallace St

Broadway

Marstrand Av
Salal Dr
Cranberry

University of British Columbia

Stadium

street names here not described in main text

Fisheries

South Campus

Nurseries

16 Av

Camosun Park

Tolmie St
Sasamat St
Trimble St
Discovery St
Coutenay St
Camosun St
Crown St
Wallace St
Highbury St
Alma St
Dunbar Dr

10 Av
11 Av
12 Av
13 Av
14 Av
15 Av
16 Av
17 Av
18 Av
19 Av
20 Av
21 Av
22 Av
23 Av
24 Av

Quadra Park
Quadra
Puget
Galliano
Valdez
Questel
King Edward Av
Alamein Av

Carnarvon Park
Carnarvon St
Mackenzie St

Valley Dr

Kitsilano Div

see inset map on next page

King Edward Way
Doncaster Way
Chaldecott Park
Alma
Dunkirk

King Edward Av
26 Av
27 Av
28 Av
29 Av
30 Av
32 Av
33 Av
34 Av
35 Av
36 Av
37 Av

Chaldecott
Collingwood St
Blenheim St
Balaclava St
Carnarvon St
Macdonald St
Trafalgar St
Elm
Paton St

Oliver Cr
McBain Av
McMullen
Towhey
Trowbridge
Navaez
Yew St

Briar
Spring
Nanton
Mag 29 Av

Quilchena
Linden

Kerrisdale Park

Larch St
Balsam St
Vine St
Yew St

Southwest Marine Dr

Killarnua Dr
Sennok Cr
Semana Cr
Salish Dr
Salish Cr
Haisla Cr
Iyahun Cr

32 Av

Camosun St
Crown St
Wallace St
Dunbar St

38 Av
39 Av
40 Av
41 Av
Mayfair Av
40 Av
41 Av
42 Av
43 Av
44 Av
45 Av

Elm Park

West Boulevard
East Boulevard
Maple St

38 Av

St Clair
Olympic
Highbury St
Alma St

Collingwood
Pl

Malkin Park
Southlands
Pl

Cedarhurst
Mackenzie
Pl McCleery
Macdonald St

Elm St
Balsam Pl
Vine St
Lime

46 Av
47 Av
48 Av
49 Av

Yuculta
Musquam Dr
Staulo Cr

Stalo
Dr
Lu (7)
Holland St
Wallace St
Hum-lulsum
Wallace St (8)

Musquean Park
47 Av
48 Av
49 Av
50 Av
51 Av

48 Av

49 Av
Southwest Marine Dr

50 Av
Mathers Cr
Vine
Lime

51 Av
53 Av
54 Av

Prescott
Carrington St

Collingwood
Glengalough

51 Av
53 Av
55 Av

Beechwood

57 Av

Deering Island Pl since 1991

Celtic Av

Macdonald St

Yew St

Beechwood

53 Av
54 Av
57 Av
58 Av
59 Av
60 Av
61 Av
62 Av

Arbutus Park

Arbutus St

75 Av

Southwest Ma

see inset m on next pa

RICHMOND

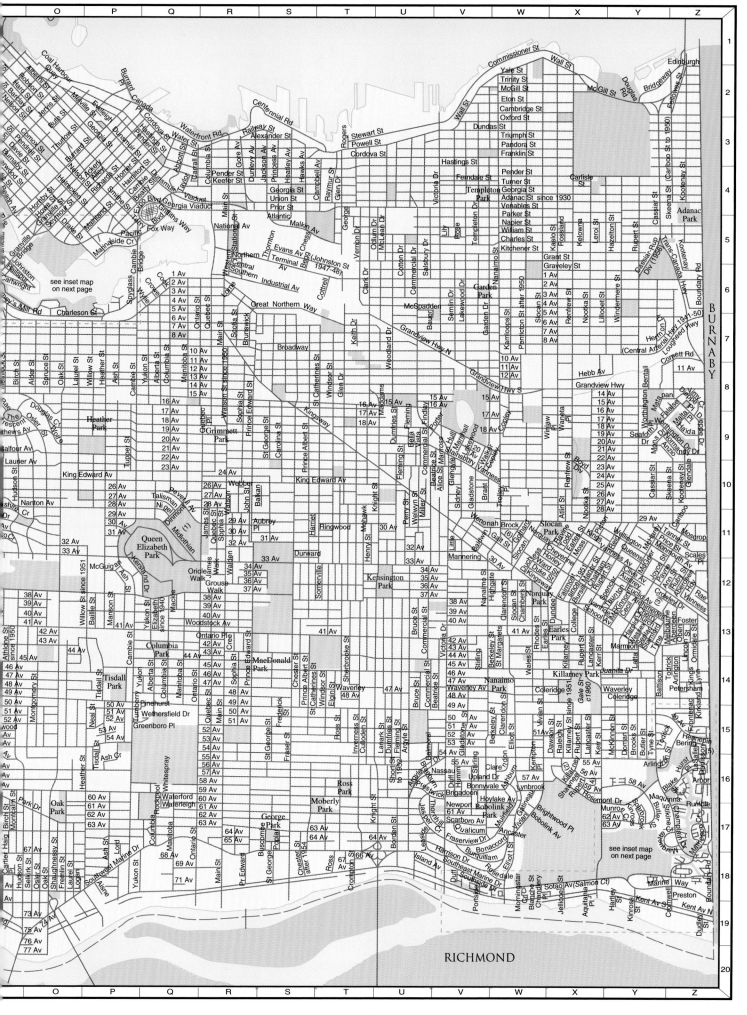

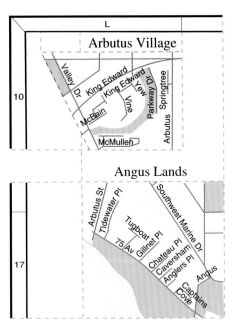

Arbutus Village

Angus Lands

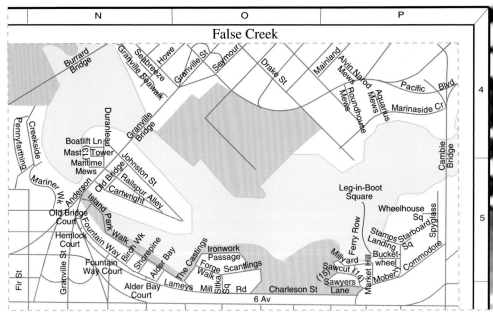

False Creek

INSET MAPS

PRIVATE THOROUGHFARES INDEX (to March 1996)
Contains only private thoroughfares not included in main 1999 index

Champlain Heights

Riverview

Fraser Lands

Street Index, 1930-1999 Map, page 82-3

MARINASIDE CRESCENT. Named 1993, By-law 7226. The name, proposed by the developers of the former Expo lands, Concord Pacific Development, describes its location near a marina on the north side of False Creek.

MARINE CRESCENT. Named by Point Grey By-law 232, 1924, after its position abutting South West Marine Drive. At the city council meeting of 18 July 1950, a delegation presented a petition objecting to a proposal to change the name to Larch Street. Consequently, no change was made.

MARINE DRIVE. Descriptive name for the road paralleling the coast on the north and south sides of the Vancouver peninsula. Within various jurisdictions it has had a series of names. In 1861-2, Hugh McRoberts had slashed a trail along the north arm of the Fraser River from New Westminster to the Musqueam Band Reserve, which, for many years, was called simply River Road.

South Vancouver Highway By-law 1, 1893, legally described but did not name "*River Road*" between present Granville Street along the north side of the river to Boundary Road. In 1910 South Vancouver By-law 141 changed River Road to River Avenue West between Ontario and Main Streets, and to River Avenue East from Main Street to Boundary Road. In 1915 River Road [sic] was changed to Marine Drive by South Vancouver By-law 421.

No Point Grey by-laws designated River Road as Marine Drive. However, the name was used in the preamble to By-law 17, 1915, which states: "Whereas it is advisable that the streets connecting with the Marine Drive ... and extending from eastern end of said Marine Drive to eastern boundary of the municipality bear the same name."

Point Grey By-law 23, 1910, extended Marine Drive, so called, across DLs 316, 317, and 325A.

The following are other Point Grey by-laws concerned with Marine Drive:

By-law 6, 1921, established Marine Drive through the northeast part of DL 315, from West 49th Avenue southeast to West 53rd Avenue between Carnarvon and Marine Crescent.

By-law 232, 1924:
- Extended Marine Drive northwest from Marine Crescent at West 49th Avenue to Cedarhurst;

- Changed West 46th Avenue between Blenheim and Dunbar Streets to Marine Drive;
- Changed Queen Avenue between Blanca and present Discovery to Marine Drive;
- Changed West 74th Avenue (formerly Eburne Avenue) between Granville and Hudson Streets to Marine Drive.

Upon amalgamation in 1929, Vancouver By-law 2014 differentiated Marine Drive by location:
- South East Marine Drive from Ontario Street east to Boundary Road;
- South West Marine Drive from Ontario Street west to Canadian government wireless station at tip of Point Grey;
- North West Marine Drive from Canadian government wireless station at Point Grey to Sasamat Street.

River Road, now Marine Drive, circa 1900. The woman in the picture is Miss M. E. McCleery "near their farm." CVA Str. P. 133, N. 91 #1.

after William Henry Eburne (1856-1924), developer of Eburne Townsite. Changed to West 74th Avenue by Point Grey By-law 17, 1914, and then to Marine Drive between Granville and Hudson Streets.

Hadden Avenue. Originally a two-block-long street between Sasamat and Imperial Streets, named 1929, By-law 2014, after Harvey Haddon, an English investor in Vancouver real estate. In 1928 he donated land for a park, now Hadden Park, and upon his death in 1931, he left to the city a bequest of $500,000, to be used for parks. The by-law spelled his name incorrectly. By 1939 Hadden between Trimble and Imperial Streets was taken over by RCAF Station Jericho and is now part of Jericho Park. In 1984, By-law 5765 changed the remnant between Sasamat and Trimble Streets to North West Marine Drive.

Queen Avenue. Named on Plan 229 (1887), probably after Queen Victoria, it lay between Blanca and Imperial (later Discovery) Streets. Changed to Marine Drive by Point Grey By-law 232, 1924, and later designated North West Marine Drive in 1929, By-law 2014.

MARINE WAY. Named 1984, By-law 5741, although the Street Naming Committee had assigned the name on 11 April 1980, to the new road south of South East Marine Drive.

MARINER WALK. Private thoroughfare in False Creek named after Mariner Point condominium development. First listed in 1986 city directory, although shown on Plan LE 5873 (1982).

MARITIME MEWS. Private thoroughfare on Granville Island, shown on Plans LE 5873 (1982) and LF 11465 (1991). Name approved by the Street Naming Committee in January 1992.

MARKET ALLEY. Named after the adjacent city market, it lay in the lane between Hastings and Pender Streets from the first lane west of Main Street to Carrall Street, as shown in *Goad's Atlas*, Plate 69. Listed in city directories from 1900 to 1973 and now unnamed.

MARKET HILL. Named 1976, By-law 5010, Plan LF 7386, after the sloping street or hill that holds the major commercial or market square in the False Creek development.

MARKHAM STREET. See Marguerite Street.

MARLBOROUGH STREET (Deleted). Named 1913 by South Vancouver By-law 251, it lay between East 65th Avenue and East 61st Avenue (later Asquith Avenue), two blocks west of Tyne Street. In the first replotting of Champlain Heights, the street was realigned to run at an angle, as shown on Plan LF 4530, attached to By-law 4770, 1970. In the final replotting of Champlain Heights, Marlborough Street was deleted by By-law 5195, 1978. Origin of name unknown, but probably British.

MARLEY ROAD. Now East 37th Avenue between Nanaimo and Wales Streets. An unofficial name shown on *Goad's Atlas*, Plate 100. George Marley and Amy Agnes Marley are shown in South Vancouver Voters Lists, 1911-5, owning property in DL 394.

MARLIN QUAY. Private thoroughfare named after large game fish, the name approved by the Street Naming Committee on 3 June 1985. The Riverside Landing Housing Cooperative suggested the name based on a nautical theme.

MARMION AVENUE. Named after *Marmion: A Tale of Flodden Field*, a novel by Sir Walter Scott. Changed from East 43rd Avenue between Joyce and Latta Streets in 1929, By-law 2028. It falls between East 42nd Avenue (if extended) and East 43rd Avenue. See page 135.

MARPOLE AVENUE. Named on Plan 4502 (1913), after Richard Marpole (1850-1920), former general superintendent and executive assistant of the Pacific Division, CPR. Shown as *Ferndale Avenue* on 1910 and 1911 map (Map 13875 and 14398). An unofficial descriptive name.

MARQUETTE CRESCENT. Named by By-law 5741, 1984, after the French missionary and explorer of the Mississippi River, Jacques Marquette (1637-75).

MARSHALL STREET. Originally Marshall Avenue, shown on Plan 2002 (1909), owner Sarah Marshall.

Goad's Atlas, Plate 92, shows *Haywood Terrace* (late), but the name is not shown elsewhere. Probably named for a real estate development; 1910 and 1911 city directories show Vicker Wallace Haywood and William Haywood in real estate.

Wallace Haywood and William Haywood in real estate.

MARSTRAND AVENUE. After Otto Marstrand, partner in the pioneer brewing firm, Doering and Marstrand. Its successor, BC Breweries Limited, built a new brewery in 1912 at 12th Avenue and Yew Street, now demolished and replaced by apartments. Named 1997 By-law 7741, Plan LF 11692.

MARTHA STREET. See St. Catherines Street.

MARTIN STREET (Proposed). See Ash Street.

MARY STREET (Deleted) (THSL). Named on Plan 1377 (1907), after the co-owner, Mary Jean Andrews (1860-1946). Later part of East 16th Avenue between Kootenay Street and Boundary Road; disappeared in the replotting of Renfrew Heights, 1947. Survey name only in association with Frederick Street (Deleted) (THSL).

MARY STREET (DL 301). Now East 18th Avenue between Main and Knight Streets. Shown on Plan 187 (1885) and named by H.V. Edmonds after his daughter, Mary Gifford Edmonds, who married C.M. Marpole. When Vancouver absorbed DL 301 in 1911, it became part of East 18th Avenue.

MAST TOWER ROAD. Private thoroughfare on Granville Island, shown on Plan LF 11405. Its name, approved by the Street Naming Committee in January 1992, is indicative of the many sailboats at moorage in False Creek.

MATAPAN CRESCENT. Name suggested in 1948 by the Vancouver Town Planning Commission after the naval battle near Cape Matapan in the Greek Peloponnesus on 28 March 1941. Approved by city council 23 March 1948 (Vancouver City Council Minutes, v. 54, p. 259.)

MATHESON CRESCENT. Named 1978, By-law 5195, Plan LE 3742B. Origin of name unknown.

MATTHEWS AVENUE. Shown on Plan 4502 (1913) and named by the CPR, developers of Shaughnessy Heights, after Wilmot Delouir Matthews (1850-1919), a director of the company.

MAXWELL STREET. Originally called Maxwell Road, it became part of Fleming Street between East 20th and East 22nd Avenues by South Vancouver By-law 141, 1910. Surveyed and named on Plan 1990 (1909).

The name "Maxwell" was transferred to the street immediately east of Fleming Street, which had been surveyed but not named on Plan 331 (1889). Vancouver city directory, 1917, shows Maxwell Street between Fleming and Welwyn Streets. Reuben Hamilton told Major J.S. Matthews on 5 June 1953 that the Maxwell family had lived on that part of Fleming Street. The 1908 Provincial Voters List, Richmond riding, shows Robert E. Maxwell, carpenter, at Cedar Cottage.

MAYFAIR AVENUE. Named by Vancouver By-law 2082, 1930, probably after the exclusive Mayfair district in London, England.

Originally called 38th Avenue South to differentiate it from 38th Avenue, and so named by Point Grey By-law 17, 1914. Point Grey council minutes 29 August 1927 reported that a postcard vote on a name for 38th Avenue South was to be laid over for a week for further returns. There was no report of results in the minutes, but on 1 November 1927 Point Grey By-law 763, 1927, changed the name to Lower 38th Avenue.

This change does not seem to have occurred, as Vancouver By-law 2082, 1930, still called it 38th Avenue South when it was renamed Mayfair. See page 135.

MEADOWLAND PLACE. Private thoroughfare in Champlain Heights, the name was approved by the Street Naming Committee on 21 June 1978. Community Builders Limited, developers of Park Place, named its thoroughfares after provincial parks.

Meadowland Park, on Trans Canada Highway east of Chilliwack (NW 1/4, Section 30, New Westminster District, Group 2), was created in 1958 but cancelled as a provincial park in 1978. Its name is descriptive name of its location.

MEARES AVENUE. Named 1978, By-law 5150, after John Meares (1756-1809), a British navigator who made two voyages to the northwest coast of North America, where he built a ship at Nootka Sound in 1788. Its seizure by the Spanish precipitated the Nootka crisis.

MELBOURNE STREET. Named on Plan 2587 (1909). On 24 October 1995 the Street Naming Committee approved its extension between Crowley Drive and Vanness Avenue (Plan LF 11676). Origin of name unknown, but probably British.

map of Vancouver, 1886. Writing to Major J.S. Matthews, 27 April 1936, L.A. Hamilton stated that he could not remember the reason for adopting the name.

On 24 May 1973 the Dunsmuir-Melville connector opened to extend the one-way flow of traffic from Dunsmuir to Pender Streets.

MIDLOTHIAN AVENUE. Named on Plan 6430 (1932) and extended on Plan 6539 (1936). First listed in 1944 city directory.

According to S.M. Montgomery, secretary of the board of works, William B. Young of the city engineering department took the name from one of Sir Walter Scott's Waverley novels, *The Heart of Midlothian*. Midlothian is a district near Edinburgh, Scotland.

MILES ROAD. Now East 47th Avenue between Ontario and Prince Edward Streets. Among the

THE

HEART OF MIDLOTHIAN

BY

SIR WALTER SCOTT, BART.

A. & C. BLACK, LTD.
4, 5 & 6 SOHO SQUARE, LONDON, W.1
1929

A suprising number of Vancouver street names were derived from Sir Walter Scott's novels: Dinmont, Durward, Ivanhoe, Marmion, Midlothian, Nigel, Glengyle, Peveril, Robsart, Talisman, Waverley, and Woodstock. In addition, Melrose Avenue takes its name from Melrose Abbey, close to the home of Sir Walter Scott, and Scott Street was probably named after him.

owners' signatures shown on Plan 1748 (1907) was that of Leonard C. Miles, born in 1882, a machinist by trade, secretary (or manager) of Equity Brokerage Company, and in real estate from 1908-14. He later became the proprietor of Albion Iron Works.

Became East 49th Avenue (now East 47th Avenue) in 1910 by South Vancouver By-law 141.

MILLBANK. Named 1976, By-law 5010, the name recalling the former sawmills along the banks of False Creek.

MILLER STREET. Originally called Miller Road, after Jonathan Miller (1836-1914), a constable, government agent, collector for the Burrard Inlet area, and participant in the drafting of the Vancouver charter. Vancouver postmaster from 1886 to September 1908. Renamed Miller Street in 1910 by South

Jonothan Miller. CVA Port P. 94, N. 75.

Vancouver By-law 141. Named on Plans 1458 and 1536 (1907). South Vancouver Voters List, 1899, shows Jonathan Miller owning property in Block 14, DL 352. In 1902-3 he owned property in Block 16, DL 352.

MILLS AVENUE. See Alice Street.

MILLSTONE STREET. A private thoroughfare shown on Plan LF 11558 (1993) and named arbitrarily by Marine Woods Developments Limited in association with Cobblestone, Cornerstone, Fieldstone, and Keystone.

MILLYARD. Named 1976, By-law 5010, to commemorate the former millyards along False Creek in its industrial heyday.

MILTON ROAD (DL 325). Now West 66th Avenue between East Boulevard and Granville Street and West 67th Avenue between Granville and Heather Streets. Point Grey By-law 1, 1910, allocated $3,100 to clearing and grading Milton Road between Granville Street and Dixon Road (now Heather Street). Point Grey By-law 17, 1914, changed the name to West 66th and West 67th Avenues. Probably named after Albert Milton (1860-1932), owner of property in DL 325 in 1905.

MILTON STREET (DL 318). Originally it extended south from the intersection of Granville Street and South West Marine Drive to the Fraser River, as shown on a 1925 plan of Point Grey Municipality (Map 14376). The name was probably transferred from the former Milton Road, which was changed in 1914 to West 66th and West 67th Avenues. Albert Milton (1860-1932) owned property in the vicinity.

Point Grey By-law 265, 1928, diverted portions of Milton Street and West 75th Avenue, so Milton Street zigzagged to the river. In 1954, By-law 3486 renamed the unused portion of Milton Street, between West 75th Avenue and the river, Bentley Street.

MILTON STREET (DL 334) (Deleted). Named by South Vancouver By-law 251, 1913, after an unidentified person. This first street west of Tyne lay between the later Asquith and East 65th Avenues. Listed in city directories from 1911 to 1924 with no residents. Last shown on a 1947 map (Map 14404). Deleted by an unidentified resurvey of the area. Now within Champlain Heights area.

MINTO CRESCENT. Shown on Plan 6011 (1921) and named by Point Grey By-law 232, 1924, after the 4th Earl of Minto, Governor-General of Canada, 1898-1904.

MINTO STREET. See Arlington Street.

MISSOULA AVENUE. Now East 36th Avenue between Culloden and Commercial Streets. Named on Plan 1522 (1907) after Missoula, Montana. Dr. S.E Fleming, care of Panton and Hutchinson, owned property in DL 700 in 1907. Samuel Panton was connected with the Montana Company, a real estate firm, hence the street name.

Changed to East 37th Avenue by South Vancouver By-law 141, 1910, and to East 36th in 1929 by By-law 2028.

MOBERLY ROAD. Named 1976, By-law 5010. According to the report submitted by the False Creek Development Group to the Street Naming Committee on 12 March 1976, the name honours Walter Moberly (1832-1915), a former assistant surveyor general of British Columbia and a Dominion government engineer in charge of exploratory surveys of the Rocky Mountain district of the CPR.

MOHAWK STREET. Surveyed in 1910, Plan 2534, but not named until 1913 by South Vancouver By-law 251, probably after the Mohawk people.

MONCTON ROAD. See Crown Street.

MONMOUTH AVENUE. Named by South Vancouver By-law 251, 1913, probably after Monmouth, Wales. Surveyed 1909-12.

Fisher Street. Named on plan 3521, 1910, likely after Edward Fisher, a farmer in the area. An unofficial name, now part of Monmouth, one-half block west of Joyce Street.

MONS DRIVE. On 23 March 1948 Vancouver City Council approved the Vancouver Town Planning Commission's recommendation that the streets in Renfrew Heights be named after personalities, battles, and events of the two world wars (Vancouver City Council Minutes, v. 54, p. 259). Mons, Belgium, was occupied by German troops in both world wars.

MONTAGUE ROAD. Now East 21st Avenue between Knight and Fleming Streets. A survey name of unknown origin on Plan 1990 (1909).

MONTANA STREET. See Culloden Street.

MONTCALM STREET. (DL 393). See St. Lawrence Street.

MONTCALM STREET. (Shaughnessy Heights). See Richelieu Street.

MONTCALM STREET. Within the original city limits of Vancouver, named on Plan 3015 (1910), after the Marquis de Montcalm (1712-59), commander of the French forces in North America until his death in 1759 on the Plains of Abraham, Quebec city.

Extended to Shaughnessy Heights, Point Grey, on Plan 4502 (1913), southeast from West 16th Avenue to Oak Street. At amalgamation this part became Richelieu Avenue, By-law 2014, 1929.

Point Grey By-law 17, 1914, named Montcalm Street between West 59th Avenue and South West Marine Drive. This same by-law changed Third Street in Eburne Townsite (Plan 1749 [1908]) to Montcalm and extended it north to West 59th Avenue.

MONTGOMERY STREET. Named by the CPR after Samuel James Montgomery (1878-1976), who was secretary to the Vancouver Board of Works, 1907-44.

First named on Plan 6339 (1931) and extended by Plans 7421 (1946) and 7908 (1948).

MONTJOY ROAD (Deleted). Origin of name unknown. Named on Plans 1733, 2061, 3025, and 3505; surveyed 1908-10. *Goad's Atlas*, Plates 108 and 109, shows East 64th Avenue (late Montjoy Road) in broken lengths between Nanaimo and Kinross Streets.

S.J. Montgomery. From a group photo of the Vancouver Board of Works, 1915. cva C.I. Dept. P. 34, N. 24.

Changed to East 64th Avenue in 1910 by South Vancouver By-law 141 and, in 1929, to East 62nd Avenue by By-law 2028. This part of East 62nd Avenue disappeared with the replotting of the Fraserview Golf Course and the Fraserview development.

MONTROSE AVENUE (Deleted). Named by South Vancouver By-law 251, 1913, probably after Montrose, Scotland. It lay between the present Duff and Nanaimo Streets, south of South East Marine Drive. The street disappeared when DL 329, Lots 37-44, was replotted about 1984.

MOOSOMIN AVENUE. Now West 73rd Avenue between Granville and Selkirk Streets. Named after Moosomin, Saskatchewan, which bears the name of a Cree chief. Named on Plan 1749 (1908), the plan of Eburne Townsite. Changed to West 73rd Avenue by Point Grey By-law 17, 1914.

MORE STREET. See Payne Street.

MORNING STAR CRESCENT. A private thoroughfare shown on Plan LS 11431 (1990) and named arbitrarily by Abbey Woods, the developer.

MORRISON STREET (Deleted). Named after an unknown person by South Vancouver By-law 251, 1913; it lay one block west of Boundary Road between East 61st (later Asquith) and East 65th Avenues. Deleted from the official street plan by By-law 4770, 1970, when Champlain Heights was replotted.

The last listing in the city directory, 1936, shows "Trail in from 7200 Boundary Road" and indicates that William H. Kierstead, fur breeder,

lived at 7754 Morrison Street.

MORTON AVENUE. First listed in the 1909 city directory, probably named after John Morton (1834-1912), one of the "three greenhorns," who, in 1862, preempted DL 185, now the West End of Vancouver. Mrs. Ruth Morton is shown in 1904 Vancouver Voters List as owning Lot 6, Block 71, DL 185.

Surveyed but unnamed on Plan 92 (1882). *Goad's Atlas*, Plate 8, shows the street or lane as unnamed but with a rooming house, "The Morton," on the north side and the Imperial skating rink on the south side.

MORTON ROAD. See Inverness Street.

MOSCROP STREET. Partially surveyed but not named on Plan 1689 (1908). In 1909, Plan 1918 showed *Bursill Road* between Boundary Road and the present Hoy Street, with owner Margaret E.D. Bursill listed in South Vancouver Voters Lists, 1907-13 inclusive. A survey name only.

Goad's Atlas, Plate 97, 1913, shows the street as East 30th Avenue. Moscrop Street was first listed in 1917 city directory. Origin of name unknown but perhaps connected with nearby Moscrop Street in Burnaby.

MOSS STREET. Origin of name unknown. In 1929, By-law 2014 renamed Maple Street (DL 37) to remove duplication with existing Maple Street in DL 526.

Maple Street (DL 37). Probably an arbitrary name. Unnamed on Plan 2376, 1909, but named by 1913. See *Goad's Atlas*, Plate 100.

MOUNTAIN VIEW ROAD (Deleted). A descriptive name used on Plans 1733, 2061, 3025, and 3505, surveyed 1908-10. Shown in *Goad's Atlas*, Plates 108 and 109, in broken lengths from Nanaimo Street to beyond Kerr Street. Changed to East 62nd Avenue in 1910 by South Vancouver By-law 141 and, in 1929, to East 60th Avenue by By-law 2028. The road disappeared with the replotting of the Fraserview Golf Course and the Fraserview development.

MUIRFIELD DRIVE. Named 1952, By-law 3330, after Muirfield Golf Links, owned by the Honourable Company of Edinburgh Golfers.

MUNROE CRESCENT. After Lawrence (Larry) Robertson Munroe (1922-70), a member of the

Vancouver Planning Department who had been involved with the planning of Champlain Heights (Street Naming Committee, 1 October 1971). Named 1978, By-law 5195, Plan LE 3742B. Formerly the three sides of the crescent were Hartley Street, East 61st Avenue, and McKinnon Street, shown on Plan LF 4530, attached to By-law 4770, 1970. They were renamed Munroe Crescent.

MURRAY ROAD (Deleted). Named by South Vancouver By-law 251, 1913, it lay between East 69th Avenue (later East 67th Avenue) and South East Marine Drive, the second street west of Boundary Road. On Plan 2713 (1910) the name *Ruxton Road*, origin unknown, was crossed out and Murray was substituted. Murray Street disappeared with the replotting of Champlain Heights. Origin of name unknown, but there are several Murrays listed in South Vancouver Voters Lists at that time.

MURTON ROAD. Now West 34th Avenue between Collingwood and Blenheim Streets. Shown on Plan 3685 (1909), with the name stamped over and 34th Avenue substituted. Origin of name unknown.

MUSQUEAM DRIVE AND CLOSE. The name "Musqueam" means "place always to get [the root] iris-like plant" (Akrigg 1997). By-law 5010, 1976, Plan LF 7356, established the name, which had been used for many years on the Musqueam Band Reserve. See also Salish Drive.

MYRTLE STREET. Now East 54th Avenue between Inverness and Argyle Streets. First named on Plan 1645 (1908) and later extended by Plans 1673, 1681, 2373, and 3085 between 1908 and 1910. South Vancouver By-law 141, 1910, changed the name to East 56th Avenue (now East 54th Avenue). All the new streets on Plan 1645 bore tree names, thus "myrtle."

N

NAIRN AVENUE. Private thoroughfare in Enclave 15, Champlain Heights. The name, submitted by the developer, Abacus Cities, was approved by the Street Naming Committee on 17 April 1979. The manager's report to city council, 27 April 1979 (Vancouver City Council Minutes, v. 132, p. 26), stated that the developers of Enclave 15 chose names of provincial parks. Nairn Falls Park is between Whistler and Pemberton. Origin of name unknown.

NANAIMO STREET. Shown on Plan 100, a resurvey of Hastings Townsite in 1906, and named by the provincial government after the Nanaimo Mining Division.
Boundary Drive. Shown in *Goad's Atlas*, Plates 78, 80, 84, and 88, formed the boundary between the city of Vancouver and Hastings Townsite and became part of Nanaimo Street when the townsite joined Vancouver in 1911.
In 1950, By-law 3195 designated the portion north of Dundas Street as Nanaimo Street North, although the name had been in use since the early 1920s.

Graham Avenue. Shown on Plan 178 (1884), now part of Nanaimo Street north of Ferndale Avenue. This survey name, the eastern boundary of DL 184, was after the original owner of DL 184, John Graham (1826-1908), in charge of the treasury department of the Colony of British Columbia, who later conveyed his grant to C.T. Dupont and P.C. Dunlevy.
In 1910, South Vancouver By-law 141 changed the following roads to Nanaimo Street: Albert, Nanaimo, and Tilley.
Albert Road. Named on Plan 2202 (1909), lay between the present East 54th and East 59th Avenues. Probably named after Albert, Prince Consort of Queen Victoria, in association with Victoria Road, shown on the same plan.
Tilley Road. Named by South Vancouver Highway By-law, 1905, lay between the present East 49th and East 54th Avenues. By 1910 it extended south from East 65th Avenue to the BCER (Eburne to New Westminster line). Frank E. Tilley is shown in 1893 South Vancouver Assessment Roll owning 19.56 acres in DL 336.

NANTON AVENUE. Surveyed 1921, Plan 6011, and named by the CPR after Sir Augustus Meredith Nanton (1860-1925), a director of the company. Name confirmed by Point Grey By-law 483, 1926. In 1961, By-law 3937 extended Nanton Avenue west from East Boulevard to Arbutus Street. It now extends to Yew Street.

NAPIER STREET. Named on Map 14267, "Plan of the City of Vancouver, Western Terminus of the Canadian Pacific Railway," compiled by H.B. Smith, 1886. It lay between the present Glen and McLean Drives in DL 182 and gradually extended to Boundary Road. Origin of name unknown.

NAPLES WAY. Private thoroughfare in Champlain Heights, first listed in 1982 city directory. Henriquez and Partners, architects, chose Mediterranean names for the enclave.

NARVAEZ DRIVE. Named by a resolution of city council, 6 March 1941 (Vancouver City Council Minutes, v. 42, p. 329, 333) and shown on Plan 6897 (1941). The name commemorates Jose Maria Narvaez, in 1791 commander of the Spanish naval schooner *Saturnina*, which made an exploratory voyage from Nootka as far as Cape Lazo and ventured into English Bay – the first European vessel to do so.

NASSAU DRIVE. Named after the Nassau Golf Club in the Bahama Islands by a resolution of city council, 18 July 1950 (Vancouver City Council Minutes, v. 57, p. 643), which renamed part of East 56th Avenue.

NATHAN AVENUE. Now East 36th Avenue between Victoria Drive and Gladstone Street. Unnamed on a 1910 map of South Vancouver (Map 14212). Listed once only in 1913 city directory, as follows: "From Victoria Road, 1700 block, Gladstone intersects." Amongst the seven residents shown is Mrs. Ellen Sherwood, society editor of BC Saturday magazine *Sunset*, which may account for the social item listed under adjacent Tattenhall Street. Nathan probably a local name. City surveyor's office has no record of the name.

NATIONAL AVENUE. Named by By-law 1803, 1926, after its location near the Canadian National Railways passenger station. It lay east from Main Street to Station Street and between two parts of Thornton Park (City Engineer Plan MC10).

In 1992 the existing National Avenue was closed to become part of Thornton Park. The part of Station Street immediately north of the northern boundary of Thornton Park was renamed National Avenue and extended westward between Main and Quebec Streets (By-law 7001, Plan LF 11492).

NAUTILUS CLOSE. Name suggested by United Properties for its development, Discovery Point, and approved by the Street Naming Committee on 28 February 1984. Nautilus derived from the Greek word for sailor.

NEAL STREET. Named 1958, By-law 3731, Plan LA 17A, after William Merton Neal (1886-1961), former chairman and president of the CPR, who became a freeman of the City of Vancouver on 16 June 1947. Neal Street between West 54th and West 57th Avenues is a private thoroughfare in Langara Garden Apartments.

NELSON STREET. Named by L.A. Hamilton after the Honourable Hugh Nelson (1830-93), who served as lieutenant-governor of British Columbia, 1887-92. First MP for New Westminster, he entered the Senate in 1879.

H. Nelson. From a group photo of Commissioners and Pilots of Vancouver Pilotage District, 1879-1916. CVA Port. P. 189, N. 138.

NEW WESTMINSTER ROAD. See Kingsway.

NEWCASTLE COURT. Private thoroughfare in Champlain Heights, the name approved by the Street Naming Committee on 21 June 1978. Community Builders Limited, developers of Park Place, called its thoroughfares after BC provincial parks. Newcastle Island Marine Park near Nanaimo, British Columbia, was named after Newcastle-upon-Tyne, England.

NEWCOMBE STREET (Deleted). Unnamed on Plan 2552 (1910) and named by South Vancouver

By-law 251, 1913, it lay immediately west of and parallel to Boundary Road between Ellis Avenue and the BCER line to New Westminster, which began service in November 1909. The road disappeared in the replotting of Marine Way in the late 1970s. Origin of name unknown.

NEWMAN STREET. Now East 32nd Avenue between Main and Prince Edward Streets. Probably named after Arthur G. Newman, owner of property in DL 634 from 1902-15, according to South Vancouver Voters Lists. Unnamed on Plan 1225 (1906). Changed to East 32nd Avenue in 1910 by South Vancouver By-law 141.

NEWPORT AVENUE. Named 1952, By-law 3330, after the Newport Golf Club, Newport, Rhode Island.

NEWTON ROAD. See Sophia Street.

NICOLA STREET. Named by L.A. Hamilton, who wrote Major J.S. Matthews, 27 April 1936, that he couldn't recall why he gave the name but he may have wandered off the map he was using and chosen names of lakes. Akrigg (1997) says that Nicola Lake was named after a famous Thompson First Nations head chief, who was given the name "Nicholas" by early fur traders.

NIGEL AVENUE. Named on Plan 6430 (1932) and extended on Plan 6539 (1936). First listed in the 1944 city directory.

According to S.M. Montgomery, secretary of the board of works, William B. Young of the city engineering department chose the name from one of Sir Walter Scott's Waverley novels, *The Fortunes of Nigel.*

NOOTKA STREET. Shown on Plan 100, a re-survey of Hastings Townsite, 1906, and named by the provincial government, probably after Nootka Sound. First listed in the 1915 city directory. The part between Broadway and Hebb Avenue was not named until 1951, By-law 3232.

NORFOLK STREET. See Commercial Street.

NORMANDY DRIVE. On 23 March 1948 Vancouver City Council approved the recom-

mendation of the Vancouver Town Planning Commission that streets in Renfrew Heights be named after personalities, battles, and events of the two world wars (Vancouver City Council Minutes, v. 54, p. 299). Normandy Drive commemorates the Normandy invasion in northwestern France in 1944.

NORQUAY STREET. Named after the nearby John Norquay School, which was named after John Norquay (1841-89), premier of Manitoba, 1878-87. First listed in 1930 city directory, although surveyed on Plans 1507 and 2372 (1907).

NORTH BOULEVARD. Now West 4th Avenue between Blanca Street and the eastern boundary of the University Endowment Lands. Unnamed on Plan 6583 (1911) and named in *Goad's Atlas,* Plate 49. Point Grey By-law 31, 1913, named it University Boulevard, but this name was not used.

NORTH ROAD. Now West 35th Avenue between East Boulevard and Marguerite Street. Shown on Plans 2975 (1909) and 3536 (1911), the name refers to its position as the northernmost street of three. A survey name only, it was used in a real estate advertisement in the *Vancouver Daily Province,* 16 May 1912, when lots were sold at $1,350 and up.

NORTH ARM ROAD. See Fraser Street.

NORTHERN STREET. Named unimaginatively after its position in Parcel A, DL 2037, Plan 5703. Laid out when the eastern part of False Creek was filled in and the Canadian Northern Pacific Railway (later Canadian National Railways) built its station and yards there. Originally between Station and Main Streets (By-law 1556, 1922), it was shortened to its present length between Station and Western Streets in 1926, By-law 1803. First listed in 1927 city directory.

NORTHUMBERLAND AVENUE. Private thoroughfare in Champlain Heights. Named by the Greater Vancouver Housing Corporation in association with the nearby Tyne Street and the Tyne River, which bisects the English counties of Durham and Northumberland.

O

OAK STREET. Officially registered on Plan 590 (1891) but named on an 1887 map (Map 14160) by L.A. Hamilton, who chose tree names.

Extended south by Point Grey By-law 6, 1910 (from 16th Avenue south to present Park Street); Point Grey By-law 17, 1912 (from 16th Avenue south to present Marine Drive); and Point Grey By-law 39, 1912 (from BCER to Fraser River).

OBEN STREET. Named after Philip Oben (1856-1933), who came to the Vancouver area in 1887 and helped clear the West End. He eventually moved to Central Park, where he acquired 7.93 acres in DL 36-49 of Burnaby and South Vancouver Small Holdings and had a small grocery store. Oben Street is shown on a 1919 map of South Vancouver (Map 14372) lying between Kingsway and Vanness Avenue. Resurveyed in 1967, Plan 12672, the street is now shorter.

Mr. & Mrs. P. Oben. CVA Port. P. 110, N. 60 #1.

O'CONNOR STREET. See Culloden Street.

ODLUM DRIVE. Named after Professor Edward Odlum (1850-1935). A large property owner in Grandview, he initiated the formation of the Grandview Ratepayers Association and served as an alderman in 1892 and 1904.

OGDEN AVENUE. Named after Isaac Gouverneur Ogden (1844-1928), vice-president of the CPR, in charge of finances. Named on Plan 2301 (1909), when the CPR opened a subdivision at Kitsilano Point. First listed in 1913 city directory. The city belatedly confirmed the name in 1958, By-law 3731.

OLD BRIDGE COURT. Named 1984, By-law 5741; a dedicated road leading from Lamey's Mill Road.

OLD BRIDGE STREET. Private thoroughfare on Granville Island. Central Mortgage and Housing Corporation suggested the name because the street follows the alignment of the now-demolished second Granville Street Bridge. Name approved by the Street Naming Committee on 9 August 1978.

OLD BRIDGE WALK. A private thoroughfare. Name approved on 15 August 1979.

OLIVER CRESCENT. Named by Point Grey By-law 294, 1928, after John Oliver (1856-1927), premier of British Columbia, 1918-27. By-law 3232, 1951, extended the crescent to include the portion of West 26th Avenue between Macdonald and Trafalgar Streets, and eastward to the intersection of West 23rd Avenue and Vine Street.

OLYMPIC STREET. Probably named after the Olympic Mountains in Washington State, according to Point Grey alderman W.H. Lembke. Shown on Plan 2182 (1909) and named by Point Grey By-law 17, 1914, the street originally lay between West 39th and West 48th Avenues. Musqueam Park absorbed the street between West 46th and West 48th Avenues.

ONTARIO PLACE. Adjacent to Ontario Street, named by South Vancouver By-law 251, 1913.

ONTARIO STREET. Named by the owner of DL 200A, Dr. I.W. Powell, after the province of Ontario.

South Vancouver Highway By-law 65, 1903, extended the street from the city limits at 16th Avenue south to the Fraser River. The eastern boundary of the huge CPR land grant of DL 526 was Ontario Street, which created the boundary between the east and west sides of Vancouver's street-numbering system.

OPPENHEIMER STREET. See Cordova Street.

ORCHARD STREET. Now East 28th Avenue between Windermere and Skeena Streets. Origin of this survey name, shown on Plan 1705 (1906) and Plan 1932 (1908), unknown but perhaps descriptive.

ORIOLE WALK. Named after the bird, perhaps in association with Grouse Walk. Private thoroughfare in the Little Mountain Housing Project. Named by Vancouver Housing Authority in 1954 without approval of city council. Street Naming Committee minutes, 15 November 1954, recorded that the deputy director of planning stated that these walks (i.e., Grouse, James, and Oriole) should not be given official street names since they were not public streets.

ORMIDALE STREET. Origin of name unknown; possibly named by Alex McDonald after the estate of Ormidale in Kilmodan parish, Argylleshire, Scotland. One of its lairds, Robert McFarlane (1802-80), became a well-known judge (Lord Ormidale). There was much confusion between the names of Bowman, Wilbers, and Ormidale Streets because three men – Joseph Bowman, John Wilbers, and Alex McDonald – owned blocks 5, 6, and 14, respectively, in DL 36-49, known as the Burnaby and South Vancouver Small Holdings. As was customary, names of owners were applied to the roads near their property.

Bowman Street. An unofficial name for a street that lay between the present East 45th and Vanness Avenues. Unnamed on Plan 3442 (1911), owner Joseph Henry Bowman (1864-1943) owned 6.63 acres in DL 36-49, Block 5. He came to Vancouver in 1888 from London, England, where he studied draughting and architecture. He was the architect for several South Vancouver schools and Point Grey municipal hall.

In 1913 South Vancouver By-law 252 changed Bowman Street between present Kingsway and Vanness Avenue to *Wilbers Street*, after John Joseph Wilbers (1861-1923), who owned 5.4 acres in Burnaby Small Holdings (DL 36-49, Block 6), was steward of the CPR hotel in Vancouver from 1890 until 1908, and was a councillor in South Vancouver in 1913.

There seems to have been some confusion about the name "Bowman." On 20 October 1915 property owners on the street called Bowman, between present East 45th Avenue and Kingsway, petitioned the South Vancouver Board of Works about changing the name. At the South Vancouver Board of Works meeting of 17 March 1916, "the communications between A. Macdonald re [sic] changing the name of Bowman Road to the former name of Ormidale Avenue" was received and filed. A. McDonald owned 7.9 acres in DL 36-49, Block 14. When South Vancouver By-law 463, 1917, changed Bowman and Wilbers Streets to Ormidale Street, the names of two South Vancouver pioneers disappeared. The street (unofficially called Ormidale), between present Kingsway and Vanness Avenue (on west side of Block 5, DL 36-49), became part of Lincoln Street by this same by-law.

ORTONA CRESCENT. Private thoroughfare in the Canadian Forces Base near Jericho Park, named after the Battle of Ortona, Italy, in December 1943, in which the Canadian First Division participated. First listed in the 1958 city directory.

OSLER STREET. Shown as Osler Avenue on Plan 4502 (1913) and named by the CPR, developers of Shaughnessy Heights, after Sir Edmund Boyd Osler (1845-1924), a director of the company. Point Grey By-law 232, 1924, changed Osler Avenue to agree with Osler Street, the extension in Point Grey.

Goad's Atlas, 1913, Plates 43 and 45, shows 6th Street between present West 73rd Avenue and Park Drive. Point Grey By-law 17, 1914, renamed it Osler Street.

OXFORD STREET. Named on Plan 100, a re-survey of Hastings Townsite, 1906, after Oxford University, the oldest university in England.

P

PACIFIC BOULEVARD. A northeast continuation of Pacific Street, named 1983, By-law 5689, Plan LF 10462. Pacific Boulevard North and South were so designated by the Street Naming Committee on 3 July 1985, when Pacific Boulevard was split to go around the new BC Place

Stadium; By-law 6781, 1991, Plan LE 11432, confirmed the designations.

In 1994, By-law 7734, Plan LF 11638, renamed Pacific Boulevard North "Expo Boulevard," and Pacific Boulevard South reverted to Pacific Boulevard.

PACIFIC STREET. Named by L.A. Hamilton in 1886, when he took the name of the Pacific Ocean from a map.

PAGE ROAD. Now East 57th Avenue between Prince Albert and Fleming Streets. Named by South Vancouver Highway By-law, 1905, probably after William Page, who owned property in DL 658 from 1893 to 1907, as shown in South Vancouver Voters Lists. Plan 3049 (1910) shows Page Road between present Elliott and Vivian Streets, since changed by the Fraserview development. South Vancouver By-law 141, 1910, changed Page Road to East 59th Avenue (now East 57th Avenue).

PAGET ROAD (Deleted). Origin of name unknown. Named on Plans 2061 and 3025 (1909), and Plan 3815 (1911), it lay between Kerr Street and Boundary Road. Also shown in *Goad's Atlas*, Plate 109.

South Vancouver By-law 141, 1910, changed it to East 65th Avenue (later East 63rd Avenue). Disappeared in the replotting for Champlain Heights.

PANDORA STREET. Named on 1902 map of Vancouver (Map 14171). Origin of name not verified but perhaps in association with adjacent Triumph Street, shown on same map. *HMS Pandora* surveyed the coast, 1846-8.

PAONESSA AVENUE (DL 707). Now East 38th Avenue between Commercial Street and Victoria Drive. Plan 3105 (1910) shows Guiseppe Paonessa as the owner of the centre three acres on north half of DL 707. Born in Italy, he died in Vancouver on 22 June 1942, aged seventy-eight. First listed in 1901 South Vancouver Voters List.

South Vancouver By-law 141, 1910, incorrectly changed Paonessa to 31st Avenue East.

PARK DRIVE (DL 185). See Lagoon Drive.

PARK DRIVE. See Commercial Drive.

PARK DRIVE (THSL). See Carlisle Street.

PARK DRIVE. Surveyed as "D" Road and listed in *B.C. Gazette*, 25 January 1900. South Vancouver Highway By-law, 1905, named *Buckberry Road* after Ed Buckberry, who owned property in DL 324A from 1905 to 1907. The city directory, 1910, lists him as a section man in Eburne.

Point Grey By-law 17, 1914, changed Buckberry Road to Park Drive when that name was transferred from Park Road (now West 59th Avenue) to the former Buckberry Road. The names of Park Road and Park Drive came from their proximity to Oak Park.

PARK LANE. See Station Street.

PARK ROAD. Now West 59th Avenue between Fremlin and Granville Streets. Named on Plan 4251 (1912), Point Grey By-law 17, 1914, made it a part of West 59th Avenue. Named after its proximity to Oak Park.

PARK ROAD (DL 712). See Sherbrooke Street.

PARK STREET. See Boundary Road.

PARKER ROAD. Changed to East 32nd Avenue between Argyle Street and Victoria Drive by South Vancouver By-law 141, 1910. Shown in *Goad's Atlas*, Plate 96. Probably named after W.H. Parker and Mrs. Hannah Parker, who both owned property in DL 706, according to South Vancouver Voters List, 1909.

PARKER STREET. Named on Map 14267, "Plan of the City of Vancouver, Western Terminus of the Canadian Pacific Railway," compiled by H.B. Smith, 1886, it lay between the present Glen and McLean Drives in DL 182. Origin of name unknown.

The aforementioned map shows *Bay Street*, a descriptive name, lying from Parker Street west to an arm of False Creek. Around 1912, when the eastern part of the creek was filled in, Bay Street became part of Parker Street.

PARKWAY AVENUE. Private thoroughfare in Arbutus Village leading into a small city-owned park – Arbutus Village Park. The name, suggested by Narod Developments Limited, was approved by the Street Naming Committee on 21 June 1978.

PATON STREET. Named 1958, By-law 3731, to recognize James Alexander Paton (1884-1946), who served Point Grey municipality as school trustee, councillor, and reeve. Upon Point Grey's amalgamation with Vancouver, he became an alderman and served on the Vancouver Town Planning Commission, 1929-35. Elected to the BC Legislative Assembly in 1931, re-elected in 1941 and 1945 (Vancouver City Council Minutes, v. 66, p. 360).

J.A. Paton. From group photo of the Reeves of Point Grey, 1908-1928. CVA Port. P. 188, N. 306 #3.

PAUL AVENUE (Deleted). Named 1970, By-law 4770, Plan LF 4530. A short street going east to Boundary Road and lying halfway between Peter and Victory Streets in Burnaby, deleted in 1978, By-law 5195. Origin of name unknown but perhaps named in association with the adjacent Peter Street.

PAYNE STREET. Named 1913, South Vancouver By-law 251, after Henry Thomas Payne (1862-1945), section hand for the BCER, and his wife, Mary Elizabeth (1867-1940), who owned property on the street in 1906. The part north of Wellington Street was called *More Street* on Plans 1975 and 1977 (1909); the name, of unknown origin, was never used.

PEACEY ROAD. See Cree Street.

PENDER STREET. Named after Pender Island, shown on the map used by L.A. Hamilton when naming streets. Pender Island commemorates Daniel Pender, RN, staff commander (later captain) of HMS *Plumper*, which surveyed the BC coast, 1857-70. By-law 573, 1907, extended Pender Street when Dupont and Princess Streets were renamed.

Dupont Street. Named in 1886 after Major Charles Thomas Dupont (1837-1923), one of the shareholders in the Vancouver Improvement Company.

Princess Street. Named 1888, By-law 72, which renamed the portion of Dupont between Main Street and Vernon Drive because of the unsavoury reputation of Dupont between Carrall and Main Streets. On 20 September 1937 Major J.S. Mathews recorded a conversation with Mrs. Stephen Ramage (née Annie Sanders, daughter

of alderman Edwin Sanders [1887]), who stated that Princess Street was named after her nickname.

PENDER-KEEFER DIVERSION (Deleted). Named 1958, By-law 3731, the diversion linked Pender Street, at Carrall, to Keefer Street, at Columbia, to improve traffic flow. The diversion disappeared prior to the completion of the Sun Yat-Sen Classical Chinese Garden, which opened in 1986.

PENDRELL STREET. Named after Pendrell Sound, shown on the map that L.A. Hamilton used when naming streets in the West End; Pendrell Sound named after Alfred Pendrell Waddington (1796-1872), who established a mule trail from the head of Bute Inlet up the Homathko River into the Chilcotin.

PENNYFARTHING DRIVE. Private thoroughfare near Granville Island named by and after the Pennyfarthing Development Corporation. Approved by the Street Naming Committee on 10 June 1982.

PENTICTON STREET. Named after the City of Penticton in 1950, when By-law 3195 renamed Clinton Street to remove duplication with Clinton Street in Burnaby. This same by-law also designated the part north of Dundas Street as Penticton Street North. Penticton is an Okanagan First Nations word meaning "the always place" (i.e., permanent abode) (Akrigg 1997).

Clinton Street. Shown on Plan 100, a resurvey of Hastings Townsite, 1906, named by the provincial government after the Clinton mining district, according to Frank Woodside, a pioneer in the area. Indirectly takes its name from Clinton, British Columbia, named in honour of Henry Pelham Clinton, colonial secretary, 1855-64.

PERCIVAL STREET. See Clark Drive.

PERRY STREET. Surveyed but not named on Plan 2332 (1909). Owner Arthur Perry listed in South Vancouver Voters Lists, 1909-12 inclusive.

PETER AVENUE (Deleted). Shown on Plan LF 4530, attached to By-law 4770, 1970; a short street crossing Boundary Road to connect with Peter Street in Burnaby. In 1978, By-law 5195 deleted the street from the official street name map.

Peter Street in Burnaby named after pioneer settler Peter Dubois, a stonecutter by trade who owned 7.9 acres in Burnaby Small Holdings. His wife was a sister of Philip Oben.

PETERS ROAD. Now West 64th Avenue between Granville and Heather Streets. Named on Plans 2277, 2526A, and 2203 (1909), after owner Thomas Richard Peters (1859-1920), first listed in 1906 South Vancouver Voters List. He spent the last ten years of his life at Cloverdale as a farmer. Point Grey By-law 17, 1914, changed the road to West 64th Avenue.

PETERSHAM AVENUE. Named after Petersham, Surrey, England, where Captain George Vancouver is buried, By-law 7590, 1996, Plan LF 11680 (Administrative Report to City Council, 30 April 1996).

PEVERIL AVENUE. Named on Plan 6430 (1932), after Sir Walter Scott's novel *Peveril of the Peak*, whose main character is Sir Geoffrey Peveril of Derbyshire. Extended on Plan 6539 (1936) and first listed in 1942 city directory.

PHILIP ROAD. See Clarendon Street.

PHILLIPS ROAD. Now East 51st Avenue between St. George and Fraser Streets. Named on Plan 1755 (1907), with one of the co-owners, George F. Phillips, carpenter for Cornish and Cooper, builders and woodworkers. Changed in 1910 by South Vancouver By-law 141 to East 53rd Avenue (now East 51st Avenue).

PICTON STREET. Named 1913 by South Vancouver By-law 251. Origin of name unknown but probably after Picton, Ontario.

PIERCE STREET (Proposed). A name suggested by the Native Sons of British Columbia, Post No. 2, for one of the new roads created by the replotting of DL 139, but it was not adopted. Those accepted were Puget and Quesnel Drives, Galiano and Quadra Streets, and Valdez Road.

Lieutenant Thomas Pierce of the Royal Marines represented the British when the British flag was hoisted at Nootka Sound on 28 March 1795.

PINE STREET AND PINE CRESCENT. Pine Street officially registered on Plan 590 (1891) but named by L.A. Hamilton on an 1887 map (Map 14160). In 1911, By-law 974 changed it to *Cherry Street*, in response to a petition by property owner and residents. However, that name only lasted until 1920, when By-law 1448 changed it back to Pine Street.

In the neighbouring Shaughnessy Heights, Plan 4502 (1913) showed Pine Crescent, which eventually extended to 33rd Avenue. The portion south of West 33rd Avenue was called Pine Street until Point Grey By-law 763, 1927, changed it to Pine Crescent at the request of several residents.

PINEHURST DRIVE. Private thoroughfare in Langara Estates, adjacent to the Langara Golf Course, named by Daon Development Company after Pinehurst, North Carolina, home to thirty-four golf courses and the Golf Hall of Fame. Name approved by the Street Naming Committee on 16 February 1978.

PINNACLE COURT. Private thoroughfare in Champlain Heights named by Community Builders, developers of Park Place, after Pinnacle Park near Quesnel, British Columbia. Name approved on 21 June 1978.

PLAYER CRESCENT (Proposed). See Tytahun Crescent.

POINT STREET. See William Street.

POINT GREY ROAD. Named after its location by By-law 573, 1907, although named on Plan 851 (1902). By-law 573 also renamed the two parts of Victoria Street: that between the present Alma and Balaclava Streets named on Plan 229 (1887), probably after Queen Victoria or the City of Victoria, and that between Macdonald and Balsam Streets, named on Plan 774 (1898) and Plan 848 (1902).

West of the present Alma Street, Point Grey Road lay in the Municipality of Point Grey, which extended the road by Point Grey By-law 17, 1914, and Point Grey By-law 232, 1924.

On 4 February 1955, the *Vancouver Sun* reported that the Kitsilano Ratepayers Association had asked the city to rename the 2400-2500 block of Point Grey Road because of the confusion caused by its location. It suggested Endacott Road after pioneer resident Colonel George Marshall Endacott (1884-1959). Later the Street Naming Committee countered with the name "McAlpine," after Dr. John Alexander McAlpine (1869-1934), a resident since 1913 at 2531 Point Grey Road.

On 14 January 1957 the board of administration recommended that no change be made, as sixteen of twenty-five property owners canvassed favoured retention of Point Grey Road. Council approved this recommendation on 16 January 1957 (Vancouver City Council Minutes, v. 66, p. 359).

POPLAR STREET. Unnamed on Plan 3021 (1909) and named in 1913 by South Vancouver By-law 251. Probably arbitrary choice of name.

PORT BAY AVENUE. Listed in city directories from 1976 to 1982 inclusive, "from Jericho Avenue west," which would have put it in the former RCAF station. Two companies – Innotech Aviation and Texaco Sky Service – were occupants. An unofficial name that may have been used for postal and delivery service. The city surveyor has no record of this name.

PORTER STREET. Named after Charles and Francis Porter, who owned property in DLs 195, 753, and 754. Originally Porter Road, surveyed but not named on Plan 811 (1900). Changed to Porter Street in 1910 by South Vancouver By-law 141.

PORTSIDE COURT, adjacent to Portside Drive, had its name assigned by the Street Naming Committee on 9 June 1986.

PORTSIDE DRIVE. Named 1984, By-law 5845. A name descriptive of its location to the port (left) side of Southside Drive in the Riverside neighbourhood.

POUND STREET (Deleted). Named by South Vancouver By-law 251, 1913, after William Alfred Pound, who came to Vancouver in 1889 as a linotype operator for the *Daily News Advertiser* and, later, for the *Vancouver Daily Province.* Served as a councillor in South Vancouver and as reeve, 1909-11. He died in Bellingham on 10 May 1938.

The street lay between Wales and Vivian Streets from 69th Avenue (later East 67th Avenue) south to River Road (later South East

W.A. Pound, as portrayed in *British Columbians as We See 'Em, 1910 and 1911,* (Vancouver: Newspaper Cartoonist Association of British Columbia, 1911).

Marine Drive). It disappeared in the replotting of the Fraserview subdivision.

POWELL STREET. Shown on Map 11427, "Plan of the City of Vancouver, Western Terminus of the Canadian Pacific Railway," compiled by H.B. Smith, 1886. Named after Dr. Israel Wood Powell (1836-1915), who had extensive land holdings in DL 200A and DL 196, was a shareholder in the Vancouver Improvement Company, the first president of the Medical Council of British Columbia, and

Israel Powell. BCARS, F-03704.

the first superintendent of Indian Affairs for British Columbia.

It lay between Carrall Street and the present Glen Drive. By 1910 it extended northeast from Semlin Drive to Renfrew Street. In 1911 By-law 842 renamed this northeast portion Wall Street. This same by-law extended Powell Street east from Semlin Drive to Boundary Road by changing Dundas Street to Powell Street. However, this part was changed back to Dundas Street in 1918 by By-law 1337.

PRESCOTT STREET. Named 1930, By-law 2082, probably after John William Prescott, JP (1867-1937), an alderman for Ward 1, 1908-9, and owner of a real estate and insurance firm.

Formerly *Stirling Street*, named by Point Grey By-law 17, 1914, and renamed Prescott in 1930 to remove duplication with Stirling Street in South Vancouver.

PRESTON AVENUE. Unnamed on Plan 4118 (1912) and named by South Vancouver By-law 251, 1913. Origin of name unknown.

PRESTWICK DRIVE. Named 1952, By-law 3330, after the Prestwick Golf Club, Prestwick, Scotland.

PRICE STREET. Shown as Price Road on Plans 1570 and 1577 (1907), it lay between Boundary Road and Joyce Street. Extended to Rupert Street, when South Vancouver Road Loan By-law 6, 1911, allocated $4,000 to it.

Mount Pleasant pioneer's shack in stump. It was built by a Mr. Berkman, and was on the east side of Seacombe Road, now Prince Edward Street, between 26th and 27th Ave. It was reached by a short forest trail from Horne Road, now 28th Avenue. The lower stump on the right was the kitchen, and the lower part of the higher stump on the left was the livingroom. The bedroom, doorless, was in the top of the higher stump and was reached by a ladder removed in daytime to the kitchen. According to Major J.S. Matthews, this photo was taken before 1910 by W.J. Moore, who lived nearby, and who also provided the particulars. CVA Bu. P. 6, N. 31 #1.

According to Spencer Robinson, councillor in 1909 for Ward 1, South Vancouver, this street was named after Mr. Price, who owned acreage there and was a janitor at Carleton School. Frank Price is listed in South Vancouver Voters List, 1908, in DL 36-51. Vancouver city directories, 1919-33 inclusive, show him as a school janitor.

PRINCE ALBERT STREET. Named 1910 by South Vancouver By-law 141, although the name appeared earlier on Plan 1369 (1907) and Plan 1797 (1908). Probably named after Prince Albert, consort of Queen Victoria.

Over the years the street had a variety of names because it lay within three jurisdictions: Vancouver, DL 301, and South Vancouver.

Burns Street (DL 264A). Named after the Scottish poet, Robert Burns. Shown on a 1902 map (Map 14171) and on Plan 1771 (1905) between East 6th and East 15th Avenues. By-law 3195, 1950, renamed it Prince Albert.

Valentine Street (DL 301). Named after its owner, Henry Valentine Edmonds (1837-97). South Vancouver By-law 141, 1910, changed it to Prince Albert. However, in 1911, Vancouver absorbed DL 301, and By-law 842 renamed that part between East 15th and East 25th Avenues Burns Street. It bore this name until 1950, when By-law 3195 changed it back to Prince Albert.

Second Street. Named on Plan 1390 (1907) and Plan 1900 (1908), between the present East 45th and East 49th Avenues. South Vancouver By-law 141, 1910, changed it to Prince Albert.

PRINCE EDWARD STREET. Named by the owner of DL 200A, Dr. Israel W. Powell, after the Canadian province of Prince Edward Island.

John Street (DL 301). Named by H.V. Edmonds, after his brother-in-law, John Alfred Webster (1838-1903), one of the first purchasers of land in Granville Townsite around 1870. He received a Crown grant of 174 acres in the Mount Pleasant area in 1877. In 1911, By-law 842 changed the street to Prince Edward between East Broadway and East King Edward Avenue.

Seacome Road. Named by South Vancouver Highway By-law, 1905, after Edward Seacome (1864-1902), a farmer who settled in the area in 1894. He cut a trail, later Seacome Road, to bring out shingle bolts. Served on the South Vancouver Council, 1898-1901. South Vancouver By-law 141, 1910, renamed the road Prince Edward Street between the present East King Edward Avenue and South East Marine Drive.

In 1954, By-law 3486 extended Prince Edward Street between South East Marine Drive and East Kent Street.

PRINCESS AVENUE (DL 196). Named when By-law 851, 1911, changed Carl Avenue. Reason for the change has not been ascertained, nor has its origin. It may have been a re-use of the name of Princess Street, which was in use until 1907, when it was changed to Pender.

Carl Avenue was on Map 14267, "Plan of the City of Vancouver, Western Terminus of the Canadian Pacific Railway," compiled by H.B. Smith, 1886. In 1897, By-law 197 renamed the street Oppenheimer Avenue, but By-law 314, 1898, changed it back. According to Gomery (1936), it was named after Carl Strouse, a wholesale merchant in Victoria and a shareholder in Hastings Mill.

PRINCESS STREET (DL 196, DL 181). See Pender Street.

PRINCESS STREET (DL 37). See Duke Street.

PRIOR STREET. Shown on Plan 196 and named after Edward Gawler Prior (1853-1920), a shareholder in the Vancouver Improvement Company and an MLA. In 1902 he became the fifteenth premier of British Columbia, and in 1919-20 he was lieutenant-governor of British Columbia.

E.G. Prior. CVA Port. T.P. 22.

PROMENADE MEWS. Private thoroughfare within the Pacifica development at 3005 Cambie Street. Shown on Plan LF 11439 (1990).

PUGET DRIVE. Named by Point Grey By-law 483, 1926, after Peter Puget, RN, a 2nd lieutenant on Captain George Vancouver's ship *Discovery* on the northwest coast in 1792. The Native Sons of British Columbia, Post No. 2, suggested this name for one of the six new roads created by the replotting of DL 139.

Q

QUADRA STREET. Named by Point Grey By-law 483, 1926, after Don Juan Francisco de la Bodega y Quadra (ca. 1744-94), Spanish naval officer exploring the northwest coast for Spain in 1775 and 1779. In 1792 he met with Captain George Vancouver at Nootka. The Native Sons of British Columbia, Post No. 2, suggested this name for one of six new roads created by the re-plotting of DL 139.

The Native Sons of British Columbia also suggested the following names derived from early explorers: Galiano, Pierce, Puget, Quesnel, Valdez, and Cayetano.

QUALICUM DRIVE. Named 1952, By-law 3330, after the Qualicum Hotel Golf Course. Qualicum is derived from "squal-li," meaning "chum salmon" in the Halkomelem language (Coull 1996; Akrigg 1997).

QUATSINO DRIVE. A private thoroughfare in Champlain Heights, named after Quatsino Sound, a Kwakwala word with various translations (Akrigg 1997). Named by the Street Naming Committee in 1979 and first listed in 1981 city directory.

QUAYSIDE COURT. A private thoroughfare near the Fraser River. A descriptive name submitted to the Street Naming Committee by Buron Construction Limited and approved 5 October 1987.

Native Sons of British Columbia at reunion of pioneers of BC, May 1925. CVA Port. P. 185.

QUEBEC PLACE. Surveyed in 1906, Plan 1167, and first listed in 1916 city directory, it lies immediately west of Quebec Street.

QUEBEC STREET. Named by the owner of DL 200A, Dr. I.W. Powell, after the province of Quebec and later extended south from East 9th Avenue to city boundary at East 16th Avenue.

South Vancouver Highway By-law, 1905, extended Quebec Street south from the boundary at East 16th to East 22nd Avenues. Between East 18th and East 20th Avenues, originally called James Street (see entry).

In 1910, South Vancouver By-law 141 extended Quebec Street south and renamed *Hay Road* from just north of East 28th to East 32nd Avenues. Hay Road, shown in *Goad's Atlas*, Plate 94, was likely named after James and William Hay, property owners in DL 632 according to South Vancouver Voters Lists, 1908-13 inclusive. Vancouver directories, 1908 and 1909, show them as builders.

For many years the northern end of Quebec Street was at East 1st Avenue. In 1976 the Quebec-Columbia Connector was built (By-law 5010, Plan LF 6373) west of Main Street to facilitate the movement of traffic into the downtown core. This connector became Quebec Street in 1978, by By-law 5161.

QUEEN AVENUE (DL 540). See Marine Drive, North West.

QUEENS AVENUE. Named 1913 by South Vancouver By-law 251, probably to harmonize with the adjacent Kings Avenue, named at the same time. Unnamed on Plans 1735 (1907) and 3333 (1911).

South Vancouver By-law 151, 1911, allocated $450 to Road Blocks 28-41, DL 37 (*Eltham Road*), from Rupert to McHardy Streets. This unofficial name, origin unknown, became part of Queens Avenue in 1913.

QUEEN'S AVENUE. Now East 29th Avenue between Nanaimo and Slocan Streets. Named on Plan 2440 (1909) in Beaconsfield Heights subdivision. Became part of East 29th Avenue when Hastings Townsite joined Vancouver in 1911. Origin of name unknown.

QUESNEL DRIVE. Named by Point Grey By-law 483, 1926, after Jules Maurice Quesnel (1786-1842), who accompanied Simon Fraser to the mouth of the Fraser River in 1808. The by-law spelled it "Quesnelle," the form used by the Native Sons of British Columbia, Post No. 2, who suggested the name for one of the six new roads created by the replotting of DL 139. This variation was in use until 1951, when the city adopted the standard spelling of "Quesnel," in spite of a protest from a resident, Mrs. E.M. Allsop, who wrote the city clerk on 28 February 1952. As of 1998 four sidewalks, including one at Quesnel and West King Edwards, still have the old name of Quesnelle stamped in the concrete.

QUILCHENA CRESCENT AND PLACE. Named by Point Grey By-law 483, 1926. The CPR opened the Quilchena subdivision in 1926, adjacent to the Quilchena Golf Club, named after Quilchena in the Nicola Valley. In the Nlaka'pamux language Quilchena means "red bluffs," the name of a former nearby village (Coull 1996, 125).

QUINTE AVENUE (Deleted). Shown on Plan GA 49, attached to By-law 3330, 1952. This part of Fraserview was replotted, and Quinte Avenue, named after the Bay of Quinte Golf Club near Belleville, Ontario, disappeared.

R

RADISSON STREET. Named 1978, By-law 5150, after Pierre Esprit Radisson (1640?-1710?), a French explorer and fur trader, probably among the first Europeans to explore north and west of the Great Lakes. On 26 January and 16 February 1978 the Street Naming Committee decided to name the streets in Enclave 1, Champlain Heights, after explorers.

RAE AVENUE. Named by South Vancouver By-law 251, 1913, after George Rae, reeve of South Vancouver in 1898, according to Mrs. Philip Oben's article in *Carleton News*, 23 July 1936. *Goad's Atlas*, Plate 101, shows the street as Union Avenue, but there is no indication on Plan 3566 (1911) of this name, which is of unknown origin.

RAILSPUR ALLEY. Named after the existing but discontinued spur line of the CPR on Granville Island, laid in the 1920s. The name of this private thoroughfare, submitted by the Central Mortgage and Housing Corporation, was approved by the Street Naming Committee on 9 August 1978.

RAILWAY AVENUE. Now East 5th Avenue between Commercial Drive and Bauer Street. Shown on Plan 722 (1894), and probably named after its proximity to the new tramline, Westminster and Vancouver Tramway, which ran from Vancouver via Park Drive (now Commercial) to the city limits and on to New Westminster.

RAILWAY STREET. Named by L.A. Hamilton after its proximity to the CPR.

RAINIER PLACE. Private thoroughfare shown on Plan LF 11622 (1994). Probably named after Mount Rainier in Washington State.

RAINTREE COURT. Private thoroughfare in Champlain Heights, named after the rain tree from tropical South America, in association with Limewood, Marchwood, and Teakwood. Name approved by the Street Naming Committee on 8 November 1979.

RALEIGH STREET. Named by South Vancouver By-law 252, 1913, which renamed *James Street*, shown as James Road on Plan 4189 (1912) (cancelled by a court order on October 1916). James Road lay between the present East 49th and East 51st Avenues. Origin of name unknown.

Raleigh Street was described in By-law 252 as being between present East 49th and East 57th Avenues, but since 1913 it has extended north to East 46th Avenue and the part south of East 54th has disappeared. Origin of name unknown.

RAND AVENUE. Named 1952, By-law 3325, in joint honour of William Rand, immediate past president of Monsato Chemical Company, which had a branch on the street, and the pioneer real estate firm Rand Brothers, as recommended in report of the Building and Town Planning Committee, 10 June 1952 (Vancouver City Council Minutes, v. 60, p. 343).

RAVINE STREET. First listed in the 1914 city directory but shown unnamed on Plan 2970 (1909). A descriptive name alluding to a deep ravine nearby.

RAYMUR AVENUE. Named by L.A. Hamilton after Captain James A. Raymur, who died 3 July 1882. He was a one-time owner of the Hastings Sawmill.

J.A. Raymur. From group photo of Commissioners and Pilots of Vancouver Pilotage District, 1879-1916. CVA Port. P. 189, N. 138.

A number of streets were named after the owners of the Vancouver Improvement Company: Alexander, Barnard, Campbell, Carl, Dunlevy, Dupont, Gore, Harris, Hawks, Heatley, Jackson, Keefer, Oppenheimer, Powell, Prior, and Raymur.

REBEKAH DRIVE. Private thoroughfare in Champlain Heights, named after the Rebekah Lodge, a female secret society, which helped fund a residential complex sponsored by the Three Links Care Society. Approved by the Street Naming Committee on 7 March 1983.

REDMOND AVENUE. See Clive Avenue.

REID STREET. Named on Plan 2197 (1909), and officially named in 1913 by South Vancouver By-law 251. Origin not verified but perhaps after Charles Gordon L. Reid (1862-1935), who is listed in South Vancouver Voters List in 1913 as owning property in DL 37.

REILLY AVENUE. Now East 20th Avenue between Lakewood Drive and Marshall Street. Named in 1913 by South Vancouver By-law 251. Plan 2573 (1910) shows E.B. Reilly (formerly E.B. Brough) as the owner, and she is so listed in South Vancouver Voters List, 1910-24. Elisa Blanche Reilly died at Gibson's Landing, British Columbia, in 1939, aged seventy-eight.

In 1949, Mrs. L.M. Watson asked that Reilly Street be renamed in view of the difficulties postal workers and others were having in locating this short street. The change was made in 1951, by By-law 3250.

REITH ROAD. Now East 55th Avenue between Main and Prince Edward Streets. Shown as Reith Street on Plan 1751 (1908) and Plan 2553 (1909). Changed to East 57th Avenue (now East 55th) by South Vancouver By-law 141, 1910. Origin of name unknown.

RENFREW STREET. Shown on Plan 100, a resurvey of Hastings Townsite, 1906, and named by the provincial government after the Renfrew Mining Division, named after Port Renfrew. The portion north of Dundas Street was designated Renfrew Street North by By-law 3195, 1950, although in use since 1924.

RHODES STREET. Named 1913, South Vancouver By-law 251. According to Thomas Winters, a police officer in South Vancouver from 1906 to 1923 who was interviewed by Major J.S. Matthews in 1938, it was named "after that South African fellow" (i.e., Cecil Rhodes [1835-1902], a British businessman prominent in South African diamond mining). See also Cecil Street.

RICE STREET. See Coleridge Street.

RICHARD STREET (Deleted). Shown on Plan 1377 (1907). Lay between Kootenay Street and Boundary Road. A survey name only, it was later part of East 17th Avenue, which disappeared in the replotting of Renfrew Heights.

Plan 1377 shows R.J. Scott, a co-owner of the property. Scott Street, three blocks north, was also named after him.

RICHARDS STREET (DL 540). See Balaclava Street.

RICHARDS STREET (DL 541). Named by L.A. Hamilton, after the Honourable Albert Norton Richards (1822-97), lieutenant-governor of British Columbia, 1876-81.

RICHELIEU AVENUE. Originally part of Montcalm Street and renamed in 1929 by By-law 2014, probably after the Richelieu River, which played a prominent part in the historical development of Quebec. Adjoining streets in Shaughnessy Heights bear names significant in Canadian history.

RIEL PLACE. Private thoroughfare in Champlain Heights named after Louis Riel (1844-85), Metis leader, founder of Manitoba, and a central figure in the two Northwest Rebellions. Name, submitted by Cartier Place development, approved by the Street Naming Committee on 8 November 1979.

RINGMORE STREET. Now East 29th Avenue between St. Catherines and Knight Streets. Shown in *Goad's Atlas*, Plate 95, as 29th Avenue East (late Ringmore). Unnamed on Plan 1546 (1907) and Plan 1983 (1909). Ringwood Street (now Ringwood Avenue) is the next street south. Origin of name unknown.

RINGWOOD AVENUE. Named as Ringwood Street by South Vancouver By-law 251, 1913. Unnamed on Plan 1983 (1909). A one-block-long avenue between East 29th and East 30th Avenues. See page 135. Origin of name unknown.

RIVER ROAD. See Marine Drive.

RIVERSIDE AVENUE (Deleted). Descriptive name given to a street on Plan 1826 (1908). Changed to East 66th Avenue (later East 64th) by South Vancouver By-law 141, 1910; lay between Victoria Drive and Nanaimo Street. Disappeared in the replotting for Fraserview.

RIVERWOOD WAY. A descriptive name, proposed by Block Brothers Realty Limited, for a private thoroughfare near the Fraser River. Approved by the Street Naming Committee on 28 July 1986 (Plan LF 11002).

ROBINSON AVENUE (DL 318). See Avery Avenue.

ROBINSON STREET (DL 394). See Slocan Street.

ROBSART AVENUE (Deleted). Named on Plan 6430 (1932), after Amy Robsart, a character in Sir Walter Scott's novel, *Kenilworth*. Absorbed by the Capilano Stadium, which opened in 1951.

ROBSON STREET. Named by L.A. Hamilton, after the Honourable John Robson (1824-92),

provincial secretary and minister of finance in 1883 and premier of British Columbia, 1889-92. Editor of the *British Columbian*, which he founded in New Westminster in 1861.

The Honourable John Robson. BCARS A-06540.

A handful of Vancouver streets are named after British Columbian Premiers: Davie, Robson, Semlin, Smithe, Turner, and Prior.

ROCKPOOLE DRIVE. Private thoroughfare shown on Plan LF 11099, approved May 1987. One of four streets within the Langara Springs development, its name is associated with the development's lagoon and waterfall. The other thoroughfares are Waterford, Waterleigh, and Whitespray.

RODGERS STREET. See Ruby Street.

ROGER STREET. See Toderick Street.

ROGERS STREET. Shown on Plan 786 (May 1899) and named July 1899, By-law 335, after the owner of the British Columbia Sugar Refining Company, Benjamin Tingley Rogers (1865-1918).

ROSE STREET. Unnamed on Plan 725 (1894) and first listed in the 1913 city directory. Shown in *Goad's Atlas*, 1913, Plate 80. Probably an arbitrary choice of name, either after the flower or a girl.

ROSEDALE DRIVE. Named 1952, By-law 3330, after the Rosedale Golf Club, Toronto.

ROSEMONT DRIVE. Shown on Plans 11415 and 11490 (1963) and first listed in the 1964 city directory. By-law 4770, 1970, extended it east to the present Champlain Crescent. Probably named after Rosemount Golf Course, Blairgowrie, Scotland.

On 21 November 1972 Vancouver City Council received a request from the Canadian Polish Congress to change Rosemont Drive to *Kopernik Drive* in honour of the 500th anniversary of the birth of Nikolaj Kopernik (1473-1543), famous Polish astronomer who is considered to be the father of modern astronomy. The request was not granted.

ROSENBERG ROAD. Now East 61st Avenue between Main and Borden Streets. Initially described but not named by South Vancouver Highway By-law 1, 1893, it lay between the present Main and Fraser Streets. South Vancouver By-law 65, 1903, and South Vancouver Highway By-law, 1905, named and extended Rosenberg Road between Fraser Street and the present Borden Street. Renamed 63rd Avenue by South Vancouver By-law 141, 1910. It is now East 61st Avenue.

Alfred Rosenberg, first listed in 1894 South Vancouver Voters List, carpenter. Born in Germany and emigrated to Canada in 1890 (Census of Canada, 1901).

ROSLYN STREET. See Ross Street.

ROSS ROAD. See Gladstone Street.

ROSS STREET. Named 1910, South Vancouver By-law 141. Origin of name unknown but perhaps after Rosshire, Scotland (many streets in the vicinity were given Scottish names), or after an unidentified person. Brattleboro Avenue, Halton Street, and Roslyn Street were renamed Ross by the same by-law.

Brattleboro Avenue. Lay halfway between East 31st and East 33rd Avenues. Likely named after Brattleboro, Vermont, in association with Bennington Avenue, both shown on Plan 1635 (1907).

Halton Street. Named on Plan 2735 (1910) and Plan 3958 (1912), it lay between present East 49th and East 51st Avenues, and East 54th and East 55th Avenues. Origin of name unknown.

Roslyn Street. Named on Plan 1369 (1907), it lay between present East 33rd and East 37th Avenues. Likely named after Roslyn, near Edinburgh, Scotland, because streets in Kensington subdivision, Plan 1369, bore British place names.

ROSSLAND STREET. Unnamed on Plan 4819 (1914) and named 1915, By-law 1230, after Rossland, British Columbia, as streets in Hastings Townsite were named after BC mining districts and cities.

ROUNDHOUSE MEWS. Private thoroughfare on the north side of False Creek named after its proximity to the Roundhouse Community Centre, housed in the former CPR roundhouse, built in 1888. Name approved by the Street Naming Committee on 3 December 1996.

ROWLING ROAD (Deleted). Named and described in South Vancouver Highway By-law, 1905, it lay between present Elliott and Kerr Streets. When South Vancouver By-law 141, 1910, changed the name to East 67th Avenue (later East 65th Avenue), the road extended to Boundary Road. With the development of Fraserview, the Fraserview Golf Course, and Champlain Heights, the street disappeared.

William Henry Rowling (1826-1905), a corporal in the Royal Engineers, received Crown grants for DL 330 and DL 258. He also bought other lots, giving him two and one-half miles of river frontage. In 1868 he moved to his farm, becoming the first settler in South Vancouver.

ROXBURGH CRESCENT. Shown on Plan 6011 (1921) and named by Point Grey By-law 232, 1924. Origin of the name, given by the CPR, is not known but it may have been after Roxburgh, a shire in Scotland.

ROYAL DRIVE. Private thoroughfare in Queen Elizabeth Park and named by the Parks Board at its 12 and 26 April 1940 meetings to commemorate the visit of King George VI and Queen Elizabeth to Vancouver in 1939. The name for the driveway around the park is not in general use.

RUBY STREET. Changed from Rodgers Street in 1929, By-law 2014, to remove duplication with Rogers Street in DL 182. Probably an arbitrary choice of name.

Rodgers Street. Shown with that spelling in city directories from 1917-30. City directories of 1916 and 1914 (first listing) show it as Rogers. Plans 2736 (1909) and 3262 (1910) show Rogers Street. South Vancouver Loan By-law 6, 1911, allocated $1,200 to Rogers Road. According to South Vancouver Voters Lists, Henry Rogers owned property in DL 36-51 in 1906 and 1907.

RUGBY AVENUE. See Argyle Street.

RUMBLE AVENUE. Named on Plan LF 4530, By-law 4770, 1970, after Rumble Street in Burnaby, which honours John Rumble, a Burnaby councillor 1903-8, 1910. It was a long curving street from Blake Street southeast to Rumble Street in Burnaby. In 1978, By-law 5195, Plan LE 3742B, shortened it to a one-block street west from Boundary Road to Matheson Crescent.

RUPERT STREET. Shown on Plan 100, a resurvey of Hastings Townsite, 1906, and named by the provincial government after the Rupert Mining District.

Rupert Street in the adjoining South Vancouver Municipality had a confusing history. In 1910, South Vancouver By-law 141 changed Collingwood Road (between Kingsway and East 29th Avenue) and Kilmarnock Street (between School Road and East 43rd Avenue) to Rupert Street.

Collingwood Road. Named by South Vancouver Highway By-law, 1905. It lay entirely within the bounds of DL 37, known as Collingwood District. The lots therein were advertised for sale 26 April 1891 in the *Daily News Advertiser.* Origin of name unknown.

Kilmarnock Street. Unnamed on Plans 1758, 1998, 2370, 2963, 3081, and 3324 (1907 to 1910) but named on Plan 4116 (1912). Origin of name unknown but probably after Kilmarnock, Scotland.

Rupert Street was gradually extended. In 1913 South Vancouver By-law 252 changed Rupert Street between Kingsway and the present East 42nd Avenue to *Churchill Street,* whose name is of unknown origin. The name lasted until 1927 when South Vancouver By-law 1388 changed it back to Rupert.

By-law 252, 1913, also changed the portion of Rupert Street between present East 49th and East 54th Avenues to *Richmond Street.* Only listed from 1917-24 in city directories, although shown on some maps as recently as 1945. Once again known as Rupert Street, although no by-law made the change. Origin of name unknown.

In 1956, By-law 3558 created the Cassiar-Rupert Diversion, allowing traffic to go onto Cassiar Street, but Rupert Street still exists as far north as East Hastings Street.

In 1960 the Rupert-Kerr Diversion was created to make a north-south highway between South East Marine Drive and the Second Narrows Bridge.

Gale Street (DL 337). *Vancouver Sun,* 31 May 1960, reported that Rupert Street between East 49th and East 54th Avenues would be changed to Gale Street after R. Harry Gale, who served four terms as mayor of Vancouver, 1918-21, and died in 1950. He owned the real estate firm of R.H. Gale and Company. However, the change was not made.

S

ST. ANDREWS ROAD. Now East 34th Avenue between Prince Edward and St. George Streets. Shown on Plan 1902 (1909), James W. Horne, the owner, named it after St. Andrew, the patron saint of Scotland. South Vancouver By-law 141, 1910, changed it to part of East 35th Avenue (now East 34th).

ST. CATHERINES STREET. It lay in two jurisdictions. The original street in Vancouver, named on Plan 899 (1903) and on Plan 1771 (1905), extended from East 6th to East 15th Avenues. Origin of name unknown.

In 1910, South Vancouver By-law 141 changed Martha, Third and Winchester Streets to St. Catherines.

Martha Street (DL 301). Shown on Plan 187 (1885), named by the owner, H.V. Edmonds, after his sister-in-law, Martha Wilhemina Webster (ca. 1840-1902). Now part of St. Catherines Street between East 15th and East King Edward Avenues.

Third Street. The third street east of the present Fraser Street on Plans 1390 and 1900 (1907), and now part of St. Catherines Street between East 45th and East 49th Avenues.

Winchester Street. Named on Plan 1211 (1906) and Plan 1369 (1907), likely after Winchester, England; the streets in Kensington Place subdivision bore British place names. Now part of St. Catherines Street between East 33rd and East 37th Avenues.

On 26 November 1945 a resolution of council extended St. Catherines Street between East 40th and East 41st Avenues.

ST. CLAIR PLACE. Unnamed on Plan 12453 (1966) but named 1967, By-law 4311. The Buscombe family owned the property. Origin of name unknown.

ST. DAVID'S ROAD. Now East 35th Avenue between Prince Edward and St. George Streets. Named on Plan 1902 (1909) by James W. Horne, the owner, after St. David, patron saint of Wales. South Vancouver By-law 141, 1910, changed it to part of East 36th Avenue (now East 35th).

ST. GEORGE STREET. Originally known as George Street in both Vancouver and South Vancouver.

In Vancouver, Plan 616 (1892) showed *Charlotte Street* from East 5th to East 15th Avenues. Probably named after Charlotte, queen consort of King George III. Renamed George Street in the resurvey of DL 264A, 1905, Plan 1771. Also shown as George on a 1902 map (Map 14171).

However, authorities soon realized that a George Street already existed in DL 182; George Street in DL 264A became known as St. George and was so listed in city directories from 1908 onwards.

In 1911, when DL 301 joined Vancouver, *Humphries Street* became part of St. George Street between East 15th and East King Edward Avenues. Shown on Plan 187 (1885) and named by the owner, H.V. Edmonds, after his son, William Humphries Edmonds (1869-1912), registrar of titles in Kamloops from 1899 to 1912.

In the adjoining municipality, South Vancouver By-law 141, 1910, named George Street and renamed Godfrey Road, St. Patrick's Road, Draper Street, and Lawson Road.

Godfrey Road. Named by South Vancouver By-law 65, 1903, and extended by South Vancouver Highway By-law, 1905. According to an undated clipping in Vancouver City Archives, "George Godfrey cut a narrow trail to his lone claim beside the fresh water stream near the present 30th Avenue and it became Godfrey Road." Shown on Plans 2149, 2462, and 3154, 1909 and 1910, between East 25th and East 31st Avenues. George Godfrey was listed in South Vancouver Voters Lists, 1894-1901.

St. Patrick's Road (DL 636). Named by the owner, J.W. Horne, after Patrick, patron saint of Ireland. Shown on Plan 1902 (1909) between present East 34th and East 36th Avenues.

Draper Street/Road. First named on Plan 1521 (1907), with J.H. Draper, one of the owners. It

eventually lay between the present East 41st and East 47th Avenues. James Harrington Draper (1845-1920) settled as a rancher at Hatzic in 1889 and came to South Vancouver in 1906, where he died on 14 January 1920.

Lawson Road (DL 313). Named on Plan 3021 (1909), probably after James W. Lawson, who owned DL 313 in 1888. A rancher and farmer, he served as the second reeve of the Municipality of South Vancouver in 1894. The road lay between the present East 63rd Avenue and South East Marine Drive.

Usona Avenue. It lay between the present East 50th and East 51st Avenues. It also became part of George Street, as shown in *Goad's Atlas*, 1913, Plate 102. Origin of this survey name, shown on Plan 2106 (1909), unknown.

In 1930, By-law 2082 changed George Street between East King Edward Avenue and Kent Avenue to part of St. George Street.

ST. GEORGE'S ROAD. Now East 36th Avenue between Prince Edward and St. George Streets. Shown on Plan 1902 (1909) and named by the owner, James W. Horne, after St. George, patron saint of England. South Vancouver By-law 141, 1910, changed it to part of East 37th Avenue (now East 36th Avenue).

ST. JOHN'S ROAD. Now East 37th Avenue between Prince Edward and St. George Streets. Shown on Plan 1902 (1909), it was named by the owner, James W. Horne, after St. John. South Vancouver By-law 141, 1910, changed it to part of East 38th Avenue (now East 37th Avenue).

ST. LAWRENCE STREET. Named after the St. Lawrence River in 1929, By-law 2014, when *Montcalm Street* (DL 393) was renamed. Unnamed on Plan 1388 (1907) but named 1913, South Vancouver By-law 251, after the Marquis de Montcalm (1712-59), commander of the French forces during the Seven Years War and until his death on the Plains of Abraham, Quebec, in 1759.

ST. MARGARET'S STREET. Shown on Plan 2737 (1909) as St. Margaret's Avenue, it lay between the present East 41st and East 45th Avenues. Became St. Margaret's Street in 1910 by South Vancouver By-law 141. Probably after St. Margaret.

In 1929, By-law 2014 changed Margate Street to St. Margaret's Street between the present East 34th and East 37th Avenues.

Margate Street. Unnamed on Plan 2911 (1910) but named by South Vancouver By-law 251, 1913, probably after Margate, Kent, England.

ST. PATRICK'S ROAD. See St. George.

ST. PAUL'S ROAD. Now East 38th Avenue between Prince Edward Street and the western boundary of Mountain View Cemetery. Shown on Plan 1902 (1909) and named by the owner, James W. Horne, after St. Paul. South Vancouver By-law 141, 1910, changed it to part of East 39th Avenue (now East 38th Avenue).

ST. ROCH AVENUE (Proposed). See Maquinna Drive.

SADDLE LANE. Private thoroughfare in Champlain Heights. Name approved by the Street Naming Committee on 27 May 1983. United Properties Limited called its project Huntingwood and chose names to fit the theme of hunting.

SAGE ROAD. Now East 26th Avenue between St. George and Fraser Streets. Named by South Vancouver By-law 65, 1903, and changed to East 26th Avenue in 1910 by South Vancouver By-law 141.

Mrs. Eliza Sage listed in 1903 South Vancouver Voters List as owning property in DL 391-2; last shown in 1939 city directory.

SALAL DRIVE. Named 1996, By-law 7626, Plan LF 11684, after the salal shrub, often found under arbutus trees.

SALERNO STREET. Private thoroughfare in the Canadian Forces Base in DL 176, first listed in the 1958 city directory. The name commemorates Salerno, Italy, where an Allied assault took place in the autumn of 1943, during the Second World War.

SALISBURY AVENUE (DL 540). See Belmont Avenue.

SALISH DRIVE. Named by By-law 4287, 1967, after the Coast Salish language group, to which the Musqueam Band belongs. Originally named Musqueam Drive, By-law 4266, 1966. Postal authorities notified the city that a Musqueam Drive already existed, so By-law 4266 was repealed and the new street renamed Salish.

SALMON COURT. See Sotao Avenue.

SALSBURY DRIVE. Named after William Ferriman Salsbury (1847-1938), who arrived in British Columbia on the first overland train. Treasurer for the CPR in Vancouver, where he served as an alderman in 1893 and 1894.

SASAMAT PLACE. Shown on Plan 6258 (1930) but not listed in city directory until 1954. Named after the adjacent Sasamat Street.

SASAMAT STREET. Named by Point Grey By-law 17, 1912, although the name had been bestowed by the provincial government in 1887, Plan 229. According to Akrigg (1997), it may have been the Halkomelem name of an early First Nations low-class village on the site of Ioco, near Port Moody. Sasamat can be translated as "lazy people," but it is not known why the inhabitants were so named.

SASKATCHEWAN AVENUE. Now West 72nd Avenue between Granville and Selkirk Streets. Named on Plan 1749 (1908) as one of the streets in Eburne Townsite; became part of West 72nd Avenue by Point Grey By-law 17, 1914. Probably named after the newly named province of Saskatchewan, as was the adjoining Alberta Street.

SAWCUT. A street in False Creek development, named 1976, By-law 5010 (Plan LF 7386), to recall the sawmills along False Creek in its industrial era.

SAWYERS LANE. Named 1976, By-law 5010 (Plan LF 7386), to recall the sawyers working in the sawmills along False Creek.

SCALES PLACE. Named 1988, By-law 6436, after John Henry Scales (1854-1948), whose father, John Scales, Royal Engineer, first settled in Vancouver in 1869.

SCANTLINGS. Named 1976, by By-law 5010, Plan LF 7386, after the scantlings, or small beams and pieces of wood, produced in lumber mills along False Creek.

SCARBORO AVENUE. Named 1952, by By-law 3330, after the Scarboro Golf and Country Club near Toronto.

SCHOOL AVENUE. Surveyed 1888, Plan 243, and named *Arbutus Lane* by the owner, George Wales. It lay between the present College and Harold Streets. South Vancouver Highway By-law, 1905, renamed it School Road, which gradually extended to Tyne Street. Probably so named because of its proximity to East Vancouver School (now Sir Guy Carleton), built in 1896-7. School Road became School Avenue in 1950, By-law 3195.

SCHOOL GREEN. Named 1976, By-law 5010, Plan LF 7386, because of its location near the planned False Creek elementary school.

SCOTIA STREET. Unnamed on Plan 197 (1885) and named by the owner, Dr. I.W. Powell, after Nova Scotia.

In 1885, Israel Powell named streets in District Lot 200A after Canadian provinces: Columbia, Manitoba, Ontario, Quebec, Scotia, Brunswick, and Prince Edward. Alberta Street was added in 1907. Saskatchewan Avenue in Eburne Townsite has disappeared.

SCOTT STREET. See Fraser Street.

SCOTT STREET. (Deleted). Named on Plan 1377 (1907), after the co-owner, R.J. Scott, as was nearby Richard Street, shown on the same plan. A survey name only, it became part of East 14th Avenue between Kootenay Street and Boundary Road, now absorbed by the Renfrew Heights development.

SEABREEZE WALK. The name is evocative of sea breezes coming in from English Bay. Named 1993, By-law 7251.

SEACOME ROAD. See Prince Edward Street.

SEAFORTH DRIVE. Named on 23 March 1948 (Vancouver City Council Minutes, v. 54, p. 259), after the Vancouver city regiment, the Seaforth Highlanders (formed in 1911), which participated in both world wars, winning many battle honours.

SEAGULL PLACE. One of the nine private thoroughfares in Enclaves 8, 9, and 10, Champlain Heights, bearing bird names submitted by Matheson Heights Co-operative and approved by the Street Naming Committee on 25 March 1981.

SEAPORT ROAD. An unofficial name listed in the city directory from 1938 to 1943 inclusive for a street that lay east from the northern foot of Victoria Drive. The city surveyor has no record of this name. Likely a name assigned by the post office for mail delivery to Seaport Agencies Limited, insurance agents connected with British Empire Dock, owned by Empire Dock Limited. President of both firms was Charles F. Millar.

SEATON STREET. See Hastings Street.

SEIGNIORY DRIVE (Deleted). Named 1952, By-law 3330. Shown on Plan 8514 (1954), it lay northeast of Lynbrook Drive to East 54th Avenue, west of Vivian Drive. When this portion of Fraserview was replotted, Seigniory Drive disappeared. Named after the Seigniory Golf Club on the Ottawa River at Montebello, Quebec.

SELBY STREET. See Woodland Drive.

SELKIRK AVENUE. See Fleming Street.

SELKIRK STREET. Shown as Selkirk Avenue on Plan 4502 (1913) and named by the CPR after Thomas Douglas, 5th Earl of Selkirk, who founded the Red River settlement in 1812.

Point Grey By-law 17, 1912, extended Selkirk Street from King Edward Avenue to West 27th Avenue. Point Grey By-law 232, 1924, changed Selkirk Avenue in Shaughnessy Heights to Selkirk Street. The last extension to Selkirk was in 1984, By-law 5741, from West 54th to West 55th Avenues.

Plan of Eburne Townsite (Plan 1749 [1908]) showed Fifth Street between West 73rd and West 70th Avenues, later extended to Park Drive. Became Selkirk Street by Point Grey By-law 17, 1914.

SEMANA CRESCENT. In Musqueam Park subdivision, leased from the Musqueam Band, named 1966, By-law 4266, after a Halkomelem word meaning "far up the river." It was the name of an old settlement (CVA, Vancouver City Clerk, Series 29 [loc. MCR 30-181, p. 502]). The name originally suggested by the city was "Casper Crescent," after well-known American golfer, William Earl "Billy" Casper, born 1931, because Musqueam Park subdivision abuts Shaughnessy Golf Course.

SEMLIN DRIVE. Named on Plan 1771, a resurvey of DL 264A (1906), after Charles Augustus

Semlin (1836-1927), premier of British Columbia, 1898-1900, who represented the Yale constituency.

SENLAC STREET. Unnamed on Plan 2426 (1909) but named 1913, South Vancouver By-law 251. Senlac Hill is near the site of the Battle of Hastings, 1066. Harold and Wessex Streets also relate to this battle.

SENNOK CRESCENT. In Musqueam Park subdivision, leased from the Musqueam Band, named 1966, By-law 4266. Sennok, meaning "entering inland," was the name of an old settlement (CVA, Vancouver City Clerk, Series 29 [loc. MCR 30-181, p. 502]). Some commercial maps spell the name incorrectly as Sennock Drive. The name originally suggested by the city was *Lema Crescent*, after well-known American golfer, Anthony David "Tony" Lema (1934-66), because Musqueam Park subdivision abuts Shaughnessy Golf Course.

SEYMOUR STREET. Named after Frederick Seymour, governor of the Crown Colony of British Columbia, 1864-9.

SHANGHAI ALLEY. First listed in the 1906 city directory and shown in *Goad's Atlas*, Plate 14. In the heart of Vancouver's Chinatown, it was named after Shanghai, China.

In December 1995, the alley was extended westward at a right angle from the end of Shanghai Alley to meet Taylor Street (Plan LF 11675), in spite of the objections of the Shanghai Alley Residents' Association (*Vancouver Sun*, 20 May 1995). The name of the extension was approved by the Street Naming Committee on 24 October 1995.

> Despite the early Asian presence here, there are only three Vancouver streets with names of Asian derivation: Canton, Shanghai, and Sotao.

SHANNON ROAD. Now West 57th Avenue from Cambie Street west to its intersection with South West Marine Drive. First mentioned in Point Grey By-law 1, 1910, which allocated $17,500 for clearing and grading. Point Grey By-law 33, 1911, established and defined Shannon Road. Point Grey By-law 17, 1912, changed it to West 57th Avenue.

William Shannon (1839?-1928) was the owner of DL 325A, Plan 711 (1893), in which Shannon

Road partially lay. A pioneer in British Columbia, he explored the Big Bend country before settling in Vancouver in 1887, where he was involved in the real estate and commission business.

SHAUGHNESSY STREET. Unnamed on Plan 3038 (1910) but named by Point Grey By-law 17, 1914, after Thomas George Shaughnessy, first Baron Shaughnessy (1853-1923), president of the CPR, 1898-1918.

SHAWNEE PLACE. First listed in 1964 city directory. Surveyed in 1963, Plan 11490. Origin of this name not verified but probably after the Shawnee people.

SHERBROOKE STREET. Named on Plan 1369 (1907), it lay between the present East 33rd and East 37th Avenues in Kensington Place subdivision, the streets of which bore English and Scottish place names. Plan 3040 (1910) shows *Park Road* between East 37th and East 41st Avenues. Origin of name unknown.

SHORE STREET. See Georgia Street.

SHOREPINE WALK. Private thoroughfare on south side of False Creek. A descriptive name approved by the Street Naming Committee on 15 August 1979.

SHORT STREET (DL 200). See Fleming Street.

SHORT STREET (DL 526, Block 187). See Greer Avenue.

SIDNEY STREET. Origin of name unknown. Named 1913, South Vancouver By-law 251. Unnamed on Plan 1552 (1907) and Plan 2707 (1910). South Vancouver Board of Works report, 4 July 1913, shows that a plank sidewalk was to be laid on Sydney [sic] Street between 27th and 29th Avenues.

SI-LU DRIVE. Private thoroughfare on Musqueam Band Reserve No. 2. According to Glen Guerin, housing officer, Musqueam Band, who submitted the name to the Street Naming Committee on 25 March 1985, "Si-lu is how you would say grandparents in our language. Some of our immediate ancestors are buried in a small cemetery adjacent to this subdivision."

SIMON AVENUE (Deleted). Shown on Plan LF 4530, attached to By-law 4770, 1970. A short street going east to Boundary Road, lying halfway between Victory and Arbor Streets in Burnaby. In 1978, By-law 5195 deleted the street from the official street name map.

Origin of name unknown but perhaps named in association with the adjacent Peter and Paul Avenues.

SIMPSON AVENUE. Probably named after John Simpson (1847-1915), who owned property in DL 540, Block 128. Listed in 1901 directory at Beach Avenue, where Simpson Brothers (his nephews, William and Zachariah) were boat builders. By 1910 he retired to Point Grey, where he died 7 January 1915, aged sixty-eight. Named by Point Grey By-law 17, 1912, which also renamed *Ash Street*, an arbitrary choice of name, shown on Plan 229 (1887).

SITKA SQUARE. Named 1976, By-law 5010 (Plan LF 7386), after the Sitka spruce sawn in the mills along False Creek and used in aircraft construction during the Second World War.

SKANA DRIVE. Private thoroughfare in Champlain Heights, named after one of the killer whales at the Vancouver Aquarium ("Skana" is the Haida word for killer whale). Submitted by the Alexander Laidlaw Cooperative, the name was approved by the Street Naming Committee on 25 March 1981. See also Hyack and Tuaq Drives.

SKEENA STREET. Named in 1950 when By-law 3195 renamed Cariboo Street (except southwest from East 29th Avenue to Moscrop Street) to remove duplication with Cariboo Road in Burnaby. This same by-law designated the part of Skeena north of Dundas Street Skeena Street North.

The name retains the pattern, established in 1906, of mining district names.

SKIPPER PLACE. Private thoroughfare; name approved by the Street Naming Committee on 3 June 1985. The Riverside Landing Housing Cooperative suggested names based on a nautical theme, hence Skipper.

SLOCAN STREET. Named on Plan 100, a resurvey of Hastings Townsite, 1906, after the Slocan Mining District. Slocan is an Okanagan First Nations word meaning "pierce, strike on the head, in reference to the First Nations practice of spearing or harpooning the salmon" (Akrigg 1997).

In South Vancouver, Ferguson Road and Robinson Street became part of Slocan Street in 1910 and 1929, respectively.

Ferguson Road. Named by South Vancouver Highway By-law, 1905, after J.F. and J.O. Ferguson, preemptors of DL 52 in 1889, as shown on a map in McDonald (1992, 23). In 1910 South Vancouver By-law 141 changed it to Slocan Street between the present East 29th Avenue and Kingsway.

Robinson Street. Named 1913, South Vancouver By-law 251. Vancouver city directory, 1913, shows James Robinson, labourer for the CPR, living at East 35th Avenue on the corner of Robinson Street and, later, at 5026 Robinson. He is last listed in 1941 city directory.

Shortly after it was named, a petition was presented to South Vancouver Board of Works, 3 March 1914, requesting that Robinson and Clarendon Streets be changed to Slocan. However, no action was taken until 1929, when By-law 2028 changed Robinson Street to Slocan Street between East 35th and East 39th Avenues.

By-law 3045, 1948, named Slocan Street between Kingsway and East 34th Avenue. In 1950, By-law 3195 renamed the part north of Dundas Street as Slocan Street North, although this form had been in use much earlier.

SMITH STREET (DL 743). See Glengyle Street.

SMITHE STREET. Named by L.A. Hamilton in 1886, after William Smithe (1842-87), then premier of British Columbia and who served as such until his death in 1887. His name often spelt incorrectly as Smythe. Richard Allen (ca. 1982) asserts that Smythe is the correct form. However, William Smithe is the signature shown on the documents and surveys he signed.

SOMERSET CRESCENT. Named by Point Grey By-law 232, 1924, probably after Somerset, England. Reconfirmed by Point Grey By-law 483, 1926. Shown on Plan 5552 (1926).

SOMERVILLE STREET. Shown on Plan 1211 (1906) between East 33rd and East 35th Avenues, and on Plan 1369 (1907) between East 33rd and East 37th Avenues. Origin of name unknown but probably an English name, as all names in the Kensington subdivision (Plan 1369) are British.

SOPHIA STREET. Shown as Sophy Street on Plan 187 (1885) and named by the owner of DL

301, H.V. Edmonds, after his sister, Sophia G. Edmonds. Listed as Sophie in 1894 and 1895 city directories, but by 1898 shown as Sophia.

In 1910, South Vancouver By-law 141 changed Welton, Newton, and Armstrong Streets and Grimmett Avenue to Sophia Street.

Welton Street. Named by South Vancouver Highway By-law, 1905, after the owner, James Welton Horne (1854-1922), a pioneer Vancouver realtor who served on Vancouver City Council, 1888-90; chaired the Parks Board, 1888-94; and was an MLA, 1890-4. First named on Plan 960 (1904), it lay between present East King Edward and East 28th Avenues.

Newton Street. Between East 28th and East 29th Avenues, named on Plan 1329 (1907). Origin of name unknown.

Armstrong Street. Between present East 36th and East 41st Avenues, and between East 43rd and East 51st Avenues. Named on Plans 1634, 1748, 2101, and 2583 (1907-9). John Armstrong was listed as owner on Plan 1634. John Charles Armstrong is listed in the 1908 Provincial Voters List as a paperhanger living on Horne Road (now East 28th Avenue).

Grimmett Avenue. Between East 63rd Avenue and South East Marine Drive, it was unofficially named after a nearby property owner, John Fletcher

Grimmett (1861-1938). Plan 4013 (1910) lists him as one of the owners, but the street is called Sophia.

SOTAO AVENUE. Private thoroughfare named by the developer and approved by the Street Naming Committee in 1996. Shown on Plan LF 11683 (1996). It is immediately south of South East Marine Drive and west of Jellicoe Street. Previously named as *Salmon Court*, Plan LF 11480 (1992).

SOUTH SHORE CRESCENT. Descriptive name for a private thoroughfare, proposed by Block Brothers Realty Limited and approved by the Street Naming Committee on 28 July 1986 (Plan LF 11002).

SOUTH VIEW ROAD (Deleted). Shown in *Goad's Atlas*, Plates 108 and 109. Named on Plans 1733, 2061, 2429, 3025, 3505, and 3451 (1908-11). A descriptive name changed in 1910 by South Vancouver By-law 141 to East 66th Avenue (later East 64th Avenue). It lay in broken lengths between Vivian and Aberdeen Streets. Deleted with the Fraserview and Champlain Heights developments.

SOUTHERN STREET. Named unimaginatively after its position in Parcel A, DL 2037, Plan 5703. It originally lay between Station and Main (Plan

Photo of Mrs. J.F. Grimmett, her son Jack, and daughter Grace, standing on old 66th Ave., now 64th, about 100 yards east of Main St. Behind them is their own large white residence, standing out in the clearing littered with stumps, roots, and boulders. Mr. Grimmett owned all this property. CVA Str. P. 119, N. 272.

Streets (By-law 1556, 1922) but was shortened to its present length between Station and Western Streets in 1926 by By-law 1803. First listed in 1927 directory.

SOUTHLANDS PLACE. Named 1961, By-law 3910, after *Southlands* (the home of W.H. Malkin, mayor of Vancouver, 1929-30), which occupied the large property subdivided in 1960, Plan 10621. The name described the location on the south slope.

SOUTHSIDE DRIVE. On the south side of South East Marine Drive, named 1984, By-law 5845.

SPARBROOK CRESCENT. Named 1978, By-law 5195, Plan LE 3742B. Origin of name unknown.

SPARROW PLACE. One of nine private thoroughfares in Enclaves 8, 9, and 10, Champlain Heights, bearing bird names submitted by Matheson Heights Cooperative and approved by the Street Naming Committee on 25 March 1981.

SPENCER STREET. Named 1913, South Vancouver By-law 251, after Spencer Robinson, in 1909 a councillor for Ward I. A chartered accountant, he died on 10 November 1953, aged seventy-nine.

In the 1914 city directory **Brittany Street** listed, but the 1916 directory shows "Brittany (Collingwood) now called Spencer." Origin of name unknown.

SPINNAKER PLACE. Private thoroughfare in Champlain Heights, named by United Properties, developers of the Compass Point project, which used nautical terms. A spinnaker is a three-cornered sail. Name approved by the Street Naming Committee on 27 May 1983.

SPRINGRIDGE AVENUE. Now East 23rd Avenue between Victoria Drive and Sidney Street. Surveyed in 1907, Plan 1552, and mentioned in South Vancouver Road Loan By-law 6, 1911, when $450 was allocated to 23rd Avenue (Springridge) from Victoria Drive to Sidney Street. Listed in the index to Volume 2 of *Goad's Atlas*, 1913, as Johnson Road (now East 23rd Avenue). See also Johnson Road (DL 743).

Changed to East 23rd Avenue in 1910 by South Vancouver By-law 141. Origin of name unknown.

SPRINGTREE DRIVE. Private thoroughfare in Arbutus Village; name, suggested by Narod Developments Limited and approved by the Street

Naming Committee on 21 June 1978. Origin of name unknown.

SPRUCE STREET. Officially registered on Plan 590 (1891) but named on an 1887 map (Map 14160) by L.A. Hamilton, who chose tree names.

SPYGLASS PLACE. Named 1984, By-law 5756, Plan 10627. Imperial Ventures Limited, 28 February 1984, submitted the name to the Street Naming Committee for its condominium development at False Creek. See also Commodore Road, Starboard Square, and Wheelhouse Square.

STADIUM ROAD, EAST. See Griffiths Way.

STADIUM ROAD, WEST. See Terry Fox Way.

STAINSBURY AVENUE (DL 195 Blocks 19-20). See Lakewood Drive.

STAINSBURY AVENUE (DL 195, Blocks 6, 7 and 8). Named by the owner, Richard Frost (1840-1912), postmaster at Epworth Post Office from 1903-9, after his wife, née Elizabeth Stainsby. Shown on Plan 1976 (1909).

The name appeared as Stainsbury in South Vancouver By-law 141, 1910, when it was changed to East 20th Avenue. However, this part of East 20th Avenue, lying at quite an angle and joining East 21st Avenue to the east, soon reverted to its original name.

Another Stainsbury Avenue in DL 195 was renamed Lakewood Drive by the same by-law in 1910.

Both avenues are shown in *Goad's Atlas*, Plate 92.

STAMFORD STREET. Unnamed on Plan 2639 (1910) but named in 1913 by South Vancouver By-law 251 in association with Harold, Senlac, Wessex, and the Battle of Hastings (1066). Harold II, killed at this battle, was making a forced march from Yorkshire, where he had defeated his brother in the battle of Stamford Springs.

STAMPS LANDING. Named by By-law 5010, 1976, Plan LF 7386, after the pioneer lumberman, Edward Stamp (1814-72), who built a mill on Burrard Inlet (later Hastings Mill) and began production in 1867.

STANLEY PARK DRIVE. Private thoroughfare in Stanley Park, federal property leased to the city

(Plan LF 11508 [1992]). Stanley Park Drive, one of the oldest drives in the city, was designated so that postal service could be provided to businesses in the park. An 1891 pamphlet, *Vancouver City: Its Wonderful History and Future Prospects* (CVA pamphlet 1891-10), states: "A carriage drive extends around the park and along the water's edge 9 miles in length."

STARBOARD SQUARE. Originally called Wheelhouse Square and renamed on 9 June 1993, Plan LF 11546, when Wheelhouse Square was relocated. The name retains the nautical flavour of Spyglass Place and Commodore Road.

STATION STREET. Named after its location in front of the Great Northern and Canadian National Railways passenger stations in 1926. By-law 1556 renamed it Park Lane. By-law 1803, 1926, repealed By-law 1556 because of a resurvey. The street lay between Prior Street and Terminal Avenue, with a short arm extending west to Main Street on the northern boundary of Thornton Park. In 1992 By-law 7001, Plan LF 11492, renamed this short arm National Avenue.

Park Lane. A short street between Prior Street and the north shore of False Creek, parallel to and east of Main Street. Vancouver Board of Works minutes, 9 February 1887, approved the calling of tenders to grub (i.e., clear) part of Park Avenue. It is shown in *Goad's Atlas, 1893*, Plate 12. According to J.S. Matthews, Park Lane was a rather fashionable residential district near a beautiful beach on False Creek, hence Park Lane (à la Park Lane in Mayfair, London).

STAULO CRESCENT. Named 1976, By-law 5010, Plan LF 7356. Extended in 1996 when By-law 7590, Plan LF 11682, changed West 51st Avenue between Staulo Crescent and Salish Drive to Staulo Crescent. Staulo means "small river" (letter from Wanona Scott, executive secretary, Musqueam Band, 17 July 1996).

STAUTLO AVENUE. Named 1976, By-law 5010, Plan LF 7356. Stautlo means "slough" (letter from Wanona Scott, executive secretary, Musqueam Band, 17 July 1996).

STEPHENS STREET. So named on Plan 774 (1898); should have been called Stephen Street because it was named after George Stephen, 1st Baron Mount Stephen, (1829-1921), first president of the CPR.

STEPHENS ROAD. Now East 46th Avenue between Elliott and Vivian Streets. Origin of this unofficial name, shown on Plan 2484 (1910), unknown.

STEWART ROAD. See Arbutus Street.

STEWART STREET. Named after William James Stewart (1863-1925), the first chief hydrographic surveyor for Canada. In 1891 he resurveyed Burrard Inlet and installed the first Pacific tide gauges on the CPR wharf. The street lies on land belonging to the Vancouver Port Corporation.

STEWART STREET. See Fleming Street.

STIKINE PLACE. Named 1984, By-law 5741, after the Stikine River, as suggested by the developer, Moodie Consultants. Stikine is a Tlingit word meaning "the river" (in the sense of "the great river") (Akrigg 1997).

STIRLING ROAD (DL 194, between Blocks 8 and 9). See Balaclava Street.

STIRLING STREET (DL 194, within Block 8). See Prescott Street.

STIRLING STREET. Shown as Stirling Road on Plan 2202 (1909), DL 727, it lay between present East 54th and East 59th Avenues. Named after Archibald William Stirling, MA, BCL (Bachelor of Civil Law), who matriculated from Lincoln College, Oxford, in 1875, aged eighteen, and began to practise as a solicitor in 1893 with Maddison, Stirling, Humm and Davies, the law firm entrusted with the estate of T.W. Duff, former owner of DL 727, shown in South Vancouver Voters List, 1910. In 1910, South Vancouver By-law 141 changed it to Stirling Street and also renamed Armytage Road between East 65th and East 67th Avenues.

Armytage Road. Named on Plan 2415 (1909), probably after Henry Dodson Green-Armytage (1848-1938), first listed in 1908 South Vancouver Voters List. Previously postmaster at Coutlee, British Columbia, 1898-1907, as well as a merchant and rancher there. Later moved to North Vancouver, where he was president of the wholesale dry goods firm, McKay, Smith and Blair, until 1930.

When Fraserview was replotted in the early 1950s, most of Stirling Street disappeared. In 1961, By-law 3937 extended the street between East 41st and East 42nd Avenues.

STOVELL ROAD. Now East 58th Avenue between Ontario and Quebec Streets. South Vancouver By-law 6, 1911, allocated $2,600 to East 60th Avenue (including Stovell Road). Plan 2452 (1909) shows Emily Augusta Stovell (Mrs. John Stovell) as the owner of Block 3, DL 656. An unofficial name.

STRATHCONA ROAD. Now East 22nd Avenue between Nanaimo Street and Boundary Road. Named on Plans 1381, 1503, 1745, and 1769, all of which were surveyed in 1907. When Hastings Townsite joined Vancouver in 1911, it became East 22nd Avenue.

Probably named after Donald A. Smith, Lord Strathcona and Mount Royal (1820-1914), one of the men chiefly responsible for the building of the CPR.

STRAUSS DRIVE. Private thoroughfare in Champlain Heights, named after the Strauss family of composers, by Community Builders, developers of Ashleigh Heights, and approved by the Street Naming Committee on 25 March 1981.

STRETCH ROAD. See Durward Avenue.

STUART STREET. See Beaver Street.

STUDD ROAD. See Lanark Street.

SUFFOLK STREET. See Beatrice Street.

SUMMIT AVENUE. Now East 28th Avenue between Ontario and Main Streets. A survey name only. Shown on Plan 632 (1890), probably descriptive of its location near the summit of a small hill northeast of Little Mountain.

SWALLOW PLACE. One of nine private thoroughfares in Enclaves 8, 9, and 10, Champlain Heights, bearing bird names submitted by Matheson Heights Cooperative and approved by the Street Naming Committee on 25 March 1981.

SWANSACRE. Private thoroughfare in Champlain Heights, named by the Kinross Creek Housing Cooperative after a street so named in the Scottish town of Kinross. Approved by the Street Naming Committee on 8 July 1982.

SWEET ROAD (Deleted). Named on Plan 2415 (1909) and unnamed on Plan 2564 (1910). South Vancouver By-law 141, 1910, changed the road to East 69th Avenue (later East 67th Avenue) between Gladstone and Nanaimo Streets. Since absorbed by the Fraserview development.

Probably named after John Hales Sweet, b. 1878. A graduate of the University of New Brunswick, 1899, and called to the bar in 1902, he joined the firm of Bodwell and Duff in Victoria and later moved to Vancouver, where he was in a partnership with Lambert Bond from 1907 to 1916. After that he is listed as "on active service."

T

TABER ROAD. Now West 36th Avenue between Crown and Dunbar Streets. Named on Plan 2439 (1909). The map accompanying Point Grey By-law 17, 1912, shows Taber Road between Crown and Dunbar Streets changed to West 36th Avenue. Origin of name unknown.

TALISMAN AVENUE. Shown on Plan 6430 (1932) and Plan 6539 (1936) and first listed in the 1942 city directory. According to S.M. Montgomery, secretary of the board of works, William B. Young, who was with the City Engineering Department, took the name from Sir Walter Scott's novel, *The Talisman.*

TALON SQUARE. Private thoroughfare in Champlain Heights, first listed in 1979 city directory. Named after Jean Baptiste Talon (1625-94), first intendant of justice and finance in the colony of New France, 1665-72.

TAMARIND DRIVE. Private thoroughfare in Champlain Heights, first listed in 1979 city directory. Named after the large tree *Tamarindus indica*, derived from an Arabic word *tamr-hindi* (i.e., the date of India).

TAMATH CRESCENT. In Musqueam Park subdivision, leased from the Musqueam Band, named

1966, By-law 4266. Tamath means "painted" (CVA, Vancouver City Clerk, Series 29 [loc. MCR 30-181, p. 502]). The city originally suggested the name *Locke Crescent*, after the well-known South African golfer, Arthur D'Arcy "Bobby" Locke (1917-84) because Musqueam Park subdivision abuts Shaughnessy Golf Course.

TANNER STREET (DL 36 and 51). Probably named after Charles Marsh Tanner (1866-1933), who owned several blocks in DL 36 and 51, according to plans 1570 and 1577 (1907). Born in England, he was a tea merchant.

Goad's Atlas, Plate 97, 1913, shows **Bell Road**, but the name was not adopted. Likely named after Henry Allyrdice Bell (1840-1925), who first owned property in DL 52 in 1906. He came to Vancouver in 1885 and was on the first Vancouver Voters List, 1886. He built the Dun-Miller block

House built by Mr. Tanner, at 2634 Tanner Street. CVA 192-6.

(the first one built after the fire of 1886) as well as the Fairfield and McKinnon blocks. In 1908 he served as a councillor in South Vancouver, where he built a fine home.

TANTALUS LANE. Private thoroughfare, named 1972, By-law 4636. The United Cooperative Housing Society named it after the Tantalus Range. Early mountaineers, tantalized by the views of the range across the Squamish River, named it after Tantalus, a king in Greek mythology.

TATTENHALL ROAD. Changed to East 36th Avenue (now East 35th Avenue), between Gladstone and Nanaimo Streets, in 1910 by South Vancouver By-law 141. Shown on a 1910 map of South Vancouver (Map 14272) as Tettenhall. Tattenhall is a town southeast of Chester, England. An item in *B.C. Saturday Sunset*, 22 July 1911, page 7, states: "A pleasant reception was held on Wednesday evening last week at Mrs. E.E. Bell's home, Tetenhall [sic] Road, South Vancouver."

TAUNTON STREET. Named 1913, South Vancouver By-law 251. Unnamed on Plan 2220 (1909). Origin unknown, but probably after Taunton, England.

TAYLOR ROAD. See Welwyn.

TAYLOR ROAD (DL 648-649). Now East 48th Avenue between Ontario and Fraser Streets. Changed in 1910 to East 50th Avenue (now East 48th Avenue) by South Vancouver By-law 141. Plan 1748 (1907) named it Falconer Road and Plans 2696 and 2946 (1910) named it Taylor Road. It lay between Ontario and Prince Edward Streets.

South Vancouver Council minutes, 17 January 1910, authorized the opening of the road, known as Taylor Road, from present Fraser Street to present St. George Street.

Among the owners on Plan 1748 was William Taylor, not yet identified.

Residence and estate of H.A. Bell. CVA Pan N. 26.

TAYLOR ROAD (DL 326A). Now East 60th Avenue between Prince Edward and Fraser Streets. Shown on a 1910 map of South Vancouver (Map 14272) as Taylor Road (62nd Avenue), which became East 60th Avenue in 1929 (By-law 2029). Whether it was a survey name or one of local usage has not been ascertained, nor has Taylor been identified.

TAYLOR STREET. Probably named after Louis Denison Taylor (1857-1946), a former mayor of Vancouver. According to Major J.S. Matthews's files, Thomas E. Price of the CPR Engineering Department stated that there had been nego- tiations between the city and the CPR over the road, known locally as False Creek Road, and the city engineer named it after Mayor Taylor.

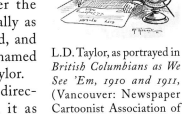

L.D. Taylor, as portrayed in *British Columbians as We See 'Em, 1910 and 1911,* (Vancouver: Newspaper Cartoonist Association of British Columbia, 1911).

The 1930 city direc- tory first listed it as lying south from Pender Street and beyond the Georgia Viaduct. Shown on a 1930 map produced by Dominion Map and Blueprint Company (CVA map 903).

In 1984 By-law 5741, Plan LF 9511, extended it from Keefer to Pender. With the redevelopment of the north side of False Creek little remains of Taylor – only the sections between Pacific and Expo Boulevards (soon to be deleted), and Keefer Place and Pender Street.

False Creek Road. Named unofficially after its location on the north side of the creek within and alongside the CPR yards. Not to be confused with the False Creek Trail from New Westminster in the 1870s and 1880s.

TEAKWOOD PLACE. Private thoroughfare in Champlain Heights. Name approved by the Street Naming Committee on 8 November 1979. Associated with Limewood, Marchwood, and Raintree.

TECUMSEH AVENUE. Shown on Plan 4502 (1913) and named by the CPR, developers of Shaughnessy Heights, after Tecumseh, a Shawnee First Nations

chief who allied his forces with those of the British and Canadians in the War of 1812.

TECUMSEH STREET (DL 393). See Wenonah Street.

TEMPERLEY STREET (Deleted). Named on "Plan of provincial government property to be sold at Victoria by public auction, Monday, January 18, 1886, J.P. Davies and Co., auctioneers" (CVA Map 143). The street lay between present Point Grey Road and West 1st Avenue from Collingwood to Alma Streets. However, it is not shown on Plan 229 (1887), the official survey of this part of DL 540. Origin of this paper survey name is unknown.

TEMPLETON DRIVE. Named after William Templeton (1853-98), mayor of Vancouver from 1897 until his death in 1898, on Plan 1771 (1905), a resurvey of DL 264A. Shown on Hermon and Burwell's 1902 "Plan of the City of Vancouver, British Columbia" (Map 14171).

TERMINAL AVENUE. Named after its location near the terminus of the Great Northern and Canadian National Railways. Named in 1922 by By-law 1556 and repealed in 1926 by By-law 1803 in order to give a more exact legal description. By-law 2526, 1938, extended it east as far as Glen Drive, and in 1976 By-law 5010 extended it one block west to Quebec Street.

TERRA VITA PLACE. Private thoroughfare off Cassiar Street, near Adanac Street, shown on Plan LF 11674 (1995). Located on the site of the former Girls Industrial School, built in 1914, now used as part of a condominium complex.

Terra Vita is Latin for "living earth."

TERRY FOX WAY. Named 1995, By-law 7474, Plan LF 11638, after Terrance Fox (1958-81), who ini- tiated the Marathon of Hope run to raise funds for cancer research. The Terry Fox Memorial, built in 1984 to honour him, is nearby.

Formerly *Stadium Road West,* named 1991, By-law 6781, as part of the ring road around BC Place Stadium.

THELLAIWHALTUN AVENUE. Named 1976, By-law 5010, Plan LF 7356, after the First Nations name Thellaiwhaltun, given to Willard Sparrow (1927-67), former chief and Musqueam

Band agent (letter from Wanona Scott, executive secretary, Musqueam Band, 17 July 1996). Originally, the name "Willard Sparrow Avenue" had been proposed.

THETA STREET. See Aberdeen Street.

THISTLE STREET (Deleted). Named by the CPR in 1909, Plan 2301. It ran north from the present Cornwall Avenue between Arbutus and Yew Streets to the then existing street car tracks. Never opened, it is now part of Kitsilano Park.

THOMAS ROAD (Deleted). Named after Owen W. Thomas, first listed in 1909 South Vancouver Voters List; he owned Block 29 and 30, DL 329. Named on Plan 2745 (1910), the street lay between South East Marine Drive and East 65th Avenue, two blocks east of Victoria Drive. It disappeared with the replotting of Fraserview.

THOMAS STREET (DL 301). See Inverness Street.

THORNHILL DRIVE. Named 1952, By-law 3330, after the Thornhill Golf Club, near Toronto.

THORNTON STREET. Named 1954, By-law 3486, as Thornton Avenue, after Sir Henry Worth Thornton (1871-1933), president of Canadian National Railways, 1922-32.

In 1979, By-law 5267 exchanged the location of Thornton Avenue with that of Cottrell Street at the request of the Cottrell Forwarding Company, which had moved its warehouse there. Later that year Thornton Avenue was renamed Thornton Street by By-law 5299 to conform to the pattern of streets running north and south.

THREADNEEDLE STREET. Now East 34th Avenue one-half block west of Prince Edward Street. Named on Plan 1719 (1908), probably after Threadneedle Street, London, England, site of the Bank of England. Named in association with Throgmorton Street, site of the stock exchange. South Vancouver By-law 141, 1910, changed it to East 35th Avenue (now East 34th Avenue).

> Among the many indications of the British influence on Vancouver street names are those named after London streets: Bayswater, Highbury, Highgate, Kingsway, Mayfair, Park Lane, Threadneedle, Throgmorton, and Watling.

THREE CEDARS DRIVE. Private thoroughfare in Champlain Heights, a descriptive name chosen by the Cedar Mill Housing Cooperative and first listed in the 1987 city directory.

THROGMORTON STREET. Now East 35th Avenue between Sophia and Prince Edward Streets. Named on Plan 1719 (1908), probably after Throgmorton Street, London, England. South Vancouver By-law 141, 1910, changed it to East 36th Avenue (now East 35th Avenue).

THRUSH PLACE. One of nine private thoroughfares in Enclaves 8, 9, and 10, Champlain Heights, bearing bird names submitted by Matheson Heights Cooperative and approved by the Street Naming Committee on 25 March 1981.

THURLOW STREET. Named after the Thurlow Islands, shown on the map that L.A. Hamilton used when naming the streets in DL 185. Captain George Vancouver named the islands in 1792 after Lord Chancellor Edward Thurlow (1732-1806).

THYNNE ROAD. See Dumfries Street.

TIDEWATER PLACE. Private thoroughfare; the name, chosen by Riverfront Properties Limited, reflects the tidal nature of the nearby Fraser River. Approved by the Street Naming Committee on 17 February 1987.

TILLEY ROAD. See Nanaimo Street.

TISDALL STREET. Named by By-law 3731, 1958, Plan LA 17A, after Charles Edward Tisdall (1867-1936), former alderman and mayor of Vancouver, 1922-3.

Tisdall Street south of West 54th Avenue is a private thoroughfare in Langara Gardens Apartments.

TOBA PLACE. Private thoroughfare in Champlain Heights, named by the Street Naming Committee in 1979, after Toba Inlet, which was explored and named by Spanish naval explorers in 1792. These men found a strange table (tabla) of planks that had been carved by the Native people. An engraver's error changed the word to Toba.

TODD STREET. Named 1954, By-law 3415, after Eric Dundas Todd (1881-1927), South Vancouver engineer and building inspector, 1923-7. By-law 3558, 1956, extended it south to Euclid Avenue.

TODERICK STREET. Named by South Vancouver By-law 251, 1913, as Todrick, after James

Banks Todrick (1858-1936), who came to Vancouver in 1905, where he was in the real estate and insurance business. Served as a councillor in South Vancouver, 1910 and 1911. Misspelled as Toderick since the first directory listing in 1917.

In 1913 the street lay between the present East 49th and East 54th Avenues, but that section was altered by the Champlain Heights replotting and now consists of two short sections.

Another section of Toderick Street lies between East 43rd and East 45th Avenues. Plan 3373 (1911) shows it as *Roger Street*, but this survey name, of unknown origin, was not used.

TOLBOOTH. Private thoroughfare in Champlain Heights, named by the Kinross Creek Housing Cooperative after Tolbooth, a street in the Scottish town of Kinross. Approved by the Street Naming Committee on 8 July 1982.

TOLMIE STREET. After Dr. William Fraser Tolmie (1812-1886). A surgeon for the Hudson's Bay Company, he served five years as a member of the Legislative Assembly in Victoria. Named by Point Grey By-law 17, 1912, although the name was bestowed by the provincial government in 1887, Plan 229, according to E.B. Hermon, pioneer land surveyor, in correspondence with Major J.S. Matthews, 24 August 1934.

TOWNLEY STREET. Named 1954, By-law 3457, after Thomas Owen Townley (1862-1935), mayor of Vancouver in 1901. After being registrar of land titles for the Vancouver district, 1901-10, he resumed his law practice.

T.O. Townley, first commanding officer of militia in Vancouver, 1894. CVA Port. P. 15, N. 79 #1.

TOWNSEND ROAD. Now West 70th Avenue between Heather and Granville Streets. Named by South Vancouver Highway By-law, 1905, after Willis Noah Townsend (1862-1935), who owned property in DL 325 in 1901. Councillor in South Vancouver in 1901 and school trustee and secretary for Eburne School in 1903, he spent the last fifteen years of his life in Delta, where he died 1 April 1935. His name was usually listed as William N. Townsend. Changed to West 70th Avenue by Point Grey By-law 17, 1914.

TRACY ROAD. Now East 30th Avenue between St. George and Fraser Streets. Named on Plan 1220 (1906), after the surveyor of the plan, Lieutenant-Colonel Thomas Henry Tracy (1843-1925), who served as Vancouver city engineer from 1891 until 1905, when he entered private practice as a land surveyor and consulting engineer. Survey name only.

T.H. Tracey. CVA Port. P. 146, N. 245.

A handful of Vancouver street were named after city surveyors: Dawson, Garden, George, Hamilton, Hermon, Herbert, Stewart, and Tracy.

TRAFALGAR STREET. Named by By-law 573, 1907, after the British naval battle at Trafalgar in 1805, as suggested by Miss Dora Bulwer (see Alma Street). Previously called Boundary Street, being on the western boundary of DL 526, the huge CPR land grant.

Kaye Rd., 1912, now Trafalgar St., looking south from 18th Ave. west. This area was so wet that it was better and cheaper to plank the muskeg rather than gravel it, as the gravel would sink out of site. CVA Str. P. 207, N. 149.

Point Grey By-law 17, 1912, changed the adjoining street, *Kaye Road*, between West 16th Avenue and Wilson Road (now West 41st Avenue), to Trafalgar Street. Named after Alexander Kaye (1873-1951), an assayer at Atlin and Rossland before joining the Canadian government assay office in Vancouver. See also MacDonald Street.

TRAMWAY AVENUE. See McSpadden Avenue.

TRIMBLE STREET. After Dr. James Trimble, a surgeon in the Royal Navy who took up practice in Victoria in 1858. He became mayor of Victoria, and was speaker of the provincial legislature, 1872-8. He died 1 January 1885. Named by Point Grey By-law 17, 1912, although the name had been bestowed by the provincial government in 1887, Plan 229, according to E.B. Hermon, pioneer land surveyor, in correspondence with Major J.S. Matthews, 24 August 1934.

In 1984 By-law 5765, Plan LF 10605, changed the portion of Trimble north of its junction with North West Marine Drive to North West Marine Drive.

TRINITY STREET. Named on Plan 100, a resurvey of Hastings Townsite, 1906, after Trinity College, Dublin, Ireland.

TRIUMPH STREET. Named on a 1902 map of Vancouver (Map 14171). Origin of name not verified but perhaps after HMS *Triumph*, which visited Vancouver for the first Dominion Day celebrations, 1 July 1887.

TROLLEY PLACE. Named 1992, By-law 7047, after its location near the former Central Park trolley line, now the right-of-way for the SkyTrain.

TROUNCE ALLEY. Named officially 1972, By-law 4636, Plan LF 5892, when a Gastown beautification project was developed, although the alley had been shown in the 1896 city directory and in *Goad's Atlas*, 1913, Plate 3.

Why Trounce Alley was named after Trounce Alley in Victoria is told in the correspondence between Frank W. Hart and Major J.S. Matthews, 4 September 1933. As a young man, Hart visited Victoria, where Weiler Brothers entertained him so royally in Trounce Alley that, on returning to Vancouver, he talked about it so much that he acquired the nickname "Hart of Trounce Alley." His store and undertaking establishment on Cordova Street backed onto an alley.

Thomas Trounce was a Victoria businessman,

and he built the Weiler furniture factory on Trounce Alley.

TRUTCH STREET. Named on "Plan of provincial government property to be sold at Victoria by public auction, Monday, January 18, 1886" (Map CVA 743). This preliminary plan was superseded by Plan 229 (1887), which showed Trutch Street between the present Point Grey Road and West 16th Avenue.

Point Grey By-law 483, 1926, extended the street from West 16th Avenue to West 19th Avenue, but in 1951 Vancouver By-law 3250 shortened it to West 18th Avenue.

Named after Sir Joseph William Trutch (1826-1904), first lieutenant-governor of British Columbia, 1871-6.

TUAM PLACE. Private thoroughfare named 1972, By-law 4636, at the suggestion of the United Cooperative Housing Society, after Tuam Mountain on Salt Spring Island. Tuam means "flanked by the sea" or "facing the sea" (Akrigg 1997).

TUAQ DRIVE. Private thoroughfare in Champlain Heights, named after one of the killer whales in the Vancouver Aquarium. The name "Tuaq," an Inuktitut word meaning "the first one, the only one," was submitted by Alexander Laidlaw Cooperative and approved by the Street Naming Committee on 25 March 1981. See also Hyack and Skana Drive.

TUGBOAT PLACE. Private thoroughfare. The name, submitted by Riverfront Properties Limited and approved by the Street Naming Committee on 17 February 1981, is indicative of the tugboats plying the nearby Fraser River.

TUPPER STREET. Named by South Vancouver Highway By-law, 1905, probably after Mrs. Mary Tupper, property owner in DL 472 from 1893 to 1897. Mountain View Cemetery Register shows that Mary Tupper, a widow, born in Ireland, had died 27 January 1897. The street lay between West 18th and West 22nd Avenues. Point Grey By-law 17, 1912, extended it to West 24th Avenue.

TURNBERRY CRESCENT. Private thoroughfare in Langara Estates, adjacent to the Langara Golf Course. Daon Development Company chose golf course names. Turnberry, Scotland, has two golf course names. Turnberry, Scotland, has two golf courses at the Turnberry Hotel. Name approved by the Street Naming Committee on 16 February 1978.

TURNER STREET. Named on Plan 1771, a re-survey of DL 264A (1905), after John Herbert Turner (1834-1923), premier of British Columbia, 1895-8.

TYNE STREET. Named after the Tyne River, England, in 1910 by South Vancouver By-law 141, which renamed Grant Road, from Vanness Avenue south to the present East 65th Avenue, Tyne.

Grant Road. Named by South Vancouver Highway By-law, 1903, lay between the present Kingsway and Vanness Avenue. Named after John Grant, owner of 5.84 acres in DL 36-49, the Burnaby Small Holdings. Provincial Voters List, 1898, shows him as a gardener.

By-law 5195, 1978, deleted Tyne south of East 54th Avenue when Champlain Heights was replotted. A new road connection with Tyne was surveyed and named Champlain Crescent.

Some people were dissatisfied with this name because they felt two names for one length of road was confusing. At a meeting of the Champlain Heights Planning Advisory Committee, 14 April 1980, a motion was passed requesting that city council change the name of Champlain Crescent back to Tyne Street. At its next meeting on 27 May 1980, the chairman observed a lack of support for the change and no further action was taken.

On 24 October 1995 the Street Naming Committee approved the extension of Tyne Street between Euclid Avenue and Crowley Drive (Plan LF 11676).

TYTAHUN CRESCENT. In Musqueam Park sub-division, leased from the Musqueam Band, it was named by By-law 4266, 1966. Tytahun, meaning "upper end," was the name of an old settlement (CVA, Vancouver City Clerk, Series 29 [loc. MCR 30-181, p. 502]). The city originally suggested *Player Crescent*, after a then well-known South African golfer, Gary Player, because Musqueam Park abuts Shaughnessy Golf Course.

U

UNION STREET. Named 1911, when By-law 806 renamed Barnard Street because it sounded too much like Burrard Street. Origin of name unknown.

Barnard Street. Shown on "Plan of the City of Vancouver, British Columbia," compiled by H.B. Smith, 1886 (Map 14267), named after Francis Stillman Barnard (1856-1936), MP for the Cariboo in 1880. He was shown in the first Vancouver Voters List, 1886 and was a shareholder in the Vancouver Improvement Company, the largest landowner in the city next to the CPR.

On 20 November 1918, Alderman Joseph Hoskins gave notice of a by-law to change the

name of Union Street to *Victory Street*. At the council meeting of 2 December 1918, a letter from C.C. Delbridge and J.D. McNeill protesting the change was read. The matter was referred to the By-laws Committee, but no change was made.

In 1930, By-law 2082 changed Union between Vernon Drive and Boundary Road to Adanac Street.

UPLAND DRIVE. Named 1952, By-law 3330, after Uplands Golf Course in Oak Bay, near Victoria, British Columbia.

UPLAND STREET see Gladstone Street.

V

VALDEZ ROAD. Named by Point Grey By-law 483, 1926, after Cayetano Valdés, a Spanish naval officer with Galiano while exploring the area between Vancouver Island and the Mainland in 1792. The Native Sons of British Columbia, Post No. 2, suggested this name for one of the six new roads created in the replotting of DL 139.

> There are a number of Vancouver street names derived from Spanish names (some of which were suggested by the Native Sons of British Columbia): Blanca, Camano, Cardero, Cordova, Galiano, Haro, Langara, Narvaez, Quadra, Toba, and Valdez.

VALENTINE STREET. See Prince Albert Street.

VALLEY DRIVE. Named by Point Grey By-law 232, 1924, after its location in a valley. When the Quilchena Golf Course closed in 1953, Valley Drive east of Arbutus Street was developed, with Arbutus Gardens complex opening in 1967. Bruce Macdonald (1992) mentions that the diagonal route of a former logging railway became the location of Valley Drive.

VANNESS AVENUE. Origin of name unknown. Named and delineated by South Vancouver Highway By-law, 1905, as Van Ness Avenue, it lay the length of the north side of DL 37.

By-law 3325, 1952, and By-law 3937, 1961, created slight extensions to the street.

The name was in use before 1905, as shown by a large advertisement in the *Daily News Advertiser*, 26 April 1891.

VENABLES STREET. Named after Captain Cavendish Venables, 74th Highlanders, who, around 1861, secured a military grant to the land in Venables Valley west of the Thompson River between Aschroft and Spences Bridge. He probably knew some of the early land owners in DL 182, who were also prominent businessmen in the Cariboo – Peter Dunlevy and Francis Barnard. Named on "Plan of City of Vancouver, British Columbia," compiled by H.B. Smith, 1886 (Map 14267), it lay between the present Glen and Odlum Drives.

In 1957 By-law 3618 linked Venables to Prior Street between Raymur and Campbell Streets.

VERNON DRIVE. Named after Forbes George Vernon (1843-1911), chief commissioner of lands and works, who, in 1883, was one of the original owners of DL 182. Forbes and George Streets also named after him. Vernon Drive later extended to East 4th Avenue when False Creek was filled in.

VIA GARIBALDI (Proposed). see Commercial Drive.

VICTORIA DRIVE originally lay in two jurisdictions: the Municipality of South Vancouver and the City of Vancouver. Probably named after the City of Victoria and, indirectly, after Queen Victoria.

South Vancouver Highway By-law 1, 1893, established a road north from the present East 59th Avenue to the City of Vancouver's southern boundary. Although not named in clause 8 of this by-law, other clauses mention Victoria Road.

In 1910, South Vancouver By-law 141 changed Victoria Road to Victoria Drive south from the BCER right-of-way to East 59th Avenue.

Statue of Queen Victoria in front of the Legislature Building, Victoria. BCARS I-20956.

Hill Street. Named by South Vancouver By-Law 141, 1910, for a section of the street that jogged west between Stainsbury and the BCER

> A large number of street names in Vancouver were derived from royalty: Albert, Alexandra, Balmoral, Beatrice, Elizabeth, Guelph, King Edward, Kingsway, Prince Albert, Prince Edward, Kings, Queen and Queens, Royal, Rupert, and Victoria.

Hastings St. East, at Victoria Rd., circa 1900. At this point there was only forest beyond Victoria Rd. The road was planked. The logs were hauled by teams of ten horses from the forest to the south, and then rolled into a salt water just west of Cedar Cove. The fine large logs had been taken out 20 or 30 years earlier. CVA Str. P. 227, N. 292 #2.

right-of-way. Although shown in *Goad's Atlas*, Plate 92, 1913, and on a 1930 Vancouver Town Planning Commission map (Map 14337), the name, of unknown origin, was not in common use. Deleted with the replotting of the Victoria Diversion in 1954.

In 1948, By-law 3081 standardized the use of Victoria Drive throughout the city at the request of the Victoria Drive Ratepayers Association.

In 1953, the Central Park line of the BCER closed, and there was a change in the street pattern as the right-of-way became accessible. By-law 3487, 1954, made the following changes:

(a) Section running southeast from the northern end of Commercial Street to Victoria Drive was designated Victoria Diversion;

(b) Section between the BCER and Stainsbury Avenue was changed to part of Beatrice Street.

VICTORIA STREET (DL 264A). See Guelph Street.

VICTORIA STREET (DL 540). See Point Grey Road.

VICTORY STREET (Proposed). See Union Street.

VIEW STREET. Now East 62nd Avenue between Cambie and Columbia Streets. A descriptive name shown on Plan 1765 (1908), it became East 64th Avenue (now East 62nd Avenue) in 1910, South Vancouver By-law 141.

VIMY CRESCENT. Named after the Battle of Vimy Ridge, France, April 1917. Canadian forces played a major role in its capture.

VINE STREET. Named on an 1887 map surveyed by L.A. Hamilton (Map 14160) and registered on Plan 590 (1891). Point Grey By-law 17, 1912, named the part between West 33rd and West 45th Avenues. The part extending south from King Edward Avenue into the Arbutus Village complex is a private thoroughfare. Name suggested by the Vancouver Town Planning Commission and approved by city council on 23 March 1948 (Vancouver City Council Minutes, v. 54, p. 259).

VIVALDI PLACE. Private thoroughfare in Champlain Heights, named by Community Builders, developers of Ashleigh Heights, after the Italian composer, Antonio Vivaldi (1678-1741), and approved by the Street Naming Committee on 25 March 1981.

VIVIAN STREET. Named Vivian Road after William Thomas Vivian (1856-1947), shown in 1893 South Vancouver Assessment Roll as owner of SE 1/4, DL 336 (39.25 acres), as well as lots in DL 338, by South Vancouver Highway By-law, 1905. Changed to Vivian Street in 1910 by South Vancouver By-law 141.

WALDEN ROAD. Now East 37th Avenue between Victoria Drive and Nanaimo Street. Surveyed but not named on Plan 1700 (1907), with owners Henry Wright Walden and Robert Walden. Changed to East 37th Avenue by South Vancouver By-law 141, 1910.

WALDEN STREET. Named by South Vancouver By-law 141, 1910. First named on Plan 1329 (1907), with one of the owners, Henry Wright Walden, having extensive holdings in the area. Several other Waldens also owned property in the area.

Tyson Road. Changed in 1910 by South Vancouver By-law 141 to Walden Street between East 33rd and East 36th Avenues. Unnamed on Plan 1192 (1906), with owner T.M. Tyson. Named on Plan 1438 (1907). Thomas Mann Tyson (1867-1923), born in Scotland, was a moulder with firms such as Letson and Burpee, Wilson Brass Foundry, and Wallace Shipyards.

WALES STREET. Originally called Wales Road by South Vancouver By-law 65, 1903, after George Wales (1847-1919), born in Ontario of Irish parentage. He preempted DL 50 in 1878 and subdivided it in 1888, Plan 243. Renamed Wales Street in 1910 by South Vancouver By-law 141.

Cedar Lane. Shown on Plan 243 as the western boundary of DL 50; a survey name only.

Balmoral Road. Shown in *Goad's Atlas*, 1913, Plate 108, as Wales Road (late Balmoral Road), south from the present East 54th Avenue to East 59th Avenue. Named on Plan 3049 (1910), it was a survey name only – a Scottish one – probably named in association with Glencoe Street, shown on the same plan.

The replotting of Fraserview deleted Wales Street below East 56th Avenue.

WALKER ROAD. Now East 31st Avenue between St. George and Fraser Streets. Named on Plan 1220 (1906), with owner Thomas Allan. South Vancouver Voters Lists show a Mrs. C.K. Walker as property owner in DL 391-2. The 1909 listing shows Mrs. C.K. Walker, care of Allan Brothers. A survey name only.

WALKER STREET. Named 1913, South Vancouver By-law 251. Mr. Pleming, long-time resident of Cedar Cottage, told Major J.S. Matthews, former city archivist, he thought it was named after William George Walker, who served as municipal clerk for South Vancouver from May 1901 to March 1908.

WALL STREET. Named 1911, By-law 842, which renamed the portion of Powell Street angling northeast between Semlin Drive and Renfrew Street. In 1954, By-law 3415, Plan LA 42, extended it to Eton Street. Origin of name unknown.

WALLACE CRESCENT. Named 1934, By-law 2326, which renamed Wallace Street between 8th and 10th Avenues. Surveyed on Plan 6188 (1929), an addition to Jericho Heights Estates, in accordance with a request from Point Grey municipality that the provincial government, in its survey, contour the streets to the slope rather than set them up according to a rectangular grid. See also Crown Crescent.

WALLACE PLACE. A cul-de-sac at the southern end of Wallace Street named 1979, By-law 5275, Plan LF 9221.

WALLACE STREET. Named by Point Grey By-law 32, 1919, probably after Sir William Wallace (ca. 1272-1305), Scottish patriot and compatriot of Robert Bruce. The map attached to this by-law shows the name "Wallace" superimposed in red over the name "Bruce." Point Grey By-law 232, 1924, confirmed Wallace Street between West 48th and West 51st Avenues and extended it from West 42nd Avenue to Point Grey Road.

Bruce Street, named by Point Grey By-law 17, 1912, probably after Robert Bruce (1274-1329), king of Scotland and a champion of Scottish independence. Point Grey By-law 17, 1914, extended it to the Fraser River.

Plan 2439 (1909) shows *St. John's Road* between West 35th and West 37th Avenues, a survey name only. Origin of name unknown but it may have been after St. John, New Brunswick or St. John's, Newfoundland, as an adjacent street in the same plan was named Moncton.

"The Birth of Water Street." According to Major J.S. Matthews, this photo was taken circa May 1886. However, judging from the photo on the following page, also of Water Street and also dated May 1886, but clearly taken at a later date, this photo must have been taken some time in 1885. It is hard to make out, but in the distance on the right one can just see the same Maple tree in the foreground of the photo on the next page. CVA Str. P. 8, N. 29.

WALNUT STREET. Shown on Plan 2301 (1909), the name continued the pattern of tree names.

WALTER STREET. Now East 19th Avenue between Main and Knight Streets. Shown on Plan 187 (1885) and named by the owner, H.V. Edmonds, after his son Walter Freth Edmonds (1877-1951). When DL 301 joined Vancouver, the street became part of East 19th Avenue.

WANETA PLACE. Surveyed in 1970, Plan 14122, but not shown in city directories until 1974. Probably named after Waneta, British Columbia, to continue the pattern of streets named after BC towns and places. An Okanagan First Nations word, possibly meaning "burned area" (Akrigg 1997).

WARD STREET. Named 1929, By-law 2104, it is a contraction of *Howard Street*, which was named in 1913 by South Vancouver By-law 251. South Vancouver Voters Lists, 1897-1906, show H. Howard as owner of Block 6, DL 50. Henry Howard, born in England, was a rancher until his death on 29 March 1906 at age thirty-nine. He served as a school trustee for East Vancouver School, 1897-8.

WATER STREET (OGT). see Carrall Street.

WATER STREET. Named after its location and shown, unnamed, on Plan 168 (1885), it lay within Old Granville Townsite between the present Carrall and Cambie Streets. It now extends west to Homer Street.

Front Street. Named arbitrarily on a fire insurance plan of Granville, British Columbia, August 1885, published by Sanborn Map and Publishing Company Limited (Map 14258), it lay where the present Water Street is.

WATERFORD DRIVE. A private thoroughfare shown on Plan LF 11099, approved May 1987. One of four streets within the Langara Springs development, its name is associated with the development's lagoon and waterfall, as are Rockpoole, Waterleigh, and Whitespray.

WATERFRONT ROAD. A private thoroughfare on land belonging to the Vancouver Port Corporation, shown on Plan LF 11501, approved 7 August 1992. The name describes its location paralleling the waterfront of Burrard Inlet, east from the SeaBus terminal to Dunlevy Street.

The new "City of Vancouver," May 1886. The "Maple Tree," at the corner of Carrall and Water Street, where pioneers sheltered from sun and shower, held meetings or impromptu concerts in the evening, tied horses... Here, "Gassy Jack" squatted in 1867 and candidates spoke to the few of "Gastown" in the first civic election, 3 May. It was also used as a notice board, note the white proclamation posted. The tree was destroyed six weeks after this picture was taken in the great Fire, 13 June. Note the dirt roads and wooden planked sidewalks. CVA Str. P. 83, N. 107.

Water Street looking east from Richards and Cordova, July 1886, four weeks after the great Fire. Note the wooden planked roads and sidewalks. CVA Str. P. 129, N. 89.

WATERLEIGH STREET. A private thoroughfare on Plan LF 11099, approved May 1987. One of four streets within the Langara Springs development, its name is associated with the development's lagoon and waterfall, as are Rockpoole, Waterford, and Whitespray.

WATERLOO STREET. Named 1907, By-law 573, after the Battle of Waterloo, 18 June 1815, as suggested by Miss Dora Bulwer (see Alma Street). Originally called *Lansdowne Street*, after the 5th Marquess of Lansdowne (1845-1927), who was Governor-General of Canada at the time. Shown on Plan 229 (1887).

WATERS ROAD. See Dumfries Street.

WATERSIDE AVENUE. A descriptive name for a private thoroughfare near the Fraser River, submitted by the Marin Vista development and approved by the Street Naming Committee on 21 January 1985.

WATLING AVENUE (Deleted). Shown on Plan LF 4530, attached to By-law 4770, 1970. A short street running east to Boundary Road and connecting with Watling Street in Burnaby. By-law 5195, 1978, deleted the street and plan from the official street name map. Watling Street in Burnaby was probably named after Watling Street in London, England.

WATSON STREET (DL 301, DL 302). Named 1950, By-law 3195, when *Howard Street* renamed to remove duplication with Howard Avenue in Burnaby. Origin of name of Howard Street, first listed in 1901 city directory, is unknown, as is that of Watson.

WAVERLEY AVENUE. After *Waverley*, a novel by Sir Walter Scott, at the suggestion of William B. Young of the city's engineering department. Named 1929, By-law 2028, which changed East 49th Avenue between Victoria and Nanaimo, Elliott and Killarney, Kerr and Doman Streets to Waverly because the avenue falls between East 47th and East 48th Avenues. See page 135.

East 49th Avenue between Elliott and Wales Streets had been named *Edinburgh Road* on Plan 2484 (1910), but this survey name, probably after the Scottish city, was not adopted.

WEAVER COURT. A private thoroughfare in Champlain Heights, named by Community Builders, developers of Park Place, after Weaver Creek Park near Harrison Lake. Name approved 21 June 1978.

WEBBER AVENUE. Unnamed on Plan 2193 (1909) and named on Plan 3300 (1911), probably after George H. Webber, first listed in 1912 South Vancouver Voters List. In 1916 he is listed at 40 Webber Street. Last listed in 1922.

WEEKS ROAD. See Hoy Street.

WELLINGTON AVENUE. Origin of name unknown, but perhaps after the Duke of Wellington. Named by South Vancouver Highway By-law 65, 1903, it lay between the present Boundary Road and Manor Street. Extended from Manor Street northwest to East 29th Avenue by South Vancouver Highway By-law, 1905.

WELLS ROAD. Listed only in 1913 city directory as running east from Earle Road, with Carlton (now Killarney) intersecting. A further check of the nine residents listed shows most were living on the present East 42nd Avenue. Probably an unofficial name used for postal or delivery services. City survey office has no record of this name.

WELTON STREET. See Sophia Street.

WELWYN STREET. Named by South Vancouver By-law 141, 1910, probably after Welwyn, Hertfordshire, England, although this has not been verified. This same by-law renamed Gartley Road and Taylor Road.

Gartley Road. Named on Plans 2044, 2170, and 2332 (1909), it lay in short sections from Kingsway south to East 30th Avenue. South Vancouver Voters Lists 1908-10 show Mrs. Margaret Jane Gartley owning property in DL 352.

Taylor Road. Unnamed on Plan 1201 (1906) and named on Plan 4369 (1912), the road lay between East 18th and East 22nd Avenues. Origin of name unknown.

WENONAH STREET. Named 1929, By-law 2014, when Tecumseh Street renamed to remove duplication with Tecumseh Street in Shaughnessy Heights.

Although some sources state that it was named after Jonathan Cornett's daughter, Winona, Major J.S. Matthews questioned that assumption. According to W. L. Woodford, former municipal clerk of South Vancouver, Winona Park was named after Reeve Cornett's daughter, but the street was named after "some eastern Indian of historic fame ... which occurs in some poem." Winona, Ontario, was named after Tecumseh's oldest daughter. We-non-ah is a Dacotah word meaning "first-born daughter." "Wenona" was the mother of Hiawatha in Henry Longfellow's poem.

Tecumseh Street (DL 393). Named in D13, South Vancouver By-law 251, after Tecumseh, a Shawnee chief who allied his forces with those of the British and Canadians in the War of 1812.

WERKS DRIVE. A private thoroughfare in Champlain Heights named by the Plumbers and Pipefitters Union, sponsors of a cooperative housing project there, after a founding member of Local 170, C. Werks, about whom nothing is known. Approved by the Street Naming Committee on 12 January 1984.

WESSEX STREET. Named 1913, South Vancouver By-law 251, after the ancient Anglo-Saxon kingdom of Wessex in southern England at the time of the Norman Conquest of 1066. Adjacent streets are Senlac and Harold.

WESTBANK PLACE. A private thoroughfare in Champlain Heights named by Community Builders, developers of Park Place, after Westbank Park on Okanagan Lake.

WESTERN STREET. An unimaginative name referring to the position of the street in Parcel A, DL 2037, Plan 5703. Named 1926, By-law 1803.

WEST BOULEVARD. See Boulevard, East and West.

WEST STREET. see Yukon Street.

WEST POINT PLACE. Private thoroughfare named after its location in the west Point Grey area of Vancouver. Approved by the Street Naming Committee on 3 July 1985.

WETHERSFIELD DRIVE. Private thoroughfare in Langara Estate, adjacent to Langara Golf Course, named by Daon Development Company after Wethersfield Country Club, near Hartford, Connecticut. Approved by the Street Naming Committee on 16 February 1978.

WEYMOOR PLACE. Private thoroughfare in Champlain Heights named by Intrawest Properties

Limited, whose development, Moorpark, bears names of moors – Dartmoor, Lynmoor, and Weymoor. Approved by the Street Naming Committee on 25 March 1981.

WHEELHOUSE SQUARE. Named 1984, By-law 5756. Imperial Ventures Limited chose a nautical theme for its condominium project on False Creek – Commodore Road, Spyglass Place, and Starboard Square.

Wheelhouse Square was originally where Starboard Square is now. Because residents had difficulty gaining access to their building from Wheelhouse Square, an access lane from Spyglass Place was named Wheelhouse Square (Plan LF 11547, 9 June 1993).

WHITEHEAD ROAD. Now West 37th Avenue between Cambie and Camosun Streets. Mentioned in Point Grey By-law 1, 1910, which allocated $23,700 for clearing, grading, and macadamizing it from Camosun Street to Granville Street. Point Grey By-law 20, 1910, extended the road from Cambie to Trafalgar Street. Point Grey By-law 17, 1912, renamed the road West 37th Avenue.

In a conversation in 1936 with J.S. Matthews, assessment commissioner J.W. Allan said that Whitehead was a New Zealand miner living in a cabin at the corner of West 37th Avenue and Wallace Street (i.e., in DL 2027) around 1907. South Vancouver Voters Lists 1906 and 1907 show George Whitehead, Fairview, owning property in DL 2027. According to his death certificate, George Whitehead (1842-1919), born in England and having spent thirty years in Vancouver, retired in 1910. He had been a miner.

WHITESIDE STREET (Proposed). *Vancouver Sun*, 31 May 1960, reported that a section of Macdonald Street between 16th and 18th Avenues would be named Whiteside. Macdonald Street angles slightly here to create a small triangle with a short one-block-long street on the east side. The name was not adopted although, in 1997, the street still existed.

Thomas J. Whiteside (1861-1935), a building contractor, served as an alderman in Vancouver, 1909-10.

WHITESPRAY DRIVE. A private thoroughfare on Plan LF 11099, approved May 1987. One of four streets within the Langara Springs development, its name is associated with the development's lagoon and waterfall, as are Rockpoole, Waterford, and Waterleigh.

WHITHORN COURT. Located in Champlain Heights, named 1984, By-law 5741, Plan LF 5741. John Northey, property developer with Polygon Group, said it was named after Whithorn Properties, one of the companies in the group.

WHITNEY PLACE. A private thoroughfare in DL 331, Lot 187, shown on Plan LF 11622 (1994), probably named after Mount Whitney in the Sierra Nevada range, California.

WHYTE AVENUE. Named after William Mehven Whyte (1843-1914), superintendent of the CPR's western division in 1886 and a vice-president by 1910. Shown on Plan 2301 (1909) and first listed in the 1913 city directory. The city belatedly confirmed the name in 1958, By-law 3731.

WILBERS STREET. See Ormidale Street.

WILLIAM STREET (DL 301). Now East 23rd Avenue between Main and Knight Streets. Shown on Plan 187 (1885) and named by H.V. Edmonds, after his son, William Humphries Edmonds (1869-1912), registrar of titles in Kamloops, 1899-1912. Became part of East 23rd Avenue when DL 301 joined Vancouver in 1911.

WILLIAM STREET. Named on Map 14267, "Plan of the City of Vancouver, Western Terminus of the Canadian Pacific Railway," compiled by H.B. Smith, 1886. Origin of name unknown.

Around 1913, when the eastern portion of False Creek was filled in, Point Street became part of William Street west of Glen Drive, as shown in *Goad's Atlas*, Plate 83.

Point Street, also shown on the aforementioned 1886 plan, was probably named after its location looking due west to a point of land extending to False Creek.

An article in the *Vancouver Sun*, 7 July 1964, reported that sign painters made William the street of indecision: twenty-one signs bore the correct form of William, twenty-two spelled it "Williams," and eight said Williams East.

WILLINGDON PLACE. See Athlone Street.

WILLOW STREET (OGT). See Cordova Street.

WILLOW STREET. Officially registered on Plan 590 (1891) but named on an 1887 map (Map 14160) by L.A. Hamilton, who chose tree names. Point Grey By-law 17, 1912, extended it from West 16th Avenue to West 26th Avenue. In 1951 By-law 3232 changed Connaught Drive between West 32nd and West 41st Avenues to Willow Street.

WILSON ROAD. Now East 41st and West 41st Avenue. Named by South Vancouver Highway By-law, 1905, after Charles Henry Wilson (1854-1947), who came to Vancouver in 1886 and became an important contractor with the firm Crowe and Wilson. The road extended from the present Blenheim Street to the present Granville Street.

C.H. Wilson. From a group photo of the Capilano Water Works Dam, circa 1903, Annual official visit. CVA C.I. Dept. P. 33, N. 5.

Point Grey By-law 21, 1910, extended Wilson Road from Granville to the eastern boundary of the municipality at Cambie Street. Soon, Point Grey By-law 17, 1912, renamed it 41st Avenue.

In 1910 South Vancouver By-law 141 renamed Wilson Road (from Cambie Street to Victoria Drive) East and West 43rd Avenues. Not until the amalgamation of Point Grey, South Vancouver, and Vancouver in 1929, By-law 2028, did that length of road become East and West 41st Avenue.

WILTSHIRE STREET. Named arbitrarily after Wiltshire, England, in 1950, By-law 3199, which renamed Sperling Street to remove duplication with Sperling Avenue in Burnaby.

Sperling Street. Named by Point Grey By-law 17, 1914, after Rochfort Henry Sperling (1876-1956), general manager of the BCER and subsidiary companies, 1897-1914. Reconfirmed by Point Grey By-law 232, 1924, it lay between West 41st and West 57th Avenues.

"Magee Street" had been proposed to replace Sperling Street but residents were opposed to this name, thinking it would be called "Maggie." There had been a Magee Road in Point Grey from 1893 to 1912, when it was renamed West 49th Avenue (Point Grey By-law 17, 1912). Hugh Magee (1821-1909), one of the pioneers of the area, preempted DL 194 in 1867 and DL 321 in 1873.

WINDERMERE STREET. Shown on Plan 100, a resurvey of Hastings Townsite, 1906, named after the Windermere Mining Division, British Columbia, and indirectly after Windermere Lake, England.

WINDSOR STREET. Originally lay in South Vancouver municipality. Plan 1369 (1907), a plan of Kensington subdivision, showed this English place name between East 35th and East 39th Avenues. South Vancouver By-law 141, 1910, established this name and also changed Gray Road between East 26th and East 33rd Avenues, as well as Fourth Street between East 45th and East 49th Avenues, to Windsor Street.

Gray Road. Named by South Vancouver By-law 65, 1903, after David George Gray (ca. 1858-1935), who came to Granville in 1882 and appears in the first Vancouver Voters List, 1886. First listed in South Vancouver in 1901. In 1916 he donated land to South Vancouver for a park (South Vancouver Council Minutes, 7 April 1916).

Fourth Street. Named on Plans 1390 and 1900 (1907) because it was the fourth street east of Fraser Street.

In the City of Vancouver Kathleen and Dock Streets lay north of Windsor Street.

Kathleen Street (DL 301). Shown on Plan 187 (1885) and named by the owner, H.V. Edmonds, after his sister-in-law, Elizabeth Kathleen Black (née Kemp) (ca. 1843-1912). When Vancouver absorbed DL 301 in 1911, Vancouver By-law 842 changed Windsor Street to Dock Street, so perhaps Kathleen Street between East 15th Avenue and East King Edward Street had been known as Windsor.

Dock Street. It ran south from an arm of False Creek to East 15th Avenue, the city boundary, as shown in *Goad's Atlas*, 1913, Plates 86-7 and 90-1. Shown on a 1902 Map (Map 14171). Probably in the early days there would have been small docks or piers along False Creek. Changed to Windsor Street in 1914, By-law 1168. In 1997 the north end of Windsor Street was at Glen Park on a bluff high above where False Creek used to lie.

WINDSOR STREET (Deleted). A popular name reflecting the British background of most settlers. Shown in *Goad's Atlas*, 1913, Plate 108. It lay, in broken lengths, between Elliott and Rupert Streets. Surveyed in 1909-10, Plans 2274 and 3049. Changed to East 60th Avenue (later East 58th Avenue) by South Vancouver By-law 141, 1910. Disappeared with the replotting of Fraserview. A survey name.

WINLAW PLACE. Named 1969, By-law 4417, after the settlement of Winlaw on the Slocan River, which commemorates John Winlaw, sawmill operator and first postmaster (1903) (Akrigg 1997).

WINNIFRED AVENUE. See Inverness Street.

WINTER STREET (Deleted). Named 1913, South Vancouver By-law 251, it was never developed and is now a lane between Lakewood and Garden Drives and between Blocks 21 and 22, DL 195. Shown on Plan 5027 (1921) spelled as "Winters."

Thomas Winters told Major J.S. Matthews, city archivist, that "a street was named after me down by the interurban at Gladstone" but that the "s" in his name had been dropped.

Thomas Francis Winters (1864-1954), born in Ireland, came to Vancouver in 1899. He served on the South Vancouver police force and, later, with the National Harbour Board police. He died 20 February 1954.

WINTERS ROAD (DL 50). See Earles Street.

WOLFE AVENUE. Named by the CPR, developers of Shaughnessy Heights, after General James Wolfe, commander of the British expedition, who died on the Plains of Abraham while capturing Quebec on 13 September 1759. Surveyed 1913, Plan 4502.

WOLFE STREET. See Galt Street.

WOOD STREET (OGT). see Abbott Street.

WOODLAND DRIVE. Shown on a 1902 map surveyed by Hermon and Burwell (Map 14171) and on Plan 1771 (1905), a resurvey of DL 264A. A descriptive name.

Selby Street. An unofficial name for a very short portion of Woodland Drive south of East 15th Avenue, shown unnamed on Reference Plan 135 (1911). Named in *Goad's Atlas*, 1913, Plate 91. Listed in 1922 and 1924 city directories: "From 1238 East 16th Ave., runs 1 block south." Probably named after Albert Edward Selby (1870-1948), conductor for the BCER, who lived nearby at 1336 East 17th Avenue.

WOODSTOCK AVENUE. Named 1929, By-law 2028, after *Woodstock*, a novel by Sir Walter Scott. Formerly East and West 42nd Avenue in the Municipality of South Vancouver. Named Woodstock to differentiate it from West 40th and West 41st Avenues, between which it falls. See page 135.

WORCESTER STREET (DL 330) (Deleted). Named by South Vancouver By-law 251, 1913, probably after Worcester, England. The fourth street west of Boundary Road, it lay between present East 65th Avenue and South East Marine Drive. Only listed in city directories from 1917 to 1922. Shown on maps until 1945 (CVA map 822). Deleted by an unidentified resurvey of the area. Now within Champlain Heights area.

WORTHINGTON DRIVE/PLACE. Named to honour the two sons of former alderman Dr. G.H. Worthington, who both died near Falaise, Normandy: Lieutenant-Colonel Douglas Grant Worthington was killed 19 August 1944, and his brother, Major John Robert Worthington was wounded and later died. They served in the 28th Armoured Regiment, British Columbia Regiment. Name recommended by the Vancouver Town Planning Commission and approved by Vancouver City Council, 23 March 1948 (Vancouver City Council Minutes, v. 54, p. 259).

WYLIE STREET. Named on Plan 5832 (1925), a special survey of part of DL 302. Previously known as part of Yukon Street. Three of the streets in this special survey were named after early aldermen. Peter Wylie served as an alderman for Ward 5 in 1902.

P. Wylie. From a group photo of the Capilano Water Works Dam, circa 1903. CVA C.I. Dept. P. 33, N. 5.

Y

YALE STREET. Named on Plan 100, a resurvey of Hastings Townsite, 1906, after Yale University, New Haven, Connecticut. First listed in 1913 city directory. In 1958 By-law 3731 changed part of Wall Street to Yale.

YARDLEY PLACE. A private thoroughfare shown on Plan LF 504 (1992), named by Vancouver Land Corporation after Yardley, near Birmingham, England.

YEW STREET. Officially registered on Plan 590 (1891) but named on an 1887 map (Map 14160) by L.A. Hamilton, who chose tree names.

Point Grey By-law 17, 1912, extended it from West 41st and West 45th Avenues, and Point Grey By-law 232, 1924, extended it from West 16th to West 23rd Avenues.

Point Grey By-law 32, 1919, changed Barton Road to Yew Street.

Barton Road and *Barton Road North.* named after Eveline Barton, shown on Plan 3856 (1912) as one of the owners of part of DL 316. A daughter of Samuel McCleery, she married Heber Beriam Barton (1871-1934), a school teacher at Eburne, who became secretary of Eburne Cannery, 1901-2 and was associated with the Greenwood Cannery. Point Grey By-law 37, 1911, established Barton Road North from present West 49th Avenue south to the intersection of South West Marine Drive and West 54th Avenue. Barton Road extended from the intersection of West 57th Avenue and South West Marine Drive into Marine Drive Golf Course.

Hobson Street. Named by Point Grey By-law 17, 1914, after Edward Hobson, who ceded a half-road allowance, shown on Plan 3898 (1911). A builder, contractor, and realtor, he died 26 January 1917, aged sixty-one. Changed to Yew Street between West 40th and West 41st Avenues by By-law 2082, 1930.

YEWBROOK PLACE. A private thoroughfare, first listed in 1981 city directory, abuts Yew Street. There is a brook nearby.

YORK AVENUE. Named by the CPR to commemorate the 1901 visit to Vancouver of the Duke and Duchess of York (later King George V and Queen Mary). Named as York Street between Yew and Balsam on Plan 848 (1902). By 1909 it lay between Chestnut and Trafalgar Streets. In 1958, By-law 3731 changed York Street to York Avenue to conform with the pattern of avenues running east and west.

Half Avenue. In 1913, a one-block-long street between Trafalgar and Stephens – half the width of the property on Plan 774 (1898) – became part of York Street, By-law 1070.

YORK ROAD. See Carnarvon Street.

YUCULTA CRESCENT. Named 1976, By-law 5010, Plan LF 7356. Description of what is referred to as a "fiery surface in the water," especially at the entrance at Seymour Narrows (letter from Wanona Scott, executive secretary, Musqueam Band, 17 July 1996).

YUKON STREET. Named after Yukon Territory, which entered Confederation in 1898. Originally surveyed but not named on Plan 177 (1884), (DL 200 A), it lay between the present West 2nd Avenue and Broadway. In 1907 it was named on Plan 1530 between Broadway and West 16th Avenue and was first listed in Henderson's 1907 Vancouver directory. In 1945 By-law 3081 changed Yukon Street to Alberta Street between West 37th and West 41st Avenues.

West Street. So named on Plan 1765 (1908) due to its westernmost position on the plan. South Vancouver By-law 141, 1910, changed it to Yukon Street between West 59th and West 62nd Avenues.

The Street Numbering System

The use of numbers to designate the roads running east and west in the original City of Vancouver was first shown on Plan 197, amended 1885 – a plan of parts of DL 200A, which showed 5th Avenue to 9th Avenue. Smith's 1886 "Plan of the City of Vancouver, Western Terminus of the Canadian Pacific Railway" (Map 14267) shows avenues numbered from 1st to 9th in DL 200A and DL 540. In the resurvey of DL 264A (Plan 1771 [1905]) the east-west avenues were numbered 1st Avenue to 15th Avenue, the southern boundary of the city. Further west the southern boundary was 16th Avenue.

Bruce Macdonald, in *Vancouver: A Visual History*, gives a clear explanation of the street numbering system:

> The origin of the hundred block system used for Vancouver's street address system lies in the original settlement of Gastown. The north-south zero axis runs along Carrall Street and through the site of the first small business, Gassy Jack's saloon, where a statue of Gassy Jack now stands in Maple Tree Square. From here Vancouver streets run 49 blocks west and 38 blocks east. Thus an address such as 3800 East Hastings is a location 38 blocks east of Maple Tree Square. The east-west zero axis is on the waterfront a few hundred feet north of Maple Tree Square. The hundred blocks run south from here 93 blocks to the 9300 block (93 times 100) in the southern tip of Vancouver. However, further south on the False Creek waterfront, the intersection of First Avenue and Main Street lies not in the 100 block of Main but in the (100 plus 1600) 1700 block of Main...
>
> The eastern boundary of DL 526, the land grant to the CPR, is today's Ontario Street, created the boundary between Vancouver's east side and west side that exists today. Ontario Street is a southward extension of Gastown's Carrall Street, and it continues the zero hundred block for east-west streets that started by Gassy Jack's saloon. (MacDonald 1992, 23)

In 1911, after Hastings Townsite joined the city, there were many streets that lay north of the above-mentioned east-west zero axis that had been established on the waterfront. It was not until 1950 that By-law 3195 gave the designation "North" to all streets north of Dundas Street between Lakeview Drive and Boundary Road (although in city directories these streets had been so called unofficially as early as 1913).

The adjoining municipalities of Point Grey and South Vancouver had their own systems of naming and numbering their streets. Point Grey By-law 17, 1912, adopted Vancouver's avenue numbering system south of West 16th Avenue and renamed its roads (e.g., Bodwell Road became 33rd Avenue, Whitehead Road became 37th Avenue, and Wilson Road became 41st Avenue).

South Vancouver's street system was chaotic due to scattered development and inaccurate surveys. In 1910 South Vancouver By-law 141 changed more than 200 street names in order to bring conformity to its system. All roads running east and west were designated as avenues. However, its numbering did not jibe with that of adjoining Point Grey from 33rd Avenue south. What was called 33rd Avenue in

Point Grey was called 34th Avenue in South Vancouver. It was not until the 1929 amalgamation of Point Grey, South Vancouver, and Vancouver, through Vancouver By-law 2028, that avenue numbering became continuous.

Changing all east-west roads to numbered avenues was not possible because of irregular surveys and jogs in the two municipalities. The following are "named" avenues lying among the "numbered" avenues: Aubrey, Coleridge, Dogwood, Durward, Ivanhoe, Mannering, Marmion, Mayfair, Ringwood, Waverley, and Woodstock. Over the years portions of the numbered avenues have had various names, as is shown below. For information about the changes see the alphabetical section.

PRESENT NUMBERED AVENUE	FORMER NAMES
1st Avenue	Front St. (Cambie-St. George)
2nd Avenue	Dufferin St. (Cambie-St. Edward)
3rd Avenue	Lorne St. (Alberta-Main)
4th Avenue	North Boulevard (Blanca-UEL) Kingsway (Alma-Discovery) Lansdowne St. (Yukon-Scotia) Electric Ave. (Commercial-Bauer)
5th Avenue	Railway Ave. (Commercial-Bauer)
9th Avenue	Still exists between Courtenay and Blanca, Remainder now called Broadway
10th Avenue	Lockin St. (Main-Prince Edward)
11th Avenue	Kemp St. (Main-Prince Edward)
12th Avenue	Freth St. (Main-Prince Edward)
13th Avenue	Dublin St. (Main-Prince Edward)
14th Avenue	Clifford St. (Main-Prince Edward) Scott St. (Kootenay-Boundary)
15th Avenue	George St. (Main-Knight) Boundary Ave. (Knight-Commercial) Frederick St. (Kootenay-Boundary)
16th Avenue	Fortune St. (Main-Knight) Mary St. (Kootenay-Boundary)
17th Avenue	Jane St. (Main-Knight) Dawson Road (John Hendry Park-Nanaimo) Richard St. (Kootenay-Boundary)
18th Avenue	Mary St. (Main-Knight) Flett Rd. (Knight-Commercial)
19th Avenue	Walter St. (Main-Knight)
20th Avenue	Beechie St. (Main-Knight) Gibson Rd. (Knight-Commercial) Reilly Ave. (Marshall-Lakewood)

PRESENT NUMBERED AVENUE	FORMER NAMES
21st Avenue	Arthur St. (Main-Knight)
	Montague Rd. (Knight-Fleming)
22nd Avenue	Henry St. (Main-Clark)
	Agnes Rd. (Knight-Victoria)
	Strathcona Rd. (Nanaimo-Boundary)
23rd Avenue	William St. (Main-Knight)
	Johnson Rd. (Victoria-Sidney)
	Springridge Ave. (Victoria-Sidney)
	Arnold St. (Rupert-Cassiar)
24th Avenue	Edmonds St. (Main-Knight)
	Ambrey Rd. (Gladstone-Brant)
	Hanbury Ave. (Gladstone-Brant)
	Donnelly St. (Rupert-Cassiar)
25th Avenue	Hanley St. (Rupert-Cassiar)
26th Avenue	McMullen Ave. (Cambie-Ontario)
	Sage Rd. (St. George-Fraser)
	Maple St. (Windermere-Skeena)
27th Avenue	McKendry Rd. (Victoria-Penticton)
	Castle St. (Windermere-Skeena)
28th Avenue	Summit Ave. (Ontario-Main)
	Horne Rd. (Main-Knight)
	Alves Rd. (Welwyn-Commercial)
	Orchard St. (Windermere-Skeena)
29th Avenue	Buckland Rd. (Camosun-Trafalgar)
	Allan Rd. (St. George-Fraser)
	Humblecroft Rd. (Fraser-Prince Albert)
	Ringmore St. (St. Catherines-Knight)
	Queen's Ave (Nanaimo-Slocan)
	Government Rd. (Nanaimo-Boundary)
30th Avenue	Bath Rd. (Blenheim-Carnarvon)
	Tracy Rd. (St. George-Fraser)
	Lee Rd. (Prince Edward-Fraser)
	George Ave. (Nanaimo-Baldwin)
31st Avenue	Devon Rd. (Blenheim-Balaclava)
	Walker Rd. (St. George-Fraser)
	Burrows Rd. (Fraser-Knight)
32nd Avenue	Newman St. (Main-Prince Edward)
	Bartlett Rd. (Fraser-St. Catherines)
	Johns Ave. (Victoria-E. 30th Ave.)
	Parker Rd. (Argyle-Victoria)
33rd Avenue	Bodwell Rd. (Camosun-Victoria)
	Arnold Ave. (Victoria-Slocan)

PRESENT NUMBERED AVENUE	FORMER NAMES
34th Avenue	Murton Rd. (Collingwood-Blenheim) Threadneedle St. (Walden-Prince Edward) St. Andrews Rd. (Prince Edward-St. George) Helena Ave. (Culloden-Commercial) Bodwell Rd. (Victoria-Wales)
35th Avenue	Leonard Rd. (Crown-Dunbar) Cecil Rd. (Blenheim-Collingwood) North Rd. (East Blvd.-Marguerite) Throgmorton St. (Sophia-Prince Edward) St. Davids Rd. (Prince Edward-St. George) Kensington Ave. (Fraser-Culloden) Anaconda Ave. (Culloden-Commercial) Tattenhall Rd. (Gladstone-Nanaimo)
36th Avenue	Taber Rd. (Crown-Dunbar) Centre Rd. (East Blvd.-Marguerite) St. Georges Rd. (Prince Edward-St. George) Missoula St. (Cullodden-Commercial) Nathan Avenue (Victoria-Gladstone)
37th Avenue	Whitehead Rd. (Camosun-Cambie) St. Johns Rd. (Prince Edward-St. George) Augusta Ave. (Culloden-Commercial) Walden Rd. (Victoria-Nanaimo) Marley Rd. (Nanaimo-Wales)
38th Avenue	St. Paul's Rd. (Prince Edward-Fraser) Chaplin Rd. (Fraser-Ross) Paonessa Ave. (Commercial-Victoria) McArthur Rd. (Gladstone-Nanaimo)
39th Avenue	McGarrigle St. (Fraser-Commercial) Latimer Rd. (Victoria-Clarendon)
40th Avenue	Donard St. (St. Catherines-Ross)
41st Avenue	Wilson Rd. (Camosun-Victoria) Janes Rd. (Victoria-Kerr)
42nd Avenue	Manor Rd. (Balaclava-Mackenzie)
43rd Avenue	Harcourt Rd. (Balaclava-Macdonald)
45th Avenue	Angus Rd. (Macdonald-Victoria) No. 1 Rd. (Victoria-Boundary)
46th Avenue	Haddock St. (Ontario-Prince Edward) Jersey Rd. (Prince Edward-Fraser) Argyle Place (Argyle-Bruce) Stephens Rd. (Elliot-Vivian)
47th Avenue	Miles Road (Ontario-Prince Edward) Hinkley St. (Fleming-Argyle) George Rd. (Argyle-Bruce, Elliot-Vivian)

PRESENT NUMBERED AVENUE	FORMER NAMES
48th Avenue	Falconer Rd. (Alberta-Prince Edward) Taylor Rd. (Alberta-Prince Edward) Dublin Rd. (Elliott-Vivian)
49th Avenue	Magee Rd. (Carnarvon-Granville) Ferris Rd. (Granville-Boundary) Government Rd. (Prince Edward-Fraser)
51st Avenue	Dominion Rd. (Prince Edward-Fraser) Phillips Rd. (St. George-Fraser) Madrona St. (Inverness-Argyle)
53rd Avenue	Linden St. (Inverness-Argyle)
54th Avenue	Myrtle St. (Inverness-Argyle) No. 2 Rd. (Victoria-Boundary)
55th Avenue	Reith Rd. (Main-Prince Edward)
56th Avenue	Kemball Rd. (Main-Fraser) Glencoe St. (Elliot-Dawson)
57th Avenue	Shannon Rd. (SW Marine Drive-Cambie) Page Rd. (Prince Albert-Fleming, Elliot-Vivian)
58th Avenue	Stovell Rd. (Ontario-Quebec) Creery Rd. (Prince Edward-Fraser) Discovery Rd. (Prince Edward-Fraser) Windsor St. (Elliot-Rupert) Champlain Ave. (Kerr-Boundary)
59th Avenue	Park Rd. (Granville-Fremlin) Essex St. (Fremlin-Heather) Clough Ave. (Ontario-Main) Davies Rd. (Victoria-Elliot) Ellerslie St. (Elliot-Dawson)
60th Avenue	David Rd. (location unknown) Taylor Road (Prince Edward-Fraser) Kemp Rd. (Victoria-Nanaimo) Mountain View Rd. (Nanaimo-Aberdeen)
61st Avenue	Rosenberg Rd. (Main-Borden)
62nd Avenue	Lawrence St. (location unknown) View St. (Cambie-Columbia) Jensen Rd. (Ontario-Fraser) Highland Ave. (Victoria-Nanaimo) Montjoy Rd. (Nanaimo-Kinross)
63rd Avenue	Hance Rd. (Prince Edward-Prince Albert) Grandview Ave. (Victoria-Vivian) Paget Rd. (Kerr-Boundary)

PRESENT NUMBERED AVENUE	FORMER NAMES
64th Avenue	C Road (Granville-Ash)
	Peters Rd. (Granville-Heather)
	Riverside Ave. (Victoria-Nanaimo)
	South View Rd. (Vivian-Aberdeen)
	Grauer Road (St. George-Fraser)
65th Avenue	Rowling Rd. (Kerr-Boundary)
66th Avenue	Milton Rd. (East Blvd.-Granville)
	Henry Rd. (Elliot St.-east one block)
67th Avenue	Milton Rd. (Granville-Heather)
	Sweet Rd. (Gladstone-Nanaimo)
69th Avenue	Lorne Rd. (location unknown)
70th Avenue	A Street (Granville-Ash)
	Townsend Rd. (Granville-Heather)
71st Avenue	Alberta Ave. (Granville-Selkirk)
	Ellis Ave. (Cromwell-Boundary)
72nd Avenue	Saskatchewan Ave. (Granville-Selkirk)
73rd Avenue	Moosomin Ave. (Granville-Selkirk)
75th Avenue	Griggs St. (Hudson St. East-Railway)
76th Avenue	E Road (Hudson-Selkirk)
	Clinton St. (Hudson St. East-Railway)
77th Avenue	Goodmurphy Rd. (Hudson-Oak)

NUMBERED STREETS

The few numbered streets that ran north and south were shown on survey plans and were not in general use. They were:

All in DL 662-663, changed 1910 by South Vancouver By-law 141

1st Street now Chester (E. 45th-E. 49th Ave.)

2nd Street now Prince Albert (E. 45th-E. 49th Ave.)

3rd Street now St. Catherines (E. 45th-E. 49th Ave.)

4th Street now Windsor (E. 45th-E. 49th Ave.)

5th Street now Elgin (E. 45th-E. 49th Ave.)

6th Street now Ross (E. 45th-E. 49th Ave.)

All in DL 318-319 (Eburne Townsite) and DL 318

1st Street now French St. (W. 72nd Ave.-Park Dr.)

2nd Street now Cartier St. (W. 73rd Ave.-Park Dr.)

3rd Street now Montcalm St. (W. 73rd Ave.-Park Dr.)

4th Street now Hudson St. (SW Marine Drive-Park Dr.)

5th Street now Selkirk (W. 73rd Ave.-Park Dr.)

6th Street now Osler St. (SW Marine Drive-Park Dr.)

Select Articles, Books, and Theses

Akrigg, G.P.V., and Helen B. 1997. *British Columbia Place Names.* 3rd ed. Vancouver: UBC Press.

Allen, Richard Edward. 1982. *Origin of Street and Place Names.* Winnipeg: Josten's.

Barford, Jeremy C. 1966. "Vancouver's Interurban Settlements: Their Early Growth and Functions – The Changes and Legacy Today." BA essay, University of British Columbia.

Bartley, George. 1938. *An Outline History of Typographical Union No. 226, Vancouver, BC, 1887-1938.* Vancouver: Typographical Union.

British Columbia. 1997. *British Columbia Death Index, 1872-1976.* British Columbia Archives and Records Service, (Microforms). Victoria: Micro Com Systems.

British Columbia Lands and Works Department. 1890. "Return to an order of the House for a return showing the last official report on the Condition of the Burnaby Small Holdings." Victoria: BC Legislative Assembly, Sessional Papers.

Burkinshaw, Robert K. 1984. *False Creek: History, Images and Research Sources.* Vancouver: City of Vancouver Archives.

Cail, Robert E. 1974. *Land, Man and the Law: The Disposal of Crown Lands in British Columbia, 1871-1913.* Vancouver: UBC Press.

Claydon, Peter S.N. 1994. *Vancouver Voters, 1886: A Biographical Dictionary.* Richmond, BC: British Columbia Genealogical Society.

Cotton, H. Barry. 1995. *First in the Field: The Pioneer Years of Garden, Hermon, and Burwell.* Saltspring Island, BC: Cranberry Eclectics.

Coull, Cheryl. 1996. *A Traveller's Guide to Aboriginal BC.* Vancouver: Whitecap.

Cumberland, Stuart. 1887. *The Queen's Highway: From Ocean to Ocean.* London, England: Sampson Low, Martson, Searle, and Rivington.

Davis, Chuck, ed., 1997. *The Greater Vancouver Book: An Urban Encyclopedia.* Surrey, BC: Linkman.

Ewert, Henry. 1986. *Story of the BC Electric Railway Company.* North Vancouver: Whitecap.

Fountain, G.F. 1961. *The History of Land Surveying in Vancouver.* Vancouver: Self-published.

Gibson, E.M.W. 1972. "The Impact of Social Belief on Landscape Change: A Geographical Study of Vancouver." PhD diss., University of British Columbia.

Gomery, Darrell. 1936. "A History of Early Vancouver." BA Essay, University of British Columbia.

Green, George. 1947. *History of Burnaby and Vicinity.* North Vancouver, BC: Shoemaker, McLean, and Veitch.

Hale, Linda Louise. 1986. *Vancouver Centennial Bibliography.* Vancouver: Vancouver Historical Society.

Hamilton, Reuben. 1957. *Mount Pleasant Early Days: Memories of Reuben Hamilton, Pioneer, 1890.* Vancouver: City of Vancouver Archives.

Howay, F.W. 1937. "Early Settlement on Burrard Inlet." *British Columbia Historical Quarterly* 1 (April): 3-20.

Imredy, Peggy, and Elizabeth Walker. 1986. "Kitsilano Street Names." *British Columbia Historical News* 14 (Fall): 17-8.

Kerr, J.B. 1890. *Biographical Dictionary of Well-Known British Columbians.* Vancouver: Kerr and Begg.

Lewis, Alfred Henry. 1920. *South Vancouver: Past and Present.* Vancouver: Western.

McCririck, Donna. 1981. "Opportunity and the Working Man: A Study of Land Accessibility and the Growth of the Blue Collar Suburbs in Early Vancouver." MA thesis, University of British Columbia.

Macdonald, Bruce. 1992. *Vancouver: A Visual History.* Vancouver: Talon.

MacDonald, Norbert. 1977. "The Canadian Pacific Railway and Vancouver's Development to 1900." *BC Studies* 35 (Autumn): 3-36.

————. 1973. "A Critical Growth Cycle for Vancouver, 1900-1914." *BC Studies* 17 (Spring): 26-42.

Marlatt, Daphne, and Carole Itter. 1979. *Opening Doors: Vancouver's East End.* Victoria: Provincial Archives of British Columbia.

Matthews, J.S. 1931. *The Fight for Kitsilano Beach: The Celebrated Greer Case.* Vancouver: City of Vancouver Archives.

————. 1956 *Early Vancouver: Narratives of Pioneers of Vancouver, BC, 1932-56.* Vancouver: City of Vancouver Archives.

Melvin, George H. 1972. *The Post Offices of British Columbia, 1858-1970,* Vernon, BC: self-published.

Nelson, Denys, 1927. *Place Names of the Delta of the Fraser, British Columbia.* Vancouver: Self-published.

Parker, C.W., ed. 1912. *Who's Who and Why: a Biographical Dictionary of Notable Men and Women of Western Canada.* Vancouver: Canadian Press.

————. 1911. *Who's Who in Western Canada: A Biographical Dictionary of Notable Men and Women of Western Canada.* Vancouver: Canadian Press.

Paton, J.A. 1911. "The Story of Point Grey, Vancouver": *British Columbia Magazine* 7 (7): 734-7.

Picken, M., ed. 1887. *City of Vancouver, Terminus of the Canadian Pacific Railway: British Columbia Handbook,* Vancouver: Daily News Office.

Proctor, Sharon, ed. 1978. *Vancouver's Old Streams.* Vancouver: Vancouver Public Aquarium Association.

Roy, Patricia E. 1980. *Vancouver: An Illustrated History.* Toronto: James Lorimer.

Scholefield, E.O.S., and F.W. Howay. 1914. *British Columbia: From the Earliest Times to the Present.* Vols. 3 and 4. Vancouver: S.J. Clarke.

Sorden, Leyland George, and Jacques Vallier. 1986. *Lumberjack Lingo.* Madison, WI: NorthWord.

Turner, Michael, *Kingsway.* Vancouver: Arsenal Pulp Press, 1995.

Vancouver Harbour Commissioners. 1920-9. Annual Reports of the Harbour Commissioners. Vancouver: Vancouver Harbour Commission.

Vancouver. 1914. *Vancouver Social Register and Club Directory.* Vancouver: Welch and Gibbs.

Walbran, John T. 1909. *British Columbia Coast Names, 1592-1906: Their Origin and History.* Ottawa: Government Printing Bureau.

White, Howard. 1987. *Spilsbury's Coast: Pioneer Years in the Wet West.* Madeira Park, BC: Harbour.

Whittaker, John, ed. 1990. *Early Land Surveyors of British Columbia (P.L.S. Group).* Victoria: Corporation of Land Surveyors of the Province of British Columbia.

Directories

BC Directories, *Vancouver City Directory, 1950–*

Henderson's, *British Columbia Gazetteer and Directory, 1899-1910.*

Henderson's, *Vancouver Directory, 1905-1923.*

Sun Directories Ltd., *British Columbia Directory, 1934-1948.*

Sun Directories Ltd., *Greater Vancouver and New Westminster City Directory, 1949.*

Williams, R.T., ed., *British Columbia Directory 1882/83, 1884/85-1899.*

Wrigley Directories Ltd., *British Columbia Directory, 1918-1933.*

Select Bibliography: Maps

Entry number refers to entry in *Vancouver Centennial Bibliography* (Hale 1986).

If stated as CVA, map found in City of Vancouver Archives.

7159. CVA 209. *A Student Today: A Citizen Tomorrow*
[Vancouver, BC]: Town Planning Commission, 1931. -1 folded sheet: col. map; 61 x 48 cm. folded to 24 x 15 cm. Includes map "City of Vancouver, British Columbia, Zoning Diagram".

13875. CVA 144. *Archibald Moir & Co.*
Point Grey municipality - Scale [1:6 000] - Vancouver, BC: Archibald Moir & co., [1910]. -1 plan: photocopy.

13905. *British Columbia. Department of Lands and Works*
[Granville-Burrard Peninsula] / F.G. Richards, draughtsman, Lands & Works Dept.; Victoria Steam Lith. - Scale [1:12 672]. -Victoria, BC: Lands & Works Department, [1875]. -1 plan: photocopy.

13907. CVA 2. *British Columbia. Department of Lands and Works*
Map of New Westminster district, BC, 1876 / drawn by F.G. Richards Jnr. -Scale [1:126 720]. -Victoria, BC: Lands and Works Dept., [1877]. -1 map.

13914. British Columbia. Department of Lands and Works
Plan of Hastings, Burrard Inlet, showing lots to be sold at auction at Victoria, BC -Scale [1:3 168]. -Victoria, BC: The Department, [1884]. -1 plan: part. col.

CVA 956. Challenger Cartographers Ltd.
Street map of Greater Vancouver, BC / [prepared by] Challenger Cartographers Ltd. – Scale [1:49 420]. [n.p.] Shell [1948]. Cover Title: *Shell Map of Vancouver, BC and Victoria, BC.*

14039. CVA A342. *Chas. E. Goad Co.*
Goad's atlas of the city of Vancouver, British Columbia and surrounding municipalities in 4 volumes, volume one / surveyed July 1912. -Scale [1:600]. -Vancouver, BC: Chas. E. Goad Col, 1912. -1 map in 49 sheets: col. (Insurance plan of Vancouver; 2).

14040. CVA A342. *Chas. E. Goad Co.*
Goad's atlas of the city of Vancouver, British Columbia and surrounding municipalities in 4 volumes, volume two / surveyed Dec. 1912. -Scale [1:600]. -Vancouver, BC: Chas.E.Goad Col, 1912. -1 map in 49 sheets: col. (Insurance plan of Vancouver; 1).

14053 CVA 384. *Chas. E. Goad Co.*
Vancouver, BC / surveyed July 1897, revised to June 1903 – Scale [1:1 200] and [1:600]. [Toronto, Ont.:
  The Company, 1897-1903]. –1 plan in 61 sheets.

14066. CVA 131. *Coast Map and Blue Print Co.*
South Vancouver municipality. -Scale [1:4 800]. -Vancouver, BC: The Company, [ca. 1913]. -1 plan:
  photocopy.

14083. CVA 941 *Dawson, George Herbert.*
Plan of the municipality of South Vancouver, BC, - Scale 1:12 000. -Vancouver, BC: Mahon, McFarland
  & Procter Limited Liability, 1910. -1 plan.

CVA 822. *Dominion Map and Blue Print Company*
Dial map of Greater Vancouver and suburbs / [compiled by] Dominion Map & Blue Print Co, -Scale
  [1:42 240]. –[Vancouver, BC: Sectional Map & Street Directory Co. [1945].

14116. CVA 35. *Garden, Hermon and Burwell.*
Tourist guide map of Vancouver city and park. [1:14 400]. -Vancouver, BC.: Thomson Stationery Co.
  Ltd., [1898]. -1 plan.

14160. *Hamilton, Lauchlan Alexander.*
City of Vancouver Canadian Pacific town site/ [surveyed by] L.A. Hamilton, Asst. Land Commsr.
  24th Feb. 1887; -Scale [1:7 200]. -Vancouver, BC: Ross and Ceperley, [1889]. -1 map.

14171. CVA 133. *Hermon & Burwell.*
Plan of the city of Vancouver, British Columbia. -Scale [1:9 600]. -Vancouver, BC.,: Thomson Stationery
  Co. Ltd., 1902. -1plan.

14173. CVA 190; 191. *Hermon & Burwell.*
Plan of the city of Vancouver, British Columbia. -Scale [1:9 600]. -Vancouver, BC.,: Thomson Stationery
  Co. Ltd., 1907. -1 plan.

14194. CVA 749. *McHenry, George J.*
Map of Greater Vancouver. -Scale [1:47 520]. -[Vancouver, BC: The Author, ca. 1915]. -1 map.

14229. CVA 937. *Point Grey, BC Office of the Municipal Engineer.*
The municipality of Point Grey / Municipal engineer's Office, Kerrisdale, Sept. 1912. - Scale [1:21 120].
  -[Point Grey, BC]: the Office, 1912. -1 map in 2 sheets: photocopy.

CVA 1052. *Rawson, Charles H.*
Standard pocket map of Vancouver city, BC, including DL 301. –Scale not given. Vancouver, BC: The
  Author [1911].

CVA 743. *Richards, F.G.*
Plan of provincial government property to be sold at Victoria, by public auction, Monday, January 18,
  1856, J.P. Davies & Co., auctioneers / F.G. Richards, draughtsman, Lands & Works Dept. Higgins
  Lith., Victoria -Scale [1:792]. -Vancouver, BC: Department of Lands and Works, 1886.

14258. CVA 553. *Sanborn Map and Publishing Co. Ltd.*
Granville, BC, Aug 1885 / Lloyd 10/8/85. -Scale [1:600]. -New York, NY: The Company, 1885. -1 aperture
  card: b&w; 3 x 2.3 cm. on card 8 x 18.6 cm.

14267. CVA 1. *Smith, H.B.*
Plan of the city of Vancouver, western terminus of the Canadian Pacific Railway, -Scale [1:4 800]. -
  London, Ont. : Free Press Lith., 1886. -1 plan.

14270. CVA 13. *Stuart, Allan Kilbee.*
City of Vancouver, 1893. -Scale [1:180 080]. -Vancouver, BC: printed by Evans & Hastings, [1893-ca.1935]. -1 plan : photocopy.

14272. CVA *Map 13. Thomson Stationery Co.*
South Vancouver / published by G.O.S. Stores, Thomson Stationery Co., Ltd. Liability (Gaskell & Odlum, props.). –Scale not given. –Vancouver, BC: G.O.S. Stores, [1910].

14276. CVA 59. *Thomson Stationery Co.*
Vest pocket map of Vancouver. -Scale not given. -Vancouver, BC. : Business Development Co., 1902. -1 plan in 2 sheets.

14317. CVA 38. *Vancouver, BC City Engineer.*
Vancouver, British Columbia. -Scale [1: 15 840]. -Vancouver, BC : City Engineer's Office, [1930]. -1 plan: photocopy; 89 x 115 cm.

14321. *Vancouver, BC City Engineering Department.*
[Sectional maps]. -Scale [1:7 800]. -[Vancouver, BC.: City Engineering Department, 1945. -1 map in 64 sheets. Map in atlas format.

14322 CVA *atlas G3514 V3 1962. Vancouver, BC City Engineering Department.*
Sectional maps. -Scale [1:4 800]. -[Vancouver, BC.: The Department, 1962. -1 map in 90 sheets. Map in atlas format.

14337. CVA 134. *Vancouver, BC Town Planning commission.*
Vancouver, British Columbia, south easterly portion formerly South Vancouver, zoning plan. -Scale [1:4 800]. -Vancouver, BC. : Vancouver Town Planning Commission, 1930. -1 plan.

14372. CVA 569. *Vancouver Map and Blue Print Company Limited.*
Municipality of South Vancouver. -Scale [1:14 400]. -Vancouver, BC: Vancouver Map and Blueprint Co., [1919]. -1 map.

14376. CVA 145. *Vancouver Map and Blue Print Company Limited.*
Plan of Point Grey municipality. -Scale [1:7 200]. -Vancouver, BC: the Company, [ca. 1925]. -1 plan.

14398. *Williams and Murdoff Limited.*
[Point Grey municipality]. -Scale [1:21 120]. -Vancouver, BC.: Williams and Murdoff Ltd., [1911]. -1 plan.

14404. CVA 695. *Wrigley, Roy.*
Wrigley's new revised map of Vancouver including New Westminster, Burnaby, city & district of North Vancouver, West Vancouver, Richmond, university area. -Scale [1:24 000]. -Vancouver, BC: Roy Wrigley Ltd., 1947. -1 map.